Why I Hate Abercrombie & Fitch

**SEXUAL CULTURES: New Directions from the Center for
Lesbian and Gay Studies**
General Editors: José Esteban Muñoz and Ann Pellegrini

Times Square Red, Times Square Blue
Samuel R. Delany

Private Affairs: *Critical Ventures in the Culture of Social Relations*
Phillip Brian Harper

In Your Face: *9 Sexual Studies*
Mandy Merck

Tropics of Desire: *Interventions from Queer Latino America*
José Quiroga

Murdering Masculinities:
Fantasies of Gender and Violence in the American Crime Novel
Greg Forter

Our Monica, Ourselves: *The Clinton Affair and the National Interest*
Edited by Lauren Berlant and Lisa Duggan

Black Gay Man: *Essays*
Robert Reid-Pharr *Foreword by Samuel R. Delany*

Passing: *Identity and Interpretation in Sexuality, Race, and Religion*
Edited by María Carla Sánchez and Linda Schlossberg

The Queerest Art: *Essays on Lesbian and Gay Theater*
Edited by Alisa Solomon and Framji Minwalla

Queer Globalizations: *Citizenship and the Afterlife of Colonialism*
Edited by Arnaldo Cruz-Malavé and Martin F. Manalansan IV

Queer *Latinidad: Identity Practices, Discursive Spaces*
Juana María Rodríguez

Love the Sin: *Sexual Regulation and the Limits of Religious Tolerance*
Janet R. Jakobsen and Ann Pellegrini

Boricua Pop: *Puerto Ricans and the Latinization of American Culture*
Frances Negrón-Muntaner

Manning the Race: *Reforming Black Men in the Jim Crow Era*
Marlon B. Ross

Why I Hate Abercrombie & Fitch: *Essays on Race and Sexuality*
Dwight A. McBride

Why I Hate Abercrombie & Fitch

Essays on Race and Sexuality

DWIGHT A. MCBRIDE

NEW YORK UNIVERSITY PRESS

New York and London

NEW YORK UNIVERSITY PRESS
New York and London
www.nyupress.org

© 2005 by New York University
All rights reserved

Library of Congress Cataloging-in-Publication Data
McBride, Dwight A.
Why I hate Abercrombie & Fitch : essays on race and sexuality / Dwight A. McBride.
v. cm.
Includes bibliographical references and index.
Contents: Introduction : the new Black Studies, or beyond the old 'race man'—
Straight Black Studies—Why I hate Abercrombie & Fitch—It's a white man's world :
race in the gay marketplace of desire—On race, gender, and power : the case of Anita
Hill—Feel the rage : a personal remembrance of the 1992 LA uprising—Ellen's
coming out : media and public hype—Affirmative action and white rage—Speaking
the unspeakable : on Toni Morrison, African American intellectuals, and essentialist
rhetoric—Cornel West and the rhetoric of race transcending—Can the queen speak? :
sexuality, racial essentialism, and the problem of authority.
ISBN 0-8147-5685-9 (cloth : alk. paper) — ISBN 0-8147-5686-7 (pbk. : alk. paper)
1. African Americans—Study and teaching.   2. African Americans—Intellectual life.
3. African Americans—Social conditions—1975-   4. United States—Race relations.
5. Racism—United States.   6. Sex role—United States.   7. Sexual orientation—
United States.   I. Title: Why I hate Abercrombie and Fitch.   II. Title.
E184.7.M348   2004
305.896'073'00722—dc22   2004015659

New York University Press books are printed on acid-free paper,
and their binding materials are chosen for strength and durability.

Manufactured in the United States of America
c 10 9 8 7 6 5 4 3 2 1
p 10 9 8 7 6 5 4 3 2 1

for the thriving community of

African Americanist and queer studies scholars in Chicago;

and still we rise

Finally, my brethren, be strong in the Lord, and in the power of his might. Put on the whole armour of God, that ye may be able to stand against the wiles of the devil. For we wrestle not against flesh and blood, but against principalities, against powers, against the rulers of the darkness of this world, against spiritual wickedness in high places. Wherefore take unto you the whole armour of God, that ye may be able to withstand in the evil day, and having done all, to stand.   —Ephesians 6:10–13

Quiet as it's kept, whether we are "rioting" or not, most African Americans live every day with greater or lesser amounts of rage toward white people and the system that gives them the power and privilege to decimate our lives. I know I do.

—Barbara Smith, *The Truth That Never Hurts:*
Writings on Race, Gender and Freedom

Contents

Acknowledgments   xi

Preface   1

Introduction: The New Black Studies,
   or beyond the Old "Race Man"   17

Part I   Queer Black Thought

1   Straight Black Studies   35

2   Why I Hate Abercrombie & Fitch   59

3   It's a White Man's World: Race in the Gay Marketplace of Desire   88

Part II   Race and Sexuality on Occasion

4   On Race, Gender, and Power: The Case of Anita Hill   135

5   Feel the Rage: A Personal Remembrance of the
     1992 Los Angeles Uprising   143

6   Ellen's Coming Out: Media and Public Hype   149

7   Affirmative Action and White Rage   154

Part III   Straight Black Talk

8   Speaking the Unspeakable:
On Toni Morrison, African American Intellectuals,
and the Uses of Essentialist Rhetoric   163

9   Cornel West and the Rhetoric of Race-Transcending   185

10   Can the Queen Speak? Sexuality, Racial Essentialism,
and the Problem of Authority   203

Notes   227

Bibliography   235

Index   241

About the Author   251

Acknowledgments

A book such as this one accumulates many debts in its production and owes a great deal to the people and places that gave it the opportunity to come to fruition. For their support I am most grateful to the large community of African Americanist and queer studies scholars in the city of Chicago who provided a nurturing intellectual and social environment for my thinking over the past five years. I am privileged to work in this community at this historic moment in its development.

I wish to thank my colleagues in the Department of African American Studies at the University of Illinois at Chicago (UIC) for their patience, support, and friendship. They are still among the finest scholars and people I have known. At UIC, I was aided by the incredible research assistance of Darcy Thompson and Justin A. Joyce, both of whom always went above and beyond the call of duty. Their scholarly examples were reminders of the excitement of doing the work that we do as cultural critics. My debt to Mildred McGinnis—my administrative assistant during my tenure as head of the Department of African American Studies at UIC—is too great ever to repay. She made the phrase "having my back" real for me. Since my arrival at Northwestern University as chair of the Department of African American Studies, my colleagues in the department have shown me in everyday ways how possible it is to transform the discipline of African American studies into one that is more inclusive, intellectually responsible, and more vibrant in its curricular offerings. I could scarcely imagine a more collegial group with whom to engage in this important work. My research assistants at Northwestern have also been extraordinary: my undergraduate research assistant, Nicole Mash, my computer tech support coordinator, B. C. Broussard, and, with my very deepest gratitude, my graduate research assistant, Stefan Griffin. Stefan gives new meaning to clichés like dedicated, smart, efficient, and (a favorite among the AFAM office staff) "tight." Both Marilyn Williams (department assistant in the AFAM Department) and especially Marsha Figaro (assistant to the chair in AFAM) work closely with me daily to handle the myriad details of managing not only our department, but also my own scholarly and professional life and work. None of this would be possible without all that they do—again above and beyond any call of duty.

I have had opportunities to present earlier versions of some of these chapters in various contexts and have received valuable feedback. For this I am indebted to the UIC Queer Faculty Reading Group (especially Jennifer Brody, Sharon Holland, Jamie Hovey, John D'Emilio, and Gretchen Kenagy) for their comments on an early draft of the "Straight Black Studies" chapter; the Departments of African American Studies and English at Northwestern University; Jonathan Holloway, Hazel Carby, and the Department of African American Studies at Yale University; Lauren Berlant and the Center for the Study of Gender, Cathy Cohen, Ken Warren and the Center for the Study of Race, Politics, and Culture, and George Chauncey and the Lesbian and Gay Studies Project at the University of Chicago; Donald Pease and the Master of Arts in Liberal Studies Program at Dartmouth College; Darlene Clark Hine and the Ph.D. Program in Comparative Black History at Michigan State University; and T. Denean Sharpley-Whiting and the Department of Africana Studies at Hamilton College.

I am delighted to have the last three chapters of this book finally appear here together, since they represent a tripartite discussion of race discourse in the United States. My gratitude to *Modern Fiction Studies,* the *Harvard Black-Letter Law Journal,* and NYU Press and *Callaloo* for publishing earlier singular versions of these pieces.

As ever, I am grateful to my family—biological and elective. They provide me shelter in good and bad times. In this past year as this book was being completed (2002–03), I had more of the latter. Special thanks are due to those who held my hand and reminded me of who I am and of how loved I am: Bettye and James McBride, Willie Hampton and Makelia McBride-Hampton, Courtenay Isaiah Hampton, E. Patrick Johnson and Stephen Lewis, Mark Canuel, Darrell Darrisaw, Robert Blackmon, Sharon Holland and Jennifer Brody, Ken and Belinda Martin, John (Connie) Conrad, Tom Bestul and Larry McClain, Ken Dorfman and Steve Kleen, Lisa Thompson, Lisa Merrill, Bill Handley, Rachel Lee, David Blackmore, Chris Cunningham, Fred Haug, Thomas LeBien, Frank Geraci, Darieck Scott, Juan Battle and Michael Bennett, Tim Hane, John Keitel, Byron Patterson, Karen and Flora Lang, Houston A. Baker and Charlotte Pierce-Baker, Hortense J. Spillers, Cathy Cohen and Beth Richie, Gabriel Gomez, Darrell Moore, Tyrone Forman and Amanda Lewis, Jay Louser and Allen Neilsen, Toby Causby, and Father Juan Reed and the entire parish at St. Martin's Episcopal Church (a place whose very existence radically redefines for me what it can mean to be a Christian).

The chapter on Abercrombie & Fitch would not have been possible without the three former managers and assistant managers at three different Abercrombie stores (all in major urban areas) who generously shared their experiences with me in formal interviews, as well as the many other brand reps (former and current) who shared their experiences with me more informally. Also a special thanks to Chris Cunningham, Mark Canuel, Patrick Johnson, Richard Iton, and, in the home stretch, David Blackmore, all of whom endured endless discussion of the issues addressed in this book. Both Mark Canuel and Richard Iton read and commented on the entire manuscript for which I will be forever grateful.

I am grateful for the research support of the following institutions: the Humanities Institute at UIC and its director, Mary Beth Rose; the Office of the Dean of the College of Liberal Arts and Sciences at UIC and to my former dean, Stanley Fish; the Weinberg College of Arts and Sciences at Northwestern University and my dean, Daniel Linzer, and all the members of his staff; the Department of African American Studies at UIC; and the Northwestern Department of African American Studies. And for their abiding support and mentorship I am grateful to the following senior colleagues: Anne Mellor, Valerie Smith, Eric Sundquist, Emily Apter, Toni Morrison, Jonathan Arac, Hortense Spillers, Aldon Morris, Robert Gooding-Williams, Michael Hanchard, and Sandra Richards.

The first complete draft of this book was finished amidst the tranquility of the Manuel Antonio community in Costa Rica. It gave me quiet, relative comfort, and a great deal of perspective. My editor at NYU Press, Eric Zinner, and his assistant, Emily Park, keep even the process of publishing fresh and exciting. I would also like to thank Nicholas Taylor at NYU Press for copyediting the manuscript. And, finally, for Jason K. Martin who continues to inspire though he may not even know so.

I dedicate these pages to the group with which I began these acknowledgments—the incomparable community of African Americanist and queer studies scholars in Chicago who I am privileged to call my friends and colleagues—who are doing more than anyone I know to change the way we think about race and sexuality in the United States.

Why I Hate Abercrombie & Fitch

Preface

I began by remembering the most easily forgotten thing: truth telling is not simple. It is not like the Norman Rockwell painting in which a ruggedly handsome white man, whose plaid collar is literally blue, speaks to the town meeting at his white clapboard church, while other white men, wearing ties, listen in admiration. Truth telling isn't like that. Truth's speakers don't often radiate handsome honesty. They are disconcerting and diverse rather than comfortably familiar. They are rarely received with admiring attention. And what they have to say can seem beyond hearing—or bearing.   —Mark D. Jordan, *Telling Truths in Church*

Why I Hate Abercrombie & Fitch: Essays on Race and Sexuality has been in the making for some time now. Indeed, the essays contained here span more than a decade. It is not a conventional book; it willfully transgresses genres. At turns academic, journalistic, and autobiographical, the book testifies to the fact that it takes a multiplicity of genres—sometimes working together in the same essay—to effectively render the truth of our lives. This is certainly the case if you believe, as I do, that truth telling is never simple or easy.

Part I of this book advances a variety of uses to which the serious analysis of race and gender together might be put. The first essay in this section ruminates on why and how the discipline of African American studies has for so long excluded any considerable focus on sexuality. It also goes far toward challenging the discipline for the incomplete and monolithic picture of the African American community that it has for so long projected and protected. The second essay in this section takes a look at the clothier and its advertising campaign to examine what it has successfully packaged and marketed— a rarified form of elite whiteness that depends upon the racist thinking and

1

logic of its consumers for its very success. And the final essay takes the analysis from the prior essay and extends it to a reading of the place and functions of race as the salient variable in the gay marketplace of desire. Taken together with the preface and the introduction, the chapters in the opening section of this book represent an attempt to speak a version of the truth of black gay male subjectivity, a version of the truth of African American studies, and a version of the truth of the black community.

Part II shifts from the broadly cultural to the political. The occasional essays in this section allow for an analysis of race and sexuality in broad terms. It is also a commentary about where both my own thinking and the thinking of the emergent field of black queer/gay and lesbian studies find themselves at present. That is, we think primarily through the lens of race, with sexuality contributing only partly to our perspective that makes the critical difference in what we, on occasion, bring to the discussion.

This book is primarily and explicitly about pushing the boundaries of what we call the discipline (and I do call it a discipline and not a field) of African American or black studies. My interventions and investments in black queer studies to date have been about transforming African American studies. For me, African American studies represents the site and the intellectual terrain on which I am most interested in doing this work of thinking about race and sexuality. I realize that the work I do is related to, indebted to, and should have an impact on queer studies as well. But such is not the fuel that drives my thinking or my intellectual and political investments. I have often thought that queer theory has been late to come to terms with much of its own racial biases. Very able and illuminating critiques to that effect have been and continue to be made by scholars and commentators in many quarters. My own investments, however, as I understand them, are with the transformation of the discipline of African American studies as an institutional formation and as a form of analysis that takes seriously the questions, complications, and richness that serious ruminations on sexuality—in concert with race, gender, and class—bring to the table of analyzing, critiquing, and recording black life, history, cultural production, and political practices. In the provocative words of Essex Hemphill:

> It is not enough to tell us that one was a brilliant poet, scientist, educa-tor, or rebel. Whom did he love? It makes a difference. I can't become a whole man simply on what is fed to me: watered-down versions of Black life in America. I need the ass-splitting truth to be told, so I will have something pure to emulate, a reason to remain loyal.

Each of the essays in this section tries to demonstrate ways of reading that might result from taking these issues seriously, sometimes independently of each other, and at other times in concert with one another. In all ways, I hope they arc toward a way of thinking that is more inclusive and that moves us beyond some of the old paradigms for race work.

Part III shifts attention closer to the academic arena in order to give a closer examination of the very constitution of gender, sexuality, and race. Theoretical in its orientation, it lays out the academic genealogy of my think-ing about race and sexuality, and the uses to which we have put such ideas in the service of our political agendas. These essays form a three-part intel-lectual discussion of the way we talk and think about race, its uses among black intellectuals and public figures, and on the silence of black gays and les-bians in the dominant forms of African Americanist and black anti-racist dis-course.

As a black, gay, male intellectual; as a Southerner with an essentially Christian orientation—at heart I am in search of "the good" (not just "the truth"), and I am consumed with identifying and analyzing what I conceive to be "evil" (not merely "problematic") in the world—this work has always been personal for me. My investments are substantial and the stakes high. I self-disclose in this way in order to begin by forestalling one of the, by now, age-old ways of disqualifying the personal, intellectual, literary, journalistic truths that people speak from the margins of our society. It is commonplace in this age of "reverse discrimination" to believe, for example, that blacks are the least reliable witnesses as to what actually happens to them in a racist society, since their view is always already tainted by the very fact of their blackness and their "oversensitivity" to such issues. Similar claims have been made about women and issues of sexual harassment, for example. Indeed, over dinner earlier this summer on my back deck, a white gay male friend whom I have known over my five years in Chicago queried me as to whether I thought that my ready investment in seeing race at work meant that I might see it functioning in places where it might not actually be significantly present. I marveled at the ease with which my friend jumped to the ready possibility or conclusion that my "obsession" with race might produce a kind of self-fulfilling prophecy. His disinclination to believe me was amazing. But his ability to call up so readily the rhetorical form that his disbelief assumed signaled to me that something in our societal ways of thinking about black people had not only brought us to a place where this gesture was commonplace, but also where the logic undergirding it could be viewed as neither slanderous nor offensive. Such logic operates on an implied gross fundamental fallacy, of course. That is, if the people who are the most obvious victims of particular forms of discrimination (in this case racism) are also the most readily disqualified as witnesses to those same forms of discrimination, then according to such logic only those people who are not victimized by racism (i.e., whites) are the ones who are, indeed, the best and most reliable witnesses and judges to what actually happens to those racial "others" in our society. So what we have effectively done is to rhetorically de-authorize or de-legitimize the victims of discrimination in our society from ever being able to speak authoritatively about their own experiences of discrimination. We have rhetorically seized their ability to bear authoritative witness to, or even to be in the best position to know, what it is that happens to them in the world. And he who effectively controls the form of epistemology (how we come to know what it is we know) ultimately goes far toward controlling what it is we can know. It is not altogether unlike the old adage that says: Until the lions have their own historians, the hunter will always be valorized.

This is, after all, the kind of thinking that has gotten us into trouble in our attitudes about such policies as affirmative action, creating categories like "reverse discrimination." This is the kind of thinking that has gotten us into trouble in our public debates over LGBT rights, when the human rights that LGBT people seek have been labeled by the political and religious right in the United States as "special rights." Indeed, at a moment when gay and lesbian citizens seek the right to have their relationships recognized by the state in the same way that our heterosexual counterparts' relationships are recognized, the political forces of evil in this country turn this into a semantics debate. "Marriage," an institution that has (and statistics bear this out) fallen on hard times in the United States, all of a sudden becomes sacred and hallowed ground that should be reserved exclusively for heterosexual pairings. Well, I say if the forces of evil in this country want a semantics debate, let's give it to them. Let them have "marriage." Indeed, let's make marriage entirely a function of the church and leave states out of it altogether. Instead, let all relationships now recognized by the states as "marriages" be recognized as "civil unions." Under that nomenclature states could also recognize the civil unions of their gay and lesbian citizenry as well, leaving marriage a private or religious affair in which the states have no interest.

It is precisely this brand of cynicism and rhetorical game-playing over the semantics of "marriage," for example (which is ultimately about winning)—as opposed to any principled positions from real moral convictions—that has created a most lamentable state of affairs in U.S. public life. It has ushered in a kind of general malaise, a hardening of the heart, and even a glazing over of the eyes at the mere mention of that by-now-familiar triumvirate of race, gender, and class (sexuality is sometimes added as an afterthought), that one theologian has rightly called "compassion fatigue." If our deeds follow from our language, as I am convinced they do, we have spoken into existence a way of simply excusing ourselves from having to think in responsible political ways about the disparities, the deeply irksome complexities, and, indeed, the evils of our society in which we are caught up and participate. Such a position is difficult even to articulate in a society in which compassion fatigue has become more than simply the order of the day, but has achieved a kind of normalcy akin to an unspoken moral imperative.

Let me take this occasion to give institutionally marginal university programs and departments a much-deserved shout-out. I specifically want to do so for African American studies programs and departments. Though African American scholars are not always synonymous with African American studies, the two do have much in common with each other in the dominant logic of institutions of higher learning. Both—due to deep-seated histories of racism that extend, of course, to intellectuals and intellectual work—are ever in the process of having to prove to others that they belong there, a fact that consumes a great deal of energy and time that would surely be better spent doing one's work.

My African American colleagues across the country have not only had to achieve intellectually at a very high level under circumstances often far less than ideal, but they have also had to manage the mentoring, advising, committee work, political institutional work, and the constant race education work of students and faculty and administrative colleagues. The demands on those unfortunate enough to be in situations where there are too few of them to share the burdensome load of being an African American faculty member can often be crippling and detrimental to otherwise successful career trajectories.

Indeed, to disgruntled white colleagues who speak disparagingly of the few financial benefits that have—due to the sheer compelling nature of market forces, and certainly not from any sense of institutional benevolence—befallen some African American scholars working at the very highest levels of achievement in some of our nation's most prestigious colleges and universities, I offer the following sobering thoughts. Were it not for years of institutional racism that kept people of color out of our nation's most prestigious colleges and universities, we might have produced by now a cohort of faculty of color with PhDs in the United States who could fill the need we now have to diversify our nation's faculties. The same is true when we speak of the need for faculty who work in the areas of African American studies, Asian American studies, Latino/a studies, and Native American studies. Since the multicultural explosion in our nation, which took place largely in the 1980s and early 1990s, the intellectual necessity for such work that we might today classify broadly as ethnic studies has become abundantly clear to many of us in academia (and the numbers are mounting). That being the case, the need for faculty of color in our institutions should neither shock nor surprise. And that we must now provide remunerations that might be "unprecedented" to such highly sought-after faculty members should neither shock nor surprise those of us who learned as early as high school economics about the law of supply and demand.

From what I have seen as a department chair now at two major research universities (one public and one private), what we have done for a few scholars of color who we might classify as stars or rising stars (meaning they are working at the highest levels of distinction and productivity in their fields), does not exceed what institutions have done for distinguished white colleagues. And more to the point, given the amount of "diversity work" faculty of color are called upon to do—both that which is institutionally sanctioned and that which goes beyond what is—the truth of the matter is that no institution could afford to pay most of us what we are actually worth. Some of those same disgruntled white colleagues who complain about the salaries of stars and rising stars among black faculty are the very ones who become the gatekeepers of "quality" when it comes to hiring black faculty. The language of "qualified" gets bandied about in discussions of such hires in a way that it simply does not when white colleagues are being considered for faculty positions. We might speak about the caliber of a white colleague's work; we might speak about him or her not having published enough; we might even speak of his or her intellectual pedigree; but rarely would such sweeping statements as "there are just so few qualified applicants" be used with regard to a pool of white applicants for a faculty position.

Let us canvass any of the English departments (I know those best) at top universities in the United States and consider the black faculty at those institutions. What you will find—and with very few exceptions—are faculty members who by any measure of "quality" are achieving at the very highest levels of distinction in the field. Canvass those same English departments at those same top institutions and consider the white faculty members there. What one will find is a range of faculty members from the very distinguished to the mediocre or, what some call, in insider's academic administrative parlance, "dead wood." This phenomenon is likely not unique to academia, but since that is what I know best, I will limit my remarks to that institution. My contention is this: there seems to be room in academia for a broad spectrum in quality of white academics, whereas there seems to be very little tolerance for such breadth when it comes to black academics. A double standard? To be sure. So what is the answer to this conundrum? I have often said, and will repeat here, that one of the ways in which we will know when black people in the United States are truly liberated and equal to their fellow white citizens will be when there are as many mediocre blacks in academia as there are currently mediocre whites. This is not meant to denigrate the mantles of "quality" or "merit," but simply to show that even these sacred truths are subject to the vagaries of racist thinking and ideology.

But none of this is new. Those of us conversant in the institutional discourse of diversity have learned to spout off such realities with the same ease with which people rehearse the quartet of race, gender, sexuality, and class when we talk about cutting-edge scholarship today. Much of what we now understand as cutting-edge scholarship in any of the traditional social science and the humanities disciplines could scarcely have been imagined before the advent of African American studies, ethnic studies, gender studies, and so forth. In the more than three decades over which these so-called marginal disciplines and areas of inquiry have emerged in the academy and, indeed, moved to the fore in recent years, it has become possible for them to make several intellectual strides, strides that make the work of an entire new generation of scholars possible. We are now, for example, able to recognize the significance of work on race that has been proceeding relatively unnoticed in traditional disciplines. We are able to give the work of people interested in thinking about race and gender an intellectually larger—and at the same time culturally more specific—context in which that work can be appreciated. And, not to put too fine a point on the matter, we have been able to open up possibilities for the reconsideration of grand historical and cultural narratives such as citizenship, the individual, the human, and modernity, to name but a few.

Indeed, the reason that race, gender, class, and sexuality can be taken as seriously as they are and be as central to how we now produce knowledge even in traditional disciplines is a direct result of the intellectual and institutional work that has for so long proceeded at the margins of the academy in departments like African American studies. The margin forced the center to change, to alter the very ways in which we produce knowledge itself. Our early twenty-first century epistemologies, or ways of knowing and producing knowledge, are radically different from those of the middle of the last century. And we have not been fair about according much of the credit for that to those very programs, curricula, and new disciplines that have been maligned, contested, and starved for resources for so long. Still they rose and evolved new vistas from which to comprehend and make sense of our world.

We can only hope that these kinds of intellectual interventions will also point up the urgency for us to be sure that our institutions take seriously the responsibility to diversify their faculty and student populations. For while the biological significance of race has been thoroughly disqualified, I would hate to see the proverbial baby of representational politics thrown out with the bathwater of biological race. Because while the particular racial markings of bodies may not theoretically matter (as if colorblindness were either desirable or achievable), the narratives, the experiences, the social, political, and economic dramas that animate our realities, the stories we tell and produce, and the intellectual questions we pose are as vital as ever. Therefore, we need to be ever vigilant and attentive to the status of race in our work as well as in our lives.

Building our African American studies departments and programs, according them the same respect and autonomy that we accord traditional disciplines, and making the hiring of minority faculty a priority across the disciplines is not just good for black faculty, it is good business. If knowledge continues to develop in the way that it has over the last few decades, our scholarly communities, our curricula, and our institutional standings will rise and fall, at least in part, on our success in recruiting and retaining African American faculty, and on the building of strong African American studies departments. What we have been witnessing over the last several decades is not just the knowledge-corrective power of African American studies, but the institutionalization of African American studies as a discipline. Recall that it was not until 1892 at the University of Chicago that the first department of sociology was founded. And the discipline of my own training, English studies, was not a recognized discipline of study until rather late in the nineteenth century. When we remember the histories of the so-called traditional disciplines that seem to us so normative today, we begin to see what we are experiencing now as part of a much larger evolution in the production of knowledge—what Thomas Kuhn might have called a "paradigm shift." As African American scholars and as African Americanists, we should take great stock in the way African American studies occupies such a central role in that process. And our institutions would do well to support what is perhaps the most important intellectual movement of our time by strengthening African American studies, ethnic studies, and gender studies, and by diversifying our faculties in the process.

When I imagine the future of African American studies and of race discourse in the United States, I still, despite much evidence to suggest the contrary, have great hope for both these enterprises. I have hope that I, or at least my black (gay, lesbian, or straight) children, will be able to live in a world where their beauty will be publicly honored, appreciated, and celebrated alongside a variety of different kinds of beauty. I have hope that we may live in a world where the novelty of the fact of blackness might become a relic of a long-dead past. I have hope that in academia, we will no longer be constantly called upon to make the case for the importance and centrality of African American studies as a discipline because it will enjoy the kind of institutional generosity of resources that departments such as English, history, biology, or sociology currently do. Indeed, there will be no more "programs" in African American studies because they will all be departments with the same autonomy afforded other disciplines in institutions of higher learning. And gone will be the days when African American studies is called upon to staff its courses, run its curriculum, and meet its administrative, advising, and teaching obligations with shared labor in the form of jointly appointed faculty or, worse still, faculty affiliates who have no real institutional obligations to African American studies other than that which they have generously elected to have. In these ways, we cripple the enterprise of African American studies from the start, forcing it to survive—in the way that no traditional disciplines do—by frequently having to depend upon the good graces of other departments. And Tennessee Williams taught us well what happens to those whose fate it is to depend upon the kindness of strangers.

I also have great hope that someday African American studies departments will have more than the handful of faculty members currently found in most of these units in universities across the country. I have great hope that they will be places in which it will be commonplace to think not only about issues of race in conjunction with questions of diaspora, gender, sexuality, and class, but that there will also be faculty in these departments who represent the range of intellectual interests and the diversity of the African American community. When I look at my own hometown of Chicago at present and consider that four of the major research universities in our metropolitan area have a black gay or lesbian scholar at the helm of their particular race-based intellectual enterprises (Beth Richie, head of the Department of African American Studies at University of Illinois at Chicago; Cathy Cohen, director of the Center for the Study of Race, Politics, and Culture at the University of Chicago; Darrell Moore, director of the Program in Black and Diaspora Studies at DePaul University; and yours truly as chair of the

Department of African American Studies at Northwestern University), I am heartened about the future of black studies. It gives me great hope that we are not only on our way to a more inclusive and intellectually more radical—not to mention responsible—version of our discipline, but that the future of the discipline—its evolution, its coming of age, its survival—depends upon our taking careful account of the overlooked complexities of black life in the United States. Those complexities include populations, questions and considerations, institutions, histories, rhetoric, politics, and cultural productions that have been marginalized by the discipline at best or, which is more often the case, entirely ignored.

So while there is a lot of work—good work—to be done, we also could not be in a better place to face the challenges of the discipline than we are in today. We are ready to move beyond the centrality of the lone "race man" standing at the precipice between a monolithic blackness and the rest of the world broadcasting a prêt-à-porter version of black life. As the epigraph with which I began this preface reminds us, "truth telling is not simple." That is true not only of one's personal truth or testimony, but it is nowhere truer than when one tries, as we must, to tell the truths of our institutions or even of an entire people. That is not the work of the lone straight black man, be he Douglass or Walker, Du Bois or Washington, King or Malcolm, Jackson or Sharpton, or even our contemporary black public intellectual versions of the same. No, that work, the work of telling our truths as African Americans, takes a diversity of voices. Both we who would be representative speakers (race men and women) and the media bear some of the responsibility for the current state of affairs. The media wants, requires, and indeed in some cases produces, such lone individuals. It makes the work of summing up black life and experience (as if there were only one) or of getting a line on black folk much easier when there are the one or two people we can turn to for that perspective. And we race men and women don't make the situation any better by yielding to the pressure to pontificate often on matters far beyond anything resembling our expertise instead of recommending someone who might know more on a particular subject than we do.

Telling the truths of black life in the United States requires a multiplicity of voices. It takes voices invested in the stories and experiences of black men and women; black heterosexuals and black gays, lesbians, bisexuals, and transgender folk; middle-class blacks as well as the black poor, and working and upper classes; incarcerated blacks; black entrepreneurs and businessmen and businesswomen; black professionals; black artists and culture producers; black sex workers; black single parents; black adoptive parents; black families in the broadest sense of that troublesome word; black churches in their various and complicated formulations; black academics; black children and so very much more. When we allow ourselves to be summed up by sanitized versions of black life in adherence to a form of black respectability, we tell only part of our story. And I am convinced that we have finally arrived at a time when this mode of representing black life in the United States no longer serves us in the ways that it might have at an earlier point in our history. The time has come for African Americans to embrace, celebrate, and document our greatest strengths as a community—our diversity and our complexity.

If African American studies is at that proverbial fork in the road, I choose the road less traveled. It is my sincere hope that this book might serve as another modest step down that road that other fellow travelers have already begun taking. For this way lies the future of the new African American studies. Down the other: worn out, monolithic versions of black life, which serve only those who believe that their authority and legitimacy over the dispensation of black knowledge derives from the centrality and repetition of such tired narratives. I believe they are wrong. And I feel certain time will bear me out.

This book represents the evolution of the thinking of one black gay male scholar about "race" since the explosion of cultural studies in the United States. The overarching premise is that African American studies has had to evolve and, in many cases, remake itself in response to the shifting American landscape, itself a cultural and critical hybrid. Indeed, African American studies has also been shaped by the very process of its institutionalization in American universities over the course of the last thirty-five years.

The result in the field of African American studies has been a division into two large conceptual camps. One camp is what we might call the celebration and culture bearers camp; that is, those scholars and culture producers who view African American culture as an entity that needs to be celebrated, as a thing to be transmitted and presented to the world in the mode of respectable admiration. With a critical lineage, liberally understood, dating back to the Harlem Renaissance in the work of figures like Alain Locke, Langston Hughes, and Zora Neale Hurston, this same conceptual camp seems to honor the role of culture producers as primary over the role of the critic and of analysis more generally. This is evidenced most readily today, perhaps, in the form of conference programs like those of the College Language Association and the African American Literature and Culture Society, and in the work published in the *CLA Journal*.

The other camp might be called the cultural studies camp. The critical lineage of this conceptual grouping can be traced back to the scholarship of the late 1970s to mid-1980s with the likes of Henry Louis Gates Jr., Houston A. Baker Jr., Hortense Spillers, and Mae G. Henderson—who represent an avantgarde who first seriously took up poststructuralism in the examination of African American literature and culture. This has resulted in a second wave of such scholars who were trained in academia during the rise of cultural studies in the United States. The effect of this has been the production of a new African American studies influenced by cultural studies, resulting in an ever-broadening notion of African American culture. This new African American studies is also the result of more-recent challenges like those posed by scholars who have raised and continue to raise questions about the diasporic context for African American studies, those pressing us to think more critically about the role of gender in African American studies, those working in the emergent field of black queer or gay and lesbian studies questioning the role of gay and lesbian sexuality in African American studies, and those pressing the issue of class analysis in African American studies. In their own ways, each of these challenges the more traditional mode of African American studies by defying the notion of African Americans as a monolithic community, and presses to tell a truer story of our complexity, diversity, and cultural richness as a community. Put more pointedly, such challenges force us to debunk and trouble the waters of the central role that race alone has held in the analytical work of the field.

The essays collected in this volume, all written between 1991 and 2003, represent the progress, pitfalls, and possibility of race as a category of inquiry in African American studies over the course of the last crucial decade when the critical—not to mention political—landscape of the United States shifted and was radically reoriented. The essays in this book—at times occasional, sometimes theoretical, and at still other times deeply personal—taken together, I hope, will not only carry us further toward complicating and politicizing our thinking about race and sexuality, but also their deployment in our communities; our political lives; and our public, personal, and sexual lives.

Manuel Antonio, Costa Rica
July 31, 2003

Introduction

The New Black Studies, or beyond the Old "Race Man"

I can recall with alarming clarity the moment I first cast eyes on the cover of the March 3, 2003, issue of *Newsweek,* which sported a picture of pop music icon Beyoncé Knowles, talk show host Star Jones, and president of Chicago-based Ariel Mutual Funds Mellody Hobson. I saw the cover story on black women rising faster socially and economically than black men and the implications that phenomenon has for "work, family, and race relations" and I cringed. I secretly hoped—in vain, of course—that this time it might be different. I hoped that the utterly insane moment when we black gay men get lumped together with prisoners and husbands (odd bedfellows to be sure) as the reason that successful sisters have fallen on hard times in the romance department might for the first time in one of these discussions not rear its ugly head. As I read on, I did not have to wait long for my hopes to be dashed and for that fateful moment to arrive: "You're not going to find one [a black man] out here because most of them are either in jail, gay, or taken."

This time, however, instead of feeling the sting of resentment and anger that I did upon witnessing a similar declaration in that infamous roundtable of the sisters scene in Spike Lee's 1991 movie, *Jungle Fever,* I was able to step back and take a look at a much more troubling issue. In this public discussion of the black community, of black intimacy, of black class issues, and of race relations, once again the black gay man and the black lesbian were completely invisible. The view of the black community and of the issues central to it that emerges is of a community of black heterosexuals in which all the women are rich, all the men are poor, and all the blacks are straight.

I could not help but imagine for a moment how differently this story might have read had the idea of who makes up the "black community" been a more complicated version than the old, worn-out, tired, overly respectable heterosexist one that we trot out whenever we publicly take up issues of black intimacy and relationships. Black lesbians and gay men completely disappear except as fodder (specifically in the latter case) for explaining why middle- to upper-class black women have a hard time finding a good black man. Instead, if we began with the assumption that black gays and lesbians are a part of the black community—which is, in fact, the simple truth—we might ask different and, ultimately, broader and more probing questions, which might yield a more truthful view of the complexities of the "black community."

Are the problems that successful black women report having in finding a good man unique to them, or are those problems shared by middle-class black gay men? After all, finding a good man who can be, in the words of songstress and poet Jill Scott, "cool with my strength," is a topic on which I could write another book. Indeed, if anything, should not parity of reasoning make this a problem that successful black women and successful black gay men have in common instead of being something to further divide them in our community? If the logic of black women being on the rise holds, does it work in the same way for black lesbians? Are successful black lesbians, then, when it comes to finding a class-appropriate sister as a mate, in a state of relationship nirvana? These concerns represent quite a different way of considering the topic than when we assume—as we do so very often—that the only black people worth talking about, worth having and finding love are straight blacks.

The black community—to borrow the words of Walt Whitman from another context—is large; it contains multitudes. But then, again, such a rich and diverse image of the black community, true as it may be, might not make for nearly as nice a photo-op as did this *Newsweek* cover. Indeed, such truth may not be so easily assimilable to the requisite sound bite or singular perspective-driven packaging that our contemporary media seems to demand of its subjects. Still, if a holistic and true perspective on the black community is what we are after, black gays and lesbians will not disappear despite the codes of silence maintained by the social scientists, historians, journalists, and social and political commentators—many of whom were, of course, cited in the *Newsweek* article. We have to question studies that make large sweeping claims about "the black community" that do not include all of our stories and experiences.

In 2002, the Policy Institute of the National Gay and Lesbian Task Force published a study—the first of its kind and scope—*Say It Loud, I'm Black and I'm Proud: Black Pride Survey 2000*. It surveyed over 2,500 black gays and lesbians in nine major metropolitan areas in the United States. The survey ranged in issues and concerns from family structure, sexual identity, and policy priorities to political attitudes, discrimination, and religion. Part of the impetus behind producing such a study was to address the disturbing and obvious omission of black lesbians and gays from public discussions about the black community and certainly from any significant treatment by social scientists who purport to study "black families." I recall my own first course on "The Black Family" in the African American Studies Program as an undergraduate at Princeton University. Had that course alone constituted my understanding of black families, I would certainly have thought that black gays and lesbians were non-existent in such a world. Such omissions in discussions of the black family, for example, mark one of the myriad ways in which black gays and lesbians are rendered invisible when the black community is studied. Indeed, it speaks to one of the findings of the *Black Pride Survey,* which maintains that fully 66 percent of the respondents agreed that homophobia was a problem within the black community.

None of the foregoing is intended to *diss* my straight sisters and their hopes of finding a good man. That is a struggle I not only understand, but identify with as well. I just don't want to have to read, yet again, about how that is or might possibly be the fault of their black gay brothers. For such an understanding of black gay male sexuality denies the reality of our humanity and our desires. The logic of the *Newsweek* article suggests that black gay male sexuality represents one of the reasons that sisters are having a hard time finding a good man. According to such reasoning, the only black pairings that have sanction are heterosexual ones; anything else represents deviance. To list black gay men along with prisoners and husbands as the cause of sisters' romantic hardships is to understand gay sexuality in the same way that one understands imprisonment and marriage (perhaps not such strange bedfellows after all). They are all things that could be different under different circumstances. But while men may get out of prison, and men may choose whether to get married, gay sexuality does not work in the same way. You don't get out of it—contrary to the claims of some religious "conversionists"—and you don't choose it. My black gay male sexuality is every bit as integral to my life and happiness as is any straight person's heterosexuality. And it is disrespectful and a breach of my humanity for anyone to suggest otherwise. Hence the source of my resentment. Black gay men are not the pariahs of the community keeping successful sisters from happy, loving relationships. We are a part of the black community and we want as much of a chance at happiness in our lives and loves as our straight sisters do. So let's keep it real when we make broad claims in the name of the black community. It belongs to all of us.

If, as the prevailing intellectual logic of today instructs us, the world of representation (or should I say the culture industry that produces representations) is the place where we find images of ourselves reflected back to us, then my question is: Where in the popular or cultural imagination (other than as fodder or buffoonery) is the bourgeois, well-educated, fairly cosmopolitan black gay man?

I pose the question here specifically with middle-class black gay men in mind, especially recognizing that the examples to follow are drawn from my own middle-class inflected experience. I in no way mean to imply that my experience is representative of that of even the majority of black gay men in the United States. Still, the crisis of representation is for black poor and working-class gay men no less significant. To that extent, some of the observations made in this introduction have broad applicability. Still, it must be recognized that there are important differences between the everyday concerns of middle-class black gay men and their poor and working-class gay brothers. To characterize it one way: the former can afford to discuss the importance of combating homophobia in black communities and the psychic cost they pay for such homophobia, while the latter is left to negotiate the perils of everyday life in those same communities. In this way, black middle-class gay men's access to greater resources also gives them greater choice, and relative security and flexibility about where and how they live, struggle, and love. So, once again, where in the popular or cultural imagination is the bourgeois, well-educated, fairly cosmopolitan black gay man?

Look for him in Hollywood films and he is not quick to surface—though his white male counterpart has been easy to imagine in recent years (*Four Weddings and a Funeral, The Next Best Thing, Philadelphia,* and so on). Look for him in U.S. television and once again (with the exception of the character of Carter Haywood on *Spin City* and Keith Charles on *Six Feet Under,* both played, of course, by self-identified straight black actors) one comes up short, though his white counterpart is perhaps better represented today than at any other time in television's history (*Queer as Folk, Will and Grace,* and *Sex and the City,* or the more recent Bravo additions of *Queer Eye for the Straight Guy* and *Boy Meets Boy,* to name only a few). Columnist and film and television critic, Stephen Tropiano, reported that of the twenty LGBT characters featured on the broadcast networks in 2001–2002, only two were African American and one was Latino. Indeed, we seem to live in an era when straight white male actors can even play a gay man on TV and add cachet to their careers, while white gay male actors are either too afraid of outing themselves in the industry for fear of being typecast, or deemed inappropriate even to play gay male roles. If such are the representational complexities for white gay men, those of black gay men are even thornier, as we will see. If you look for the image of the middle-class, black gay man among the recently dubbed grouping of black public intellectuals who have been featured, profiled, and covered from the pages of the *New York Times* to the *Atlantic Monthly* and have appeared on shows ranging from the *Today Show* to CNN, again, his is a notable absence. And even in black television programming and films—today doing a better job at representing the black middle class—you will have to search long and hard to find him there as well. Indeed, one could begin to believe, if you look at popular shows and films of the last decade or so—*Soul Food* (though there was a troubling lesbian episode), *The Cosby Show, Cosby* (the more recent working-class incarnation of the former), *Barber Shop,* anything by Spike Lee (with the noteworthy exception of *Get on the Bus*), anything by John Singleton, *The Best Man,* or *Two Can Play That Game*—that the black gay man is not just an endangered species in the African American community, but that he is already extinct, that is if he ever existed at all. I am not suggesting here that images and representations alone have the ability to rectify the deep social, cultural, and political issues that lead to this absence of black gay sexuality from any varieties of representations of the mainstream. I contend in chapter 6 of this book that images alone do not have that kind of autonomy. I raise this issue of representation here more as an opportunity to meditate on the possibility that more than mere accident or oversight are at work with regard to the paucity of media images of black gay men. An ideology or politics of respectability that has the power to create such a deafening silence as this in our media industry is one that deserves at least our comment if not our utmost attention.

Now, lest I appear ungrateful for the relative privilege I personally enjoy in the world, let me be quick to acknowledge that fact here. For if travel beyond the so-called first world has taught me anything, it has made it impossible for me to understand myself as anything but economically privileged in a global context, which is no small matter. Still, when we speak of the U.S. context, as I do in this book, the black community, the black middle class, and black LGBT's still have many formidable systemic challenges ahead of us before "the good life" belongs to us. By the good life I do not intend the "American dream" and any of the economic understandings of success that might accompany that notion. By the good life I mean the ability—or is it a right?—to go about your life and your world in relative obscurity. I mean having it not be an event every time you show up at the erstwhile all-white function, benefit, concert, opening, or seminar. I mean not carrying with you always the burden of representing the entire race each time you enter public and institutional spaces. I mean the privilege of not having to worry about, or even to think about, what your presence in any given situation means because neither it nor you is a novelty.

Still, the question with which I began (where is the image of the black gay man?) remains and has an impact in very particular everyday ways. Let's take, for example, the notion of bourgeois vacationing. People in our urban centers often offer, as their reason for vacationing, a desire "to get away from it all." And when one visits the places where middle- and upper-middle-class whites go who say such things, some of the more popular destinations include: Cape Cod, Massachusetts; Long Island, New York; Wilmington, North Carolina; Saugatuck, Michigan; Monterrey, California; Palm Beach, Florida; and Hilton Head, South Carolina—to name but a few beach communities. Perhaps one of the most salient features of these locales is that their inhabitants (both seasonal and year-round) tend to be overwhelmingly white. Now, one might be led by such coincidence to conclude that what white bourgeois subjects mean when they say they want "to get away from it all" is all of the daily stresses of life in the city. Part of what that would undoubtedly entail, among other variables, would be the stress of diversity and difference (which we urbanites often mention right off when speaking about why we like living in cities in the first place) in favor of the relative ease and comfort of sameness—an environment that reflects one's self-image back to oneself.

Assuming such logic holds, it stands to reason that middle-class blacks have sought out such places for themselves as well—Inkwell Beach in Oak Bluffs on Martha's Vineyard being the most notable example in this regard. But such places as "black" also tend to be overwhelmingly straight. Middle-class gays and lesbians have also sought out such locales for themselves—Key West, Florida; Fire Island, New York; Provincetown, Massachusetts; Rehoboth Beach, Delaware; are a few noteworthy examples. And these spaces, when we look at them, tend to be overwhelmingly white.

I had occasion to think about this two summers ago when a friend (also a black gay academic) and I drove for the first time from Chicago to Saugatuck to spend the weekend. We both commented often on how much we stood out that weekend, the polite stares we received (not so much from any hostility as from curiosity about how we came to be there at all), and the novelty of our presence in that place. The journey began as we were checking into a "friendly" local area gay resort and we stood at the desk for what felt like at least five minutes before the clerk (fully aware of our presence from the time we first arrived at the desk) would conclude the engrossing paperwork in which he was engaged to ask if he could help us. At this point I was already ready to leave, but we were tired and had driven all this way and just wanted a quiet, drama-free place where we could "get away from it all" for the weekend. So my friend signaled me to maintain my cool. I did. The rest of the weekend we spent mostly talking about the aftermath of September 11 (this was only a week or so after that tragedy), my recent "divorce" ("break-up" always seemed woefully insufficient to the emotional depth of that experience for me but remains the only language available to gay and lesbian relationships), and how much of a novelty we were in this place and how self-conscious being here made the both of us feel.

So I return, once more, to my very pressing question: Where does the black gay man go where he can see himself reflected back to himself in all the complex ways in which he exists in the world? Where can he be comfortable in his black, gay, bourgeois subjectivity? Where does he go when he wants to "get away from it all"?

Before answering that question, however, perhaps it remains to say a word or two about the specific character of my own "bourgeois" status, since I do not want to be understood as saying that all middle- and upper-middle-class subjects are created equal. Sociologist Mary Pattillo has warned us in her excellent study of the black middle class, *Black Picket Fences,* about the dangers of making such assumptions across racial lines saying: "The one black doctor who lives in an exclusive white suburb and a few African American lawyers who work at a large firm are not representative of the black middle class overall (but neither are their experiences identical to those of their white colleagues)." The specificity of my own inhabiting of that subject position is not without its contingencies. The experience of growing up in the very small city of Belton, South Carolina (population just under 5,000), the child of good working-class black parents who always labored hard to make ends meet, left a deep impression on me about the realities of class politics in this country. Money in our lives was at times the white elephant in the room that no one could talk about, and at others the omnipresent topic that I used to wish could simply disappear. Looking back on it now, I realize that many of my childhood fantasies were centered around winning the sweepstakes—a sudden, miraculous intervention that would change the course of our lives forever. Discussions about money in my family, when they did happen, were always stressful, heated, difficult, and sometimes downright painful. For underneath these conversations (a polite nomenclature in this instance) was always the pain of accusation of some form or another. The accusation that my father was not being responsible enough, "man" enough about familial duties, or that my mother was not doing enough to stretch the family's money and to properly take care of the bills that she managed, or that my sister and I were unrealistic in our expectations of what we wanted and needed for school or just as kids. So my family's relationship to money—or the lack of it—left on me what I would now understand as some rather indelible psychological scars. As an adult, I have clearly negotiated a way of dealing with that past that involves celebrating my abilities as a consumer. The logic runs something like this: As long as I have things (lots of things) and the ability to buy more things, I cannot, it follows, be poor. "Poor," in this equation, is associated with all of those painful, hurtful, difficult family encounters around financial matters when I was growing up. So much of my own personal ambition, a fact I realized a long time ago, has been about getting as far away from that past as possible. Not getting away from my family, mind you, but from the everyday realities of being one of the have-nots.

Still, among the kids I knew growing up I was one of the luckier ones. I had parents, despite whatever their own shortcomings may have been (and all parents have them with regard to their children), who practiced an ethic that led them to want more opportunity for my sister and me than they had ever had in their own lives. They were selfless in their motivations, in this regard, in a way that I can only aspire to be if and when I ever have a child of my own. Indeed, my registered nurse sister and I have achieved things as first-generation college students, and gone to places (both geographically and conceptually), that my parents could scarcely have imagined. Or did they?

Just before I left home to start college at Princeton (the first person from my high school ever to attend an Ivy League school), my mother had a very serious heart-to-heart with me. She told me how proud of me she was and how much she loved me. But she also said something that I had not anticipated hearing from her. She said that she worried about me going off up north to that secular school, where I might possibly learn to look down on or turn my back on the very values that had (as far as she was concerned) brought me the success I was now in a position to begin reaping. She worried about my soul, my identity, my potential distance from her and the world that we all knew and shared. In retrospect, this was, I think, my mother's way of expressing a conflict that I was to come to know all too well in my life—a desire for capital, on the one hand, and the conflicting experience of the "whiteness" of capital on the other. In our world, where capital and the possibility of class ascension are concerned, African Americans are taught the same ideological lessons that their poor white and immigrant counterparts learn. The difference between them on this score is that African Americans have to come up against the whiteness of capital in U.S. society. So at the same time that one desires class ascension, one also experiences it as a kind of betrayal, a disavowal of one's own cultural and racial identity. This is one of the reasons, I suspect, that we have witnessed in recent years such a proliferation of black middle-class memoirs. Middle-class blacks in many ways feel they have a great deal to prove in terms of "keeping it real" within the African American community. Indeed, middle-class standing for blacks within the African American community can simultaneously be a source of pride for members of the community that one more person has "made it," and a source of resentment and distance from those who have not. It is from the crossroads of that particular contradiction that the politically astute black middle-class subject finds that he or she must fashion a new, complicated, and carefully negotiated identity.

Still, the "travels" of my sister and me in this way, and particularly in my own case, have filled our parents with what I now understand is both a sense of pride and of dread. Pride because they have, in all the societally measurable ways, succeeded in raising their children. Dread because one of the realities of class ascension among African Americans is that rarely does it involve ascension for everyone. Indeed, in this case my parents have been the ones left behind. A certain amount of financial, experiential, and (in my case) geographical distance has been the result of their "success." And after nearly thirty years of their living in the same house (which was probably refinanced a few times too many in order to make ends meet), putting two children through college, instilling in both those kids a belief that despite their modest beginnings they were loved and they were God's and therefore just as important as anyone else in this world, they still have a mortgage, still have a car note, are both now living on fixed incomes, and still making ends meet. Not exactly the retirement of the American dream.

Such realities—not only my mom and dad's but also my own by familial association with and responsibility for my parents—compromise my class position in important ways. Money, for the countless middle- and upper-middle-class African Americans in this country who find themselves similarly situated, does not flow "forward" to them from their parents, but rather goes "back" to help out at home in any variety of ways. To this extent, the black gay bourgeois man is not in most cases the same as his white counterpart—especially those white gay men coming from backgrounds where their parents have been and continue to be able to help them out financially, and those who eventually even stand to inherit more wealth from their parents' estates. So even while I claim my position as a bourgeois subject, I do so registering my own somewhat fraught and contingent relationship to that category.

But to return to my question about where the black, gay, bourgeois man goes when he wants to "get away from it all," the answer occurred to me on a recent trip to San Juan, Puerto Rico. The same friend and I who had traveled to Saugatuck together were once again traveling companions. We set out for spring break to "get away from it all." This time we decided that we should venture a bit farther afield to make that happen. So we settled on Puerto Rico, which he, his partner, and I had passed though two years prior while on a Caribbean cruise together. I arrived a couple of days before my friend, who had papers to grade, as the winter term had just ended. Upon my arrival at the hotel, which we had booked sight-unseen online, I knew this was not going to work for me. I had a very specific—and I will admit decidedly bourgeois—idea of the kind and caliber of vacation experience I wanted to have. I wanted to be taken care of, pampered, catered to, and treated well in every conceivable way. And this place—this dark, musty, vista-less, desperately-in-need-of-a-makeover place—was not going to cut it at all. So I phoned my friend and, after a brief conversation, we determined that I was going to pay for the night at this hotel, cancel the rest of our reservation, and this same night check us into the resort further down the street in Condado, which (though far more expensive) we both knew would take us much farther toward having the kind of vacation experience we wanted to have.

During my first full day and night in San Juan, I ventured out to one of the local popular gay establishments for an evening cocktail after dinner. There I ran into another black gay man from Chicago. We had met only briefly a couple of times through a mutual friend (another successful black gay man in Chicago), but I remembered his face and having met him before. We reintroduced ourselves and passed a very nice evening getting to know one another and the friends he was traveling with—one of them was a gay black man from California who is a minister. The man whom I had initially recognized told me that he actually had a copy of my recent book—*Black Like Us: A Century of Lesbian, Gay, and Bi-Sexual African American Fiction*—back in his hotel room. He had brought it with him to read on vacation. Needless to say, we liked each other immediately. Conversation was easy, the mood jovial, and our spirits got higher as the evening and the cocktails wore on. We ended the night by vowing to meet the next day for dinner, since they were, like I was, expecting another friend in from Chicago tomorrow (both black gay men).

The next day we ended up running into each other well before dinner, and I invited them to my hotel (it turns out they too had booked a place on-line with which they were also unhappy) to relax and have drinks by the pool. We did. They eventually moved from their hotel to the one next door to ours, which shared services with our hotel. And that was the beginning of it. We were, to be sure, one of a very small handful of blacks at the hotel. But this was the kind of establishment where people had deep respect for each other's privacy. So the place suited us well. We began creating our own little world there where it was all about us. There was strength in numbers. We reflected each other back to one another. We talked easily about politics, the concerns of black gay men, the concerns of middle-class black gay men, relationship and love issues, being black in a white-centered gay community, being gay in a heterosexist black culture, travel, property, books, movies, entertaining, restaurants, catering, family, and shopping. And after their friend arrived and my friend arrived, the five of us met up with another couple of new friends from Boston (one African American gay man and his white gay male travel companion), and yet another couple of friends also from Boston—unknown to the first couple prior to this meeting (one white gay man and one gay man of South Asian origin)—and another white gay male friend of ours from Chicago who came down for a long weekend. All of us urbane; all of us well educated; all of us clearly middle to upper middle class; and all of us on vacation for more than a week in San Juan. We created a world in which black gay men formed the center. A world that was safe for us. A world where we were the dominant image being reflected. A world that was, for the time we were all there together, a place where we were able "to get away from it all." It was the most relaxing vacation I have had to date. And it was entirely unexpected.

It seems to me that only in such individualized and private ways is it possible for black gay men to create such locales for themselves. Depending on any of the dominant communities to which we reluctantly and often by default name ourselves as belonging (gay, black)—formed as they are out of dominant white supremacist or heterosexist logic—to do the work of creating comfort zones for us, spaces where we can "get away from it all," is finally, perhaps, foolhardy. We have to be about the business of creating spaces for ourselves within those locales, and in other privatized ways that may not be so conventional. It might be my living room and a dinner party or cocktail party for a guest visiting from out of town. It might be a regular Sunday brunch at a friend's house where we all gather to be with each other and to feed each other in the life-sustaining ways that involve more than simply sharing food, though that ritual is not to be underestimated. It might be the Thanksgiving dinner that two African American lesbian friends host every year, at which we all are committed to being present no matter what else is going on in our lives. It might be the now famous dessert party that a gay African American colleague and his white partner throw every year when they open their home to friends, family, and loved ones demonstrating by their quiet example what a home (gay, straight, black, white, or otherwise) might look like when it is a place where love and respect for each other and for the people they love abound. It might be my home on Christmas Day, when I choose each year to be with my elective affinities, my chosen family, the people who make it possible in the world for me to be all of me and to continue to speak my truth. Just because these events and locales are more privatized does not mean that they are not doing important institution-building work. Every time we gather, every time we insist on the non-novelty of our particular subjectivities, every time we refuse to be silenced by the dictates of some prescribed norms, we are chipping away at the exclusions and exclusivities in our world and exposing them for what they are—forms of power and control that aid and abet racist and heterosexist ways of thinking, imagining others, and controlling others.

Part I   Queer Black Thought

1 Straight Black Studies

I speak for the thousands, perhaps hundreds of thousands of men who live and die in the shadows of secrets, unable to speak of the love that helps them endure and contribute to the race. Their ordinary kisses of sweet spit and loyalty are scrubbed away by the propaganda makers of the race, the "talented Tenth" . . .

The Black homosexual is hard pressed to gain audience among his heterosexual brothers; even if he is more talented, he is inhibited by his silence or his admissions. This is what the race has depended on in being able to erase homosexuality from our recorded history. The "chosen" history. But the sacred constructions of silence are futile exercises in denial. We will not go away with our issues of sexuality. We are coming home.

It is not enough to tell us that one was a brilliant poet, scientist, educator, or rebel. Whom did he love? It makes a difference. I can't become a whole man simply on what is fed to me: watered-down versions of Black life in America. I need the ass-splitting truth to be told, so I will have something pure to emulate, a reason to remain loyal.

—Essex Hemphill, *Ceremonies*

The sexual question and the racial question have always been entwined, you know. If Americans can mature on the level of racism, then they have to mature on the level of sexuality.

—James Baldwin, *Conversations with James Baldwin*

This chapter is in large measure descriptive in its efforts to account for a phenomenon that has been part of African Americanist discourse for as long as the study of African Americans has been of any public and institutional significance—that is, its heterosexist strain. It is also, in part, analytical, due to its efforts to describe this phenomenon by attempting to provide a usable past for black queer studies. I begin by framing its concerns with a brief interpretive gloss of Essex Hemphill's remarks in the above epigraph. From there, I move to consider the motivations of the heterosexist strain inherent in much of African Americanist discourse. This leads me to a brief reading of James Baldwin's *Giovanni's Room* as a text that provides both a challenge to traditional modes of analysis for African American literary production and suggests a broadening of what African Americanist critique might mean. This suggested broadening leads me to a consideration of the critical sensibility we have come to call black queer studies, with some attention paid to the challenges it poses to dominant constructions of African American studies as an institutional formation.

In the above epigraph, taken from Essex Hemphill's short but strident personal essay, "Loyalty," included in his book *Ceremonies*, Hemphill aptly describes not only the predicament of the black homosexual in dominant articulations of the African American community, but also goes far toward metaphorically describing the relationship of black queer identity to dominant articulations of the proper object of the analysis that has congress under the rubric of African American studies—that is, a race-centered understanding of blackness, in Hemphill's words, "riddled with omissions" (70). Indeed, elsewhere have I seldom witnessed such a fierce insistence on the impossibility of disarticulating race and sexuality as Hemphill provides in this essay. Journalistic in tone, laced with a poet's diction and phrasing, shockingly sexual, unapologetic about the centrality of sexual pleasure, politically strident (even bordering on sermonic), and all under the mockingly simple title "Loyalty"—Hemphill's essay is keen to demonstrate how the very models of intervention into racial discrimination at the heart of the analysis represented by African American studies are themselves committed to the flattening out of (if not the evisceration of) queers or queer sexuality and the challenges they pose to the heterosexist construct that is "the African American community."

Consider for a moment the rhetoric of Hemphill's essay itself: "We will not go away with our issues of sexuality. We are coming home." This rhetorical construction depends upon the separation of black gays and lesbians from the location of "home," which he posits they are "coming home to." This rendering of home as a site of contestation—as opposed to the "welcome table" or "comforting" characterization of home associated with the most dominant, public, and politically salient renderings of the African American community—signals the terms of the relationship of black queer subjectivity to African American identity for Hemphill. Indeed, "home" (a term to which I will return later) is the very nexus that has to be rethought. For Hemphill, nothing less than the "ass-splitting truth" will give him something "pure to emulate, a reason to remain loyal." In this appeal for a reason to remain loyal, the writer simultaneously recognizes the political need for the grand unifying category of "the African American community" even as he presses (to the very threat of disloyalty) for a more inclusive version of it.

Also noteworthy in Hemphill's essay is the sarcasm with which he represents "the propaganda makers of the race, the 'Talented Tenth'":

> Men emasculated in the complicity of not speaking out, rendered mute by the middle-class aspirations of a people trying hard to forget the shame and cruelties of slavery and ghettos. Through denials and abbreviated histories riddled with omissions, the middle class sets about whitewashing and fixing up the race to impress each other *and* the racists who don't give a damn. (70)

In reading this essay, I feel not altogether unlike Farah Griffin who, in the course of her search for a usable past for black feminism, arrived at her critical investigation of the sexism of W. E. B. Du Bois (a recognized early male proponent of black feminism).[1] For Hemphill, surely one of the great progenitors of black queer studies, is not without his own limitations, either. Two features of Hemphill's complaint stand out in this regard: 1) the exclusivity (or specificity) of his complaint is made on behalf of gay black men, with no explicit recognition of black lesbians, and 2) the way in which he locates the black middle class as the bearers of the ideology or politics of black respectability fails to recognize the dissemination of such ideology beyond the boundaries of that strict class construction. Still, black respectability can be said to be not only at the heart of Hemphill's critique of the African American community's conservatism, but also—as my coeditors and I argue in our 2002 literature anthology, *Black Like Us: A Century of Lesbian, Gay and Bi-Sexual African American Fiction*—at the heart a usable past for black queer studies as one of the primary objects of its analysis.[2]

For our purposes, Kali Gross, following the work of Evelyn Brooks Higgenbotham, characterizes black respectability in the following manner:

> Historically, as a form of resistance to the negative stigmas and caricatures about their morality, African Americans adopted a "politics of respectability." Claiming respectability through manners and morality furnished an avenue for African Americans to assert the will and agency to redefine themselves outside the prevailing racist discourses. Although many deployed the politics of respectability as a form of resistance, its ideological nature constituted a deliberate concession to mainstream societal values. The self-imposed adherence to respectability that permeated African American women's lives, as well as African American culture, also later impacted African American activism and the course of scholarship in African American Studies. This strict adherence to what is socially deemed "respectable" has resulted in African American scholars' confining their scholarship on African Americans to often the most "heroic," and the most successful, attributes in African American culture; it has also resulted in the proliferation of analyses which can be characterized as culturally defensive, patriarchal, and heterosexist.[3]

Indeed, the politics of black respectability, understood in this way, can be seen as laying the foundation for the necessary disavowal of black queers in dominant representations of the African American community, African American history, and African American studies.

This chapter, then, represents a set of concerns about the related state of African American studies, the state of Baldwin scholarship, the complicated relationship Baldwin exhibits to identity politics, and how that complexity presages the need for a critical sensibility I align with black queer studies. Indeed, we are in a moment now when this critical sensibility called black queer studies is self-consciously in search of a usable past to define and clarify the significance of its arrival onto the scene in its current incarnation. This is evidenced by a proliferation of recent work produced at the margins of race and sexuality. Its most self-conscious manifestations to date, perhaps, come in the form of the extraordinary Black Queer Studies conference organized by E. Patrick Johnson and Mae G. Henderson at UNC–Chapel Hill in April 2000 (and a volume of essays coedited by Johnson and Henderson that is being published as a result of that event), as well as a special issue of the journal *Callaloo,* coedited by Jennifer Brody and myself titled "Plum Nelly: New Essays in Black Queer Studies," which was launched at that same historic conference. After the Black Nations/Queer Nations conference held in New York City in 1995, the UNC conference represents the single most significant gathering of this kind to take place in the country.[4]

In my treatment of Baldwin to follow, I do not want to suggest that there have not been figures other than Baldwin who might serve as models in our search for a usable past for black queer studies. Quite the contrary, this is more of a call to further work, further intervention into and interpretation of the past of black queer studies and of the object of its analysis. In fact, one colleague responding to an earlier version of this essay usefully suggested that by moving my discussion beyond Baldwin to the generation of writers preceding him (Hughes, Locke, McKay), I might avoid essentializing black gay subjectivity.[5] My colleague's concern took me back to the process of conceptualizing *Black Like Us* with my coeditors, as we worked to construct a narrative for the tradition of queer African American literature (a term about which there will doubtless be much more dissent and drama—evidenced already in the process of obtaining permissions to reprint excerpts from certain living writers and the estates of certain dead writers who have had problems with the book's subtitle).[6] We decided that the important distinction we wanted to make with Baldwin as a kind of transition figure from that earlier generation of writers in our narrative of this literary tradition was in marking Baldwin as the first "openly gay" black writer. That is, he was the first to talk publicly about his homosexuality and purposefully to make use of it in his fiction. In an interview from the latter years of his life (captured in Karen Thorsen's 1989 documentary *James Baldwin: The Price of the Ticket*), when asked to reflect upon why he chose so early on to write *Giovanni's Room* given that he was already dealing with the burden of being a black writer in America, Baldwin's response is instructive:

> Well, one could say almost that I did not have an awful lot of choice. *Giovanni's Room comes out* of something that tormented and frightened me— the question of my own sexuality. It also simplified my life in another way because it meant that *I had no secrets,* nobody could blackmail me. You know . . . you didn't tell me, I told you. [My emphasis.]

This is not the same, of course, as saying that Baldwin embraced gay sexuality as associated with the gay liberation movement, to which he had a rather complicated relationship. Still his public "outing" of himself we regard as significant not only to the development of this particularized tradition of queer African American fiction, but also as posing a challenge to dominant, respectable, sanitized narratives of the African American literary tradition and what it can include.

My claim, in this regard, is, perhaps, finally a modest one: that the state of critical discourse which proceeds under the rubric of African American studies, with its narrow-minded embrace of a race-centered identity bias, does so at the expense of other critical forms of difference that are also rightly constitutive of any inclusive understanding of black subjectivity. Perhaps one of the clearest challenges to this kind of thinking that privileges "race" (specifically here racial blackness) as the logos of African American studies can be witnessed in the example of James Baldwin's life and work—and particularly in his second novel, *Giovanni's Room*. Through a brief consideration of Baldwin's relationship to questions of identity (both his own and his representations of it), we will come to see that his logic is emblematic of long-silent but real complexities and challenges to dominant constructions of the field of African American studies itself.

Given the advent of cultural studies in the academy—with its focus on interdisciplinarity or transdisciplinarity, critical theory, and an ever-broadening notion of "culture"—it seems more possible today than ever before to engage a prophetic Baldwin in all the complexity he represents to critical inquiry by considering the various roles he has occupied. Baldwin was no more content to be simply a black writer, a gay writer, or an activist than he was to write exclusively in the genre of the novel, drama, poetry, or the essay. And the topoi of his work and the landscape of his critical and creative imagination are broad, to say the very least.

Scholarship, however, has often tended to relegate Baldwin to one or the other of these identities, rather than moving our thinking—not only of Baldwin but of African American studies generally—in a direction that speaks to the intricate social positions African Americans occupy. This is largely because the trend in scholarship itself—prior to the advent of cultural studies—was ostensibly to identify a particular theme, a category, or a political ideology at work in a text or across an oeuvre in order to fix that variable as part of the process of examining the work in question. Neither Baldwin's life nor his work is easily given over to such an approach. Try following, for example, the deployment of a single idea like "home" or "nothingness" in the context of *Giovanni's Room* (as Kathleen Drowne does in her recent essay "'An Irrevocable Condition': Constructions of Home and the Writing of Place in *Giovanni's Room*") and one begins immediately to perceive the difficulty of reading Baldwin in such a manner. Ideas, even in the realm of his imaginative representations, are rarely static for him. Rather, they are drawn to reflect the complex experience of these ideas in our lives. This represents, perhaps, one of the reasons that the critical legacy on Baldwin's work has been relatively sparse, when viewed in proportion to his voluminous contribution to African American letters.

That is not to say that Baldwin "the man" has not been of great interest, nor that he has not appeared often in epigraphic and aphoristic ways. Baldwin's words have been used in the work of film directors ranging from Marlon Riggs to Spike Lee, alluded to and cited in popular black gay fiction of the likes of James Earl Hardy's *B-Boy Blues,* and quoted by notable African American cultural critics and race men of the likes of Henry Louis Gates Jr. and Cornel West. Still, what has gone missing is sustained, critical engagement with Baldwin's content in the thoroughly active way that the criticism has continued to engage Richard Wright, for example. This is a point that echoes with more than a little déjà vu, since a similar claim was forwarded by Trudier Harris in her groundbreaking study *Black Women in the Fiction of James Baldwin.* In 1985 Harris wrote:

On occasion I was surprised to discover that a writer of Baldwin's reputation evoked such vague memories from individuals in the scholarly community, most of whom maintained that they had read one or more of his fictional works. When I began a thorough examination of Baldwin scholarship, however, some of that reaction became clearer. Baldwin seems to be read at times for the sensationalism readers anticipate in his work, but his treatment in scholarly circles is not commensurate to that claim to sensationalism or to his more solidly justified literary reputation. It was discouraging, therefore, to think that one of America's best-known writers, and certainly one of its best known black writers, has not attained a more substantial place in the scholarship on Afro-American writers.

It is interesting to observe that in 1985 Harris could still note with authority her supposition that many read Baldwin for the "sensationalism" he and his work represented. What Harris starts to recognize here implicitly I want to be more explicit about. That is, Baldwin was read in part because for his exceptionalism, aberrance, difference from other black writers. Baldwin provided a generation of African American and non–African American readers alike with characters who were racialized, sexualized, and class inflected in complex ways; so much so that at times, in Baldwin, a reader almost yearns for an overdetermined, naturalistic protagonist like Richard Wright's "Bigger Thomas" that one can hold on to. But perhaps this point only arcs toward a larger one that will need to be fleshed out in a longer-term research project that would address the larger question of the relationship between African American literary criticism and the state and progress of racialized discourse in America over time.[7] I say all this here simply to make the point that cultural studies work and black queer studies work has shown that it is possible to think critically about African Americans and African American culture without simply essentializing the category of racial blackness, appealing to outmoded and problematic notions of an authentic blackness, or fixing, reifying, or separating race, gender, and sexuality in the name of their political serviceability to racial blackness. With the advent of cultural studies, it seems finally possible to understand Baldwin's vision of and for humanity in its complexity, locating him not as exclusively gay, black, expatriate, activist, or the like, but as an intricately negotiated amalgam of all of those things, which had to be constantly tailored to fit the circumstances in which he was compelled to articulate himself. The transdisciplinary quality of the intellectual work most closely associated with cultural studies has made it possible for those open to its lessons and trained in African American studies to arrive at a critical sensibility—the emergent black queer studies—that can begin the difficult process of thinking about the ways in which race and sexuality are so deeply imbricated.[8]

I want to suggest first—following a reading that is taken from an essay of mine first published in *Callaloo* in 1998 titled "Can the Queen Speak?"—that although Baldwin's work challenges static notions of racial identity, his awareness of the hegemony of the category of race in black anti-racist discourse nevertheless limits the terms of his possible identifications with his gay sexuality. And second, I want to briefly sketch a reading of *Giovanni's*

Room that suggests that it is Baldwin's understanding of these same identifi-catory limits that necessitate the whiteness of the characters in that novel, for reasons having to do with its broad, forward-looking, prophetic project.

Let us begin with the following question: What happens discursively when a gay black man takes up the mantle of race discourse? In Thorsen's 1989 documentary of Baldwin's life, there are at least two moments to which I want to call attention by way of addressing this question. The first is a state-ment made by Amiri Baraka, and the second is a statement made by Baldwin himself from television interview footage. I turn to these less literally textual examples to demonstrate that in our more casual or less scripted moments, our subconscious understanding of the realities of race discourse is laid bare even more clearly.

Baraka's regard for Baldwin is well documented by the film. He talks about how Baldwin was "in the tradition" and how his early writings, specifically *Notes of a Native Son,* really impacted him and spoke to a whole generation. In an attempt to describe or account for Baldwin's homosexuality, however, Baraka falters in his efforts to unite the racially significant image of Baldwin that he clings to with the homosexual Baldwin. Baraka states the following:

> Jimmy Baldwin was neither in the closet about his homosexuality, nor was he running around proclaiming homosexuality. I mean, he was what he was. And you either had to buy that or, you know, *mea culpa,* go some-where else.

The poles of the rhetorical continuum that Baraka sets up here for his un-derstanding of homosexuality are very telling. To Baraka's mind, one can ei-ther be in the closet or "running around proclaiming homosexuality" (the image of the effete gay man and the gay activist collide here, it would seem). What makes Baldwin acceptable to enter the pantheon of race men for Baraka is the fact that his sexual identity is unlocatable. It is neither here nor there, or perhaps it is everywhere at once, leaving the entire question unde-cided and undecidable. And if Baldwin is undecided about his sexual iden-

tity, the one identity to which he seems firmly committed is his racial identity. The rhetorical ambiguity around his sexual identity, according to
Baraka, is what makes it possible for Baldwin to be a race man who was "in
the tradition."

Baldwin himself, it seems, was well aware of the dangers of—indeed, the
"price of the ticket" for—trying to synthesize his racial and sexual identities.
He understood that his efficacy as race man was—at least in part—depend-
ent on limiting his public activism to racial politics. The frame of the documentary certainly confirms this in the way it represents Baldwin's own response to his sexuality. Baldwin states:

> I think the trick is to say yes to life. . . . It is only we of the twentieth cen-
> tury who are so obsessed with the particular details of anybody's sex life.
> I don't think those details make a difference. And I will never be able to
> deny a certain power that I have had to deal with, which has dealt with
> me, which is called love; and love comes in very strange packages. I've
> loved a few men; I've loved a few women; and a few people have loved
> me. That's . . . I suppose that's all that's saved my life.

It may be of interest to note that while he is making this statement, the camera pans down to Baldwin's hands, which are fidgeting with the cigarette and
cigarette holder. This move on the part of the camera undercuts the veracity
of Baldwin's statement here and suggests that Baldwin himself does not quite
believe all that he is saying.[9]

If Baldwin's statement here raises the complications of speaking from a
complex racial/sexual identity location, the following excerpt from a television interview on the *Dick Cavett Show* illustrates this point all the more
clearly:

> I don't know what most white people in this country feel, but I can only
> conclude what they feel from the state of their institutions. I don't know if
> white Christians hate Negroes or not, but I know that we have a Christian

church which is white and a Christian church which is black. . . . I don't know if the board of education hates black people, but I know the text-books they give my children to read and the schools that we go to. Now this is the evidence! You want me to make an act of faith risking myself, my wife, my woman, my sister, my children on some idealism which you assure me exists in America which I have never seen.

This passage is conspicuous for the manner in which Baldwin assumes the voice of representative race man—a category Hazel Carby complicates in her recent book.[10] In the very last sentence, when Baldwin affects the position of race man, part of the performance includes the masking of his specificity, his sexuality, his difference. And in black anti-racist discourse, when all differ-ence is concealed, what emerges is the heterosexual black man "risking [him-self], [his] wife, [his] woman and [his] children." The image of the black man as protector, progenitor, and defender of the race is what Baldwin assumes here. The truth of this rhetorical transformation is that in order to be a rep-resentative race man, one must be both heterosexual and male.[11] Again, it is not my intention to fault Baldwin for this move, but rather to say that even with his own recognition of the politics of his circumstances, he does find ways to mount a counter-discourse (usually through his fiction) to such ex-clusive racial identity constructions.

Now let me turn briefly to *Giovanni's Room* to elaborate further on the character of Baldwin's counter-discourse in this regard. Baldwin makes plain a logic in 1957 that has come to be a received part of public discourse about homosexuality in America today. That is, one of the reasons that people fear queer sexuality so violently is that it threatens an ideology in America even older and stronger than baseball or apple pie—it threatens the idea of "home." This is what Baldwin understands and presages so well in *Giovanni's Room* through the representation of the complexity of David's character, drawn as he is at the crossroads of nationality (Americanness), sexuality (ho-mosexuality, or at least bisexuality), and home (place and social responsibil-ity/respectability). In order that the themes of this work might be (to use for a moment an ugly word) "universalized," Baldwin knew enough about how race worked, and continues to work, in America to know that it was impossible to use black characters. In a letter (dated January 1954) to William Cole (the editor who first brought Baldwin and *Go Tell It on the Mountain* to the attention of Knopf), Baldwin himself wrote the following words about *Giovanni's Room* shortly after he had begun working on it:[12]

> It's a great departure for me; and it makes me rather nervous. It's not about Negroes first of all; its locale is the American colony in Paris. What is really delicate about it is that since I want to convey something about the kinds of American loneliness, I must use the most ordinary type of American I can find—the good, white Protestant is the kind of image I want to use. This is precisely the type of American about whose setting I know the least. Whether this will be enough to create a real human being, only time will tell. It's a love story—short, and wouldn't you know it, tragic. Our American boy comes to Europe, finds something, loses it, and in his acceptance of his loss becomes, to my mind, heroic.

Here we see, among other things, that only whiteness is sufficient to represent large, broad, "universal" concerns. To Baldwin's mind, black characters—in their always overdrawn specificity—could only represent in the 1950s popular imagination the problems specific to blacks and are therefore easily dismissed as irrelevant beyond those confines. Marlon Ross puts the entire business of the whiteness of the characters in *Giovanni's Room* somewhat differently, though along similar lines of thought, when he writes:

> If the characters had been black, the novel would have been read as being "about" blackness, whatever else it happened actually to be about. The whiteness of the characters seems to make invisible the question of how race or color has, in fact, shaped the characters—at least as far as most readers have dealt with the novel.

Ross continues:

> In other words, Baldwin revises W. E. B. Du Bois's question "How does it
> feel to be a problem?" For Baldwin, it is not "the strange meaning of
> being black" that is the "problem of the Twentieth Century," nor even
> "the problem of the color-line." Baldwin makes the central problem of
> the twentieth century the strange meaning of being white, as a structure
> of feeling within the self and within history—a structure of felt experi-
> ence that motivates and is motivated by other denials. In *Giovanni's
> Room,* he posits the white man as a problem and then fantasizes what it
> might mean for a particular upperclass white man to become aware of the
> problematic nature of his desire—color not as "line" of demarcation but
> instead as a point of departure. Given the invisibility of whiteness as a
> racially constricted burden of desire, however, Baldwin also shows how
> even the most deeply taboo and widely outlawed desire can be cushioned
> by the privileged invisibility of whiteness.[13]

It is important to note that Ross's essay, while it does not go so far as to make
this claim explicitly, does imply that Baldwin's novel may be among the possible progenitors of another field of inquiry that has gained a lot of attention
in the last little more than a decade—that is, whiteness studies.

Giovanni's Room is not a novel about gay sexuality as much as it is a novel
about the social and discursive forces that make gay sexuality a "problem."
Even in this context, however, Baldwin does not sacrifice the complexity of
the social and discursive forces involved in this process. Everywhere in *Giovanni's Room* national identity, for example, is sexualized. Consider the following scene from David's visit to the American Express office in Paris, and
how he describes the Americans:

> *At home,* I could have distinguished patterns, habits, accents of speech—
> with no effort whatever: *now* everybody sounded, unless I listened hard,
> as though they had just arrived from Nebraska. At *home* I could have seen

the clothes they were wearing, but *here* I only saw bags, cameras, belts, and hats, all clearly from the same department store. *At home* I would have had a sense of the individual womanhood of the woman I faced; here the most ferociously accomplished seemed to be involved in some ice-cold or sun-dried travesty of sex, and even grandmothers seemed to have no traffic with the flesh. And what distinguished the men was that they seemed incapable of age; they smelled of soap, which seemed indeed to be their preservative against the dangers and exigencies of any more intimate odor; the boy he had been shone, somehow, unsoiled, untouched, unchanged, through the eyes of the man of sixty, booking passage with a smiling wife, to Rome. (118) [My emphasis.]

David sees these Americans abroad in the new light of the foreigner's eye. The language he invokes to characterize them is not dissimilar in tone from the language Giovanni will later use to describe David in the heat of their final argument in the novel. Especially noteworthy here is the claim that Americans preserve a kind of innocence that has "no traffic with the flesh." Part of David's dilemma throughout the novel is that he views sexual identity as in need of domestication so that it can be turned into "home" (witness his despair about "wandering" [84], his "sorrow," "shame," "panic," and "great bitterness" about the "beast Giovanni had awakened in him" [110–11]).[14] This sense of home, fixity, stability—represented in the novel by America and his father—comes through most clearly in his father's letter to David where we learn of his (surely tongue-in-cheek) nickname, Butch. The father writes:

Dear Butch . . . aren't you ever coming home? Don't think I'm only being selfish but its true I'd like to see you. I think you have been away long enough, God knows I don't know what you're doing over there, and you don't write enough for me even to guess. But my guess is you're going to be sorry one of these fine days that you stayed over there, looking at your navel, and let the world pass you by. There's nothing over there for you.

You're as American as pork and beans, though maybe you don't want to think so anymore.

David's father's obsession is, in part, with time. Again, this is an obsession that Giovanni identifies as very American. To David's father's mind, if David is not being a man of action (and in accordance with a rather predetermined heteronormative script, at that), then he is wasting time, wandering. Wandering is an important theme in *Giovanni's Room*. Wandering, or lack of focus, is associated with wayward sexualities (Hella in Spain, David with Giovanni). It is dangerous. David queries at one of the moments when he faces the fear of his sexuality: "The beast which Giovanni had awakened in me would never go to sleep again . . . would I then, like all the others, find myself turning and following all kinds of boys, down God knows what dark avenues, into what dark places?" (111). Gay sexuality in the novel points up desire's ability to be unfocused. This lack of focus is ultimately one of the biggest threats to heterosexuality (in a world where heterosexuality = focus). Hearth, home, and heteronormative pairings are all impossible without the sexual focus they presuppose in the form of monogamous heterosexual coupling.

David's desire for Hella represents his desire for the idea of "home." Consider the scene when they are reunited at the train station in Paris:

I had hoped that when I saw her something instantaneous, definitive, would have happened in me, something to make me know where I should be and where I was. But nothing happened . . .

Then I took her in my arms and something happened then. I was terribly glad to see her. It really seemed with Hella in the circle of my arms, that my arms were home and I was welcoming her back there. She fitted in my arms as she always had, and the shock of holding her caused me to feel that my arms had been empty since she had been away. (158–59)

If home = heterosexuality = nationhood, then it is David's desire to fulfill the heteronormative narrative laid out for him as his American birthright that he recognizes in Hella. Indeed, the lure of it is so strong in this moment that it has the force—even if only for the moment—of erasing any and all of David's prior wayward sexual exploits. He felt as if his "arms had been empty since she had been away." Again, I want to suggest that a rather complicated relationship between home, nation, and sexuality (that I do not sort out completely here) is represented in the text and bears further consideration.

From the time we begin to hear David's story, he is, to the logic of his mind, already in trouble: an American in Paris, exiled, unfocused, wandering. David is plagued, not simply by some nebulous ideology about gay sexuality, but by the complex set of responses that arise when the young American man comes up against the overwhelming weight of what is expected of him in the world. This is the drama that drives David's psychological angst in the narrative. Giovanni names it in the final argument between the two of them in this exchange:

[David] "All this love you talk about—isn't it just that you want to be made to feel strong? You want to go out and be the big laborer and bring home the money, and you want me to stay here and wash the dishes and cook the food and clean this miserable closet of a room and kiss you when you come in through that door and lie with you at night and be your little *girl* . . . that's all you mean when you say you love me. You say I want to kill *you*. What do you think you've been doing to me?"

"I am not trying to make you a little girl. If I wanted a little girl, I would be *with* a little girl."

"Why aren't you? Isn't it just that you're afraid? And you take *me* because you haven't got the guts to go after a woman, which is what you *really* want?"

He was pale. "You are the one who keeps talking about *what* I want. But I have only been talking about *who* I want." (188–89)

51

The last word is Giovanni's here. David is still trying to explain his feelings, his sexuality in terms of a heteronormative cultural narrative. This is why he is consumed by the "what" (ideological forces), whereas, Giovanni—unhampered by such concerns—is focused on "who" he loves (David) and not on what it means.

This moment should remind us of one earlier in the same argument between Giovanni and David, when Giovanni first ruminates on why David is leaving him:

> "Giovanni," I said, "you always knew that I would leave one day. You knew my fiancée was coming back to Paris."
>
> "You are not leaving me for her," he said. " . . . You are not leaving me for a *woman*. If you were really in love with that little girl, you would not have to be so cruel to me."
>
> "She's not a little girl," I said. "She's a woman and no matter what you think, I *do* love her—"
>
> "You do not," cried Giovanni, sitting up, "love anyone! You have never loved anyone, I am sure you never will! You love your purity, you love your mirror—you are just like a little virgin, you walk around with your hands in front of you as though you had some precious metal, gold, silver, rubies, maybe diamonds down there between your legs! You will never let anybody touch it—man or woman. You want to be clean. You think you came here covered with soap and you think you will go out covered with soap—and you do not want to stink, not even for five minutes, in the meantime . . . You want to leave Giovanni because he makes you stink. You want to despise Giovanni because he is not afraid of the stink of love. You want to kill him in the name of all your lying little moralities." (186–87)

The very thing Baldwin extols here in Giovanni by contrast to David (i.e., David's obsession with being pure and clean—rendered, by association, as a very American desire complicated by his nationality in the novel) is what characterizes the topoi of Baldwin's work and art. He did not care for purity. Rather, he wallowed in the dirt of the unclean places of the psyche, the cluttered rooms where life—for him—really happened. David—not unlike the representations of an institutionalized African American studies—represents the pitfalls and suffering of a life lived in observance of the rules about what we should be, how we should love, indeed, what we should feel. While the price exacted on Giovanni for the choice to live freely in defiance of social order is high, it seems to receive Baldwin's ultimate approbation. While, on the other hand, David, though he lives, is the one who represents a more profound death—indeed, an emotional death he must live with.

As a novel with no African American characters, written by an African American, gay writer, *Giovanni's Room* itself challenges dominant understandings of what constitutes African American literature, the work that proceeds under the rubric of African American literary criticism, and the forms of analysis that would come to have congress under the institutional formation of African American studies. Given the novel's unusual status, it seems to me somewhat prophetic in its call for a criticism, a way of thinking, a critical sensibility that would not arrive on the scene until many years after its publication in 1956. In this regard, Baldwin's novel perhaps represents one of the early direct calls for a more textured conceptualization of the kind of complex formulations necessary in artistic production, criticism, and discourse to truly address anything that approximates the richness and complexity of that most politically essential and politically irksome appellation, "the African American community."

In an essay in a December 2000 issue of the *Chronicle of Higher Education,* historian Nell Irvin Painter had occasion to reflect on the state of African American studies:

> After more than a quarter-century in academe, including a couple of stints as the director of a program in African-American studies and countless conversations with colleagues around the country, I have reached

some conclusions regarding black faculty members and black studies. First, black studies: The time is right for a reassessment of the field. Last year several prominent departments and programs in African-American/Afro-American/black studies celebrated their 30th anniversaries—including Cornell University, Harvard University, the University of California at Berkeley, and my own Princeton University. (The pioneering department at San Francisco State University was founded three years earlier than those others.) Second, black faculty members: Our numbers remain small, although not inconsequential. Finally, both black studies and black faculty members, often seen in countless academic minds as kindred phenomena, still face familiar frustrations. For the widespread American assumption that black people are not intellectual affects everyone in higher education who is black or who does black studies. (B7)

It is not the particular claims that Painter makes in her essay that concern me here. Indeed, her remarks are not only sound but ring very true as a description of black faculty and of black studies in the contemporary academy. Still, what fascinates me most about this piece for our purposes is the mode in which African American studies is presented by Painter, whose perspective is quite representative of the state of African Americanist discourse. The entire article focuses on the institutional problems African American studies faced in its inception, and how many of those problems continue to plague such departments and programs in the academy to this very day. Painter's discourse represents African American studies as embattled institutionally and, once again, identifies the primacy of that crisis as one of race to the extent that the fundamental problem for her is still how "the widespread assumption that black people are not intellectual affects everyone in higher education who is black or who does black studies" (B7). Setting up her examination of African American studies in this way, Painter's remarks necessarily center on how an embattled African American studies has to respond to the racist forces of institutions that resist its presence in a variety of ways. And, indeed, in this regard Painter's rhetorical strategy is not unique but can be seen as rather representative. What this strategy does not allow, however, is space for an analysis or a critique of the internal structure and strictures of the race-based discourse of African American studies itself, which, of course, underlies and animates Painter's representation of the field. That is, Painter's reflections not only come short of addressing the limitations of the exclusionary race-based thinking necessitated when institutional location is the primary rhetorical concern for African American studies, such rhetoric often works to blind us to such realities.

Admittedly, this has much to do with the discursive history of African American studies in white academic institutions—that is, in most contexts the question of racial representation (in terms of bodies on campuses and in terms of curricula) was primary to the institutional rise of African American studies. Still, this does not fully address the traditional discursive bias in African American studies for an analysis of black culture, history, life, and politics that centers on racial blackness to the exclusion of other important categories of analysis that rightfully belong to any comprehensive understanding of black people in all our complexity.

In her essay, "Nothing Fails Like Success," Barbara Johnson discusses the discursive impact of the rise of the now-famed deconstructionism in the academy in relation to the rhetoric of "success." Her example is instructive to our case here as well. Part of how success gets defined, in terms of the institutional success of an intellectual project in the academy, has to do with its successful integration into a system that may at first have resisted its presence. This could, Johnson maintains, entail a loss of the very radicality of the subject that created the institutional resistance to it to begin with. Johnson puts the matter this way: "As soon as any radically innovative thought becomes an *ism*, its specific groundbreaking force diminishes, its historical notoriety increases, and its disciples tend to become more simplistic, more dogmatic, and ultimately more conservative, at which time its power becomes institutional rather than analytical" (11). Here we should recall Painter's institutional representation of African American studies, alongside the African American literary establishment's inability to adequately (until very recently) address Baldwin's *Giovanni's Room,* as I discussed in the second part of this chapter. Johnson's concerns about the institutionalization of deconstruction illuminate quite well our discussion of African American studies. Though African American studies is not precisely an "ism," it functions institutionally, in terms of its location and its history, much like one. And more importantly, it is based in a fundamental "ism"—"racism"—which has its own troubled past within academia.[15]

Literary and cultural critic Wahneema Lubiano, in her incisive essay, "Mapping the Interstices between Afro-American Cultural Discourse and Cultural Studies: A Prolegomenon," usefully defines "African American studies" as:

> A name for the institutionalization of a set of imperatives, approaches, political engagements, and privileged "interdisciplinariness" as paradigms and sites for counter-hegemonic cultural work. Historically, intellectuals involved in Afro-American Studies have seen their work as explicit and implicit interruptions (or attempts to interrupt) the traditional academic strangleholds on knowledge categories. The object of their interventions is to change the world by means of demystifying the relationship of "knowledge" producers to "knowledge," as well as to foreground the connection between "culture" and Afro-American "everyday life."

Again here with Lubiano, as with Barbara Johnson, there is recognition of the problem inherent in the institutional rise of African American studies. Though the specifics of my claim are not what Lubiano or Johnson had in mind, their work makes this present articulation possible. My claim, again, is that the institutional rise of African American studies necessitated the primacy of race politics with regard to its embattled and contested institutional status. It is often the case that in institutional warfare, so to speak, institutions reduce and simplify the identities of the subjects they interpellate. The political privileging of race politics on the institutional level, in this context, had the effect of privileging the category of race in the intellectual identity of African American studies. This could not help but in great measure to limit the scope and possibility of the knowledge corrective work that proceeded under the banner of African American studies. Seldom did such work allow for diversity in the very idea of, or representation of, black subjectivity. This often led to the collapsing of differences of gender, class, and sexuality into a more homogeneous, hegemonic black subjectivity.

The work I am suggesting that is underway in the emergent field of black queer studies, then, is not so much a return of the repressed as it is another phase in what Lubiano identifies as the "contestatory nature of Afro-American cultural discourse." In a reading of Alain Locke's "The Legacy of the Ancestral Arts" in his time-honored classic *The New Negro,* Lubiano offers the following words, which I hope I may be forgiven for quoting at some length:

> Following the pattern of continual reconstitution of Afro-Americanness established from as varied a group as one could imagine . . . ex-slaves, craftspersons, laborers, intellectuals, political activists, preachers, and the critics of the Harlem Renaissance rewrote African American history in order to rewrite African American identity and to transform the material conditions of African American life. They were interested in scientizing, in specialized professional discourses—something about which some later manifestations of Black Studies (as [Sinclair] Drake, [Johnetta] Cole, and [Lucius] Outlaw above note) would be suspicious, a suspicion embodied in critiques of "objectivity" and other paradigms of Western knowledge. (73–74)

If Lubiano's assessment of the "pattern of continual reconstitution" is true, then the arrival on the scene of black queer studies should neither shock nor surprise. In fact, the work of Baldwin, in the context of such a rendering of the evolution of African American studies, would make his prophetic call for a black queer studies a near inevitability.

It is because of—what I am suggesting is—the insufficiency of a tradi-tional African American studies—evidenced by the arrival onto the scene, in turn and over time, of black feminist critique, black diaspora studies (which addresses the transatlantic or global context of African American studies), and, more recently, black queer studies, which has insisted on bringing home issues of sexuality in an African American studies context—that Baldwin has only in more recent years come into a kind of critical vogue. Baldwin's early work like *Giovanni's Room* posed challenges, as I have already discussed, not only for literary studies, but for what would become black studies and queer studies. The specificity of the challenges posed are now being met by the specificity of the sensibility of black queer studies—located at the porous lim-its of both African American studies and of queer studies.[16] Baldwin's work not only reminds us again and again, but, indeed, insists on the constant rearticulation of the "complexity of racial identities."[17] He reminds us that whenever we are speaking of race, we are always already speaking about gen-der, sexuality, and class.

2 Why I Hate Abercrombie & Fitch

The astronomical growth in the wealth and cultural influence of multi-national corporations over the last fifteen years can arguably be traced back to a single, seemingly innocuous idea developed by management theorists in the mid-1980s: that successful corporations must primarily produce brands, as opposed to products. —Naomi Klein, *No Logo*

The company's [Abercrombie & Fitch's] success depends on the teenager's basic psychological yearning to belong. (Remember, the Columbine shootings happened at a school some reportedly called "Abercrombie High.") And that means more than just selling the right kinds of clothes.
—Lauren Goldstein, "The Alpha Teenager"

Although [Bruce] Weber has drawn upon a style and even content pioneered by [George] Quaintance, he has not fulfilled the promise of the earlier artist. Weber has little compunction about appropriating a style of clearly gay male sensibility, marketing it, but making small but significant changes that deny and repress its historical conditions and antecedents.

This is not all that surprising, for Bear Pond is little more than Bruce Weber advertising, a new form of reactionary art. If the earlier Weber photos were used (explicitly) to sell Mr. Klein's briefs these later photos are peddling a new—post Ronald Reagan, Ed Meese, and Bowers v. Hardwick—version of (gay) male eroticism. . . . Unable to deny the existence of (gay) male sexuality Weber has de-sexualized it and reduced it to obscured indicators and marketed it as free sexual expression.
—Michael Bronski, "Blatant Male Pulchritude: The Art of
George Quaintance and Bruce Weber's *Bear Pond*"

My interest—a polite way of labeling it perhaps—in Abercrombie & Fitch began quite a few years back. It was a rather ordinary weekend night much like countless others where friends and I were out having drinks at a bar (which bar is not important to the story, as will soon become apparent). For the first time, I noticed that easily one-third of the men in the bar were wearing some item of clothing or another that sported the label of "Abercrombie & Fitch," "A&F," or just plain "Abercrombie." I asked one of my friends, "What is Abercrombie & Fitch?" And it was with that—at the time—rather innocent question that my intellectual and political sojourn with Abercrombie began. Once I saw it, I literally could not stop seeing it in any number of the gay spaces that I frequented. Whether I was at home in Chicago or traveling in New York City, Los Angeles, Houston, or Atlanta, in any mainstream gay venue there was sure to be a hefty showing of Abercrombie wear among the men frequenting these establishments. Even at the time of this writing (in the summer of 2003), the trend has only lessened slightly among white men in the U.S. urban gay male scene. Since this label has managed to capture the imagination (to say nothing of the wallets) of young, middle-to-upper-middle-class, white gay men (well at least mostly young—there are some men who are far beyond anything resembling Abercrombie's purported target age demographic of eighteen through twenty-two wearing this stuff; and occasionally one does see gay men of color sporting the brand, though not many), I recognized this trend as a phenomenon about which it might be worth finding out more.

What is it about Abercrombie—especially with its particular practice of explicitly branding its products—that seems to have a lock on this particular population? What is it about the "brand" that they identify with so strongly? What kind of statement are the men sporting this brand in this sexually charged, gay marketplace of desire making to their would-be observers or potential . . . interlocutors? And why is it that the men of color in these same spaces have not taken to this brand with equal fervor? What about the men of color who have? The central question, put somewhat more broadly, might be: what is it that Abercrombie is selling that gay white men seem so desperate to buy in legion?

Let me be extremely clear from the outset that my quarrel with Abercrombie is not of the Corrine Wood variety (she is a former lieutenant governor of Illinois), whose conservative diatribe against the "indecency" of the company's advertising could once be found at her state-sanctioned Web site. Nor is my beef with the company and its marketing strategy to be confused with that of the American Decency Association (ADA). Indeed, I hope never in my life to be associated with anything taking a principled stance on "decency." Quite a lot of that already seems to be going on in the United States these days without much help from the likes of me. If anything, ours is a country that could stand to loosen its puritanical belt a bit and adopt more of a live-and-let-live policy when it comes to human pleasures. Dare I say that we need more of a public discussion about pleasure, a better way of talking without shame in the United States about it—where we seek it out, how it is a great common denominator, how we all (conservatives and liberals alike) want and need it? Such an open dialogue about pleasure might carry us far toward understanding some of the realities of our society, which are currently labeled "vices" and therefore banished from the realm of any "rational" discussion by "decent" people. Upon closer inspection, perhaps some of these so-called vices might be better understood as extensions of our humanity rather than deviations from some idealized form of it. Such a radical approach to conceiving of our humanity, our existence as sexual beings, might go far toward altering the circumstances of those recently much-discussed brothers on the "down low," for example, who have been newly "discovered" in the pages of the *New York Times Magazine* and elsewhere. For I remain convinced that the primary solution to the conditions that lead people to participate in unsafe sexual practices, young gay teens to commit suicide, and cultures of violence to produce and even sanction gay bashings and the like, resides in a loosening of the stranglehold that a puritanical, uncompassionate, intolerant morality (too often masking itself as Christian) has on the

61

neck of our society. So let me set aside the concerns of readers who might lump this critique with those who have cast their lot with the decency police against Abercrombie. My concerns here, I am afraid, go far beyond anything quite so facile or pedestrian.

I begin first with a brief history of the company and the label of Abercrombie & Fitch itself. Second, I want to spend some time discussing the "A&F look," especially as it is exemplified in the *A&F Quarterly*—the sexy quarterly catalog/magazine that has been the source of much controversy among the decency police, the source of great interest among its young target audience and gay men, and the source of capital for serious collectors of the volumes, which sell in some cases for as much as seventy-five dollars on eBay. This last fact my research assistant and I discovered when we began to collect them for the purposes of this book. Third, I consider some aspects of the corporate culture of Abercrombie as it is represented by its stores, managers, and brand reps (as the clerks are called in Abercrombie-speak). This might help provide some insight into the current class action lawsuit that Abercrombie is facing (at the time of this writing) on discrimination charges in their hiring practices. And, finally, I hope to refer back to these points in my analysis of how "Abercrombie" functions as an idea, in order to justify the title claim of this essay in putting forth why it is I hate Abercrombie & Fitch.

The label "Abercrombie & Fitch" dates back to 1892, when David T. Abercrombie opened David T. Abercrombie & Co., a small shop and factory in downtown Manhattan. Abercrombie, born in Baltimore, was himself an engineer, prospector, and committed outdoorsman. His love for the great outdoors was his inspiration for founding Abercrombie & Co., dedicated to producing high-end gear for hunters, fishermen, campers, and explorers. Among his early clientele and devotees was Ezra Fitch, a lawyer who sought adventure hiking in the Adirondacks and fishing in the Catskills. He came to depend upon Abercrombie's goods to outfit him for his excursions. In 1900 Fitch approached Abercrombie about entering into a business partnership with him. By 1904 the shop had relocated to 314 Broadway and was incorporated under the name "Abercrombie & Fitch."

The partnership was uneasy almost from its inception. Both men were headstrong and embraced very different ideas about the company's future. Abercrombie was content to continue to do what they were already doing well—outfitting professional outdoorsmen. Fitch, on the other hand, wanted to expand the business so that they could sell the idea of the outdoors and its delights to the general public. In retrospect, this might have been one of the very earliest cases of big business ideology winning out over small. The result of these feuds was that Abercrombie resigned from the company in 1907.

After his resignation, the company did follow Fitch's vision for its future and expanded into one of the largest purveyors of outdoor gear in the country. Abercrombie & Fitch was no ordinary retail store either. Fitch brought an IKEA-like innovation to the selling and displaying of his goods: stock was displayed as if in use; tents were set up and equipped as if they were in the great outdoors; and the sales staff was made up not of professional salesmen, but of outdoorsmen as well.

By 1913 Abercrombie & Fitch had expanded its inventory once again to include sport clothing. The company maintains that it was the first store in New York to supply such clothing to both women and men. In 1917 Abercrombie & Fitch changed locations once again, this time to a twelve-story building at Madison Avenue and Forty-fifth Street. By this point it had become the largest sporting goods store in the world. At this location, Fitch took the display tactics for which the company was by this time famous to an entirely new level, constructing a log cabin on the roof (which he used as a townhouse), an armored rifle range in the basement, and a golf school in the building. By this time the merchandise the store carried had expanded once again to include such exotic items as hot air balloons, portable trampolines, and yachting pennants, to name but a sampling.

Abercrombie's reputation was so well established by this point that it was known as the outfitter of the rich, famous, and powerful. Abercrombie outfitted Teddy Roosevelt's trips to Africa and the Amazon as well as Robert Peary's famous trip to the North Pole. James Brady recently reminded us in *Advertising Age* that Hem and Wolfie (i.e., Ernest Hemingway and Winston Frederick Churchill Guest) also shopped there. In an article bearing the title "Abercrombie & Fitch Forgets Its Days of Hem and Wolfie," Brady recounts the "real man" glory days of Abercrombie & Fitch while bemoaning the A&F of our day, when the company takes out a double-truck ad in *Rolling Stone* featuring half-naked, boxer-wearing white boys on roller skates sporting backwards baseball caps. The masculine anxiety of that writer's article notwithstanding, he does refer us back to a relevant source in Lillian Ross's 1950 *New Yorker* profile of Hemingway, where one of Hem's shopping trips to Abercrombie is recounted. Other famous early A&F clientele included such notables as Amelia Earhart, Presidents William Howard Taft and John F. Kennedy, Katherine Hepburn, Greta Garbo, Clark Gable, and Cole Porter. And apparently during prohibition, A&F was also a place to buy hip flasks.

It is evident that even in its earliest incarnation, Abercrombie was closely allied with white men (and to a lesser extent white women) of means, the life of the leisure classes, and a Norman Rockwell–like image of life in the United States, for which they were famous even then. It is not surprising that the clothier we know today developed from a company with early roots in exploration, adventure, and cultural tourism, which catered to the white upper classes. The advertising from any of its early catalogs even adopts an innocent, idealistic Rockwellian aesthetic in many instances. It was not long after Abercrombie's resignation in 1907 that the company published its first catalog, which was more than 450 pages long. Some 50,000 copies were shipped to prospective customers around the world. So A&F's legacy of an unabashed consumer celebration of whiteness, and of an elite class of whiteness at that, in the face of a nation whose past and present are riddled with racist ideas, politics, and ideology, is not entirely new. Still, I believe the particular form it has taken in our time bears our careful consideration for the harm that it does to our ways of thinking about and imagining our current racial realities in this country, as well as for the seemingly elusive difficulty it poses in our attempts to understand what about it makes many of us so uneasy.

In 1928 Fitch retired from the business. The company continued to grow and expand well into the 1960s, opening stores in the Midwest and on the West Coast. In the late 1960s, however, the store fell on economic hard times—likely due to the rapid changes in American values associated with that era—and filed for bankruptcy in 1977. The company was bought by Houston, Texas–based Oshman's Sporting Goods. The business continued to decline until Abercrombie was acquired by the Limited, Inc., in 1988. The Limited tried to position the brand as a men's clothing line and later added a preppy women's line under the label as well. These efforts, too, failed, until the Abercrombie makeover began to take shape in earnest under the hand of Michael Jeffries, the current CEO of Abercrombie & Fitch, in 1992. Jeffries was no stranger to the retail world before his arrival at Abercrombie. He had done a stint at then-bankrupt retailer Paul Harris, Inc., had a hand at running his own chain (Alcott & Andrews), and a long run at Federated Department Stores, Inc. After assuming his post with Abercrombie, Jeffries hired his own team of fashion designers. He tapped superstar fashion photographer Bruce Weber (widely known for his Calvin Klein, Ralph Lauren, and Karl Lagerfeld ads) for the playful coed shots on the walls of Abercrombie stores. Weber would go on, of course, to become the photographer for the infamous *A&F Quarterly* as well. The *A&F Quarterly* was launched in 1997 to, as one commentator puts it, "glamorize the hedonistic collegiate lifestyle on which the company built its irreverent brand image." Even the words of the commentator here are extraordinary for how "collegiate" and "irreverent" are conflated in the image of Abercrombie. Indeed, it is testimony to part of A&F's genius that it successfully produced a false radicalism by hitching its label to a "collegiate" lifestyle that is inevitably and overwhelming white and upper middle class. Whatever the case, what we do know is that Abercrombie has been a financial success since 1994, only two years after Jeffries took over and reorganized the brand with his own variety of lifestyle marketing, to which they remain thoroughly committed. In 1998, the year following the launching of the *A&F Quarterly,* Abercrombie spun off from the Limited to become once again an independent, publicly traded company.

Abercrombie & Fitch has devised a very clear marketing and advertising strategy that celebrates whiteness—a particularly privileged and leisure-class whiteness—and makes use of it as a "lifestyle" that it commodifies to sell otherwise extremely dull, uninspiring, and ordinary clothing. I am not, by the way, the first commentator to recognize this fact about the clothes themselves. The danger of such a marketing scheme is that it depends upon the racist thinking of its consumer population in order to thrive. Anyone familiar with the rise of the company and its label in recent years recognizes that it has done precisely that.

Abercrombie has worked hard to produce a brand strongly associated with a young, white, upper-class, leisure lifestyle. Nowhere is this more evident than in the *A&F Quarterly.* Since, however, I could not bring myself to ask for, only to be denied, permission to use photographs from those pages in this book, or to participate in a vicious cycle of perpetuating the lure of those images by repeating them here, I leave it to my reader to seek them out, as they relate to this analysis. They are readily available online and in any number of media venues. Instead, I would like to consider in some detail a document where the A&F look gets perhaps it clearest articulation: the *Abercrombie Look Book: Guidelines for Brand Representatives of Abercrombie & Fitch* (revised August 1996).

Affectionately known in the everyday corporate parlance of Abercrombie as the *Look Book,* this pocket-size (3.5 x 5.5–inch and approximately 30-page-long) book devotes equal time to images and text. The book contains twelve images—all photographs of model brand representatives, save one sketch (which we will come to later). Four of the eleven photos (including the cover) are group shots; the remaining ones feature individual models. Of the group shots, two include the one African American model (or even visible person of color) in these pages, while all of the rest of the photos are of male and female models who appear to be white. All of the models also appear to be solidly within Abercrombie's stated target age group of eighteen through twenty-two, and they all appear in the photographs smiling and often in various states of repose. The book divides neatly into five sections: an introductory section, which addresses the relationship between the brand representative and the A&F look; a section entitled "Our Past," which gives a brief history of the company; a section called "Our Present"; followed by an "Our Future" section; and then finally the longest section (making up more than half the book) on "The A&F Look" (with subsections titled "Discipline," "Personal Appearance," and "Exceptions"). I provide such detail so that the reader will have an image of this book as an object, as well as a sense of its formal content.

The *Look Book* begins thus:

Exhibiting the "A&F Look" is a tremendously important part of the overall experience at the Abercrombie & Fitch Stores. We are selling an experience for our customer; an energized store environment creates an atmosphere that people want to experience again and again. The combination of our Brand Representatives' style and our Stores Visual Presentation has brought brand recognition across the country.

Our people in the store are an inspiration to the customer. The customer sees the natural Abercrombie style and wants to be like the Brand Representative . . .

Our Brand is natural, classic and current, with an emphasis on style. This is what a Brand Representative must be; this is what a Brand Representative must represent in order to fulfill the conditions of employment. [Emphases appear as they do in the *Look Book*.]

The book continues in much the same vein, touting the virtues of the ideal brand representative. In the approximately seventeen pages of text in the book, the word "natural," for example, appears as a descriptor no fewer than fourteen times. In this regard, it is closely followed by its companion terms "American" and "classic" to account for what the book identifies alternately as the "A&F look" and the "A&F style." Such words in the context not only of Abercrombie, but in the context of U.S. culture more broadly, are often understood for the coded ways of delineating the whiteness that they represent. Indeed, most of us carry in our imagination a very specific image that we readily access when such monikers as "natural, classic, American" are used. That image is not likely of the Native American, who has far more historic claim to such signifiers than those whom we have learned to associate with them. This fact, I think, speaks volumes about the incredible and abiding ideological feat that we encounter in the whiteness of the idea of "America" and of "the American."

Indeed, citizenship in the United States touches upon matters of social identity, including race and gender. While the dominant rhetoric of our national identity presents a color-blind, "united-we-stand," Horatio Alger narrative of upward mobility, in reality, citizenship is raced, gendered, and classed, and the original texts that define citizenship and national identity in the United States reflect this reality. UC Berkeley ethnic studies professor Evelyn Nakano Glenn touches upon one aspect of American ideological citizenship when she discusses the importance of whiteness and autonomy in contrast with non-whiteness, subservience, and dependence:

> Since the earliest days of the nation, the idea of whiteness has been closely tied to notions of independence and self-control necessary for republican government. This conception of whiteness developed in concert with the conquest and colonization of non-Western societies by Europeans. Imagining non-European "others" as dependent and lacking the capacity for self-governance helped rationalize the takeover of their lands, resources and labor (Glenn 18).

Glenn goes on to emphasize early in her essay that it is not just whiteness but masculine whiteness that "was being constructed in the discourse on citizenship." Colonization is a key aspect of this ideology of masculine whiteness, according to Glenn:

Imagining non-European "others" as dependent and lacking the capacity for self-governance helped rationalize the takeover of their lands, resources and labor. In North America, the extermination and forced removal of Indians and the enslavement of blacks by European settlers therefore seemed justified. This formulation was transferred to other racialized groups, such as the Chinese, Japanese and Filipinos, who were brought to the U.S. in the late nineteenth and early twentieth centuries as low wage laborers. Often working under coercive conditions of indenture or contract labor, they were treated as "unfree labor" and denied the right to become naturalized citizens (18).

A commitment to masculine whiteness, with its emphasis on territoriality, exploitation of resources, and the perception of other non-whites as dependent and lacking in political and mental capacity, is part of the master narrative that formed an important foundation for our ideas of American citizenship. Indeed, we have come to a point in our history where any real variation on what we might mean when we say "American" or "America" is scarcely thinkable. The ideological work of equating American with whites and America with whiteness has been thoroughly achieved. Viewed in this way, Abercrombie's early beginnings as an outfitter of upper-class explorers, adventurers, and outdoorsmen may perhaps be more relevant to our understanding and appreciation of the label's appeal than we first imagined.

The *Look Book* is noteworthy for some of the contradictions it raises as well. For example, the A&F dress code delineates its commitment to whiteness even in terms of what it deems acceptable in the way of appearance. The investment here in whiteness is also an investment in class. Recall the earlier mention in the introduction to this book of the whiteness of capital. Consider the following guidelines:

• For men and women, a neatly combed, attractive, natural, classic hairstyle is acceptable.

- Any type of "fade" cut (more scalp is visible than hair) for men is unacceptable.
- Shaving of the head or any portion of the head or eyebrow for men or women is unacceptable.
- Dreadlocks are unacceptable for men and women.

It is also in this section of the *Look Book* that we are presented with the only sketch that appears in the book. It is a combination sketch of seven heads and faces, which carries the caption "Some Acceptable Hairstyles." Included in these drawings is an African American man with a neatly cut natural (a very short afro cut). There is also among these faces a man who appears much older than the A&F target age group. In fact, this is the only place in the book where an older person is ever pictured. Indeed, it would also be unusual to find older adults working as brand representatives in their stores or being featured as models in the *A&F Quarterly*.

What is interesting to note about the acceptable hairstyles is what is out and what is in. In the mid-90s, when this edition of the *Look Book* was published, the fade was a popular hairstyle for African American men. I confess, somewhat reluctantly, that I had one myself. Also, since shaved heads are excluded, this also would put a mounting segment (at the time) of African American men out of the running along with the odd white skinhead. Finally, dreadlocks, while considered by some to be among the most "natural" of hairstyles available to African Americans, are out. Indeed dreads, as they are often referred to, are even somewhat controversial within African American communities for their association with, among other things, Rastafarianism. So other than as a commitment to a white aesthetic, the exclusion of dreads (even in terms of A&F's own commitment to the "natural" look) seems curious.

On jewelry, the *Look Book* offers the following:

Jewelry must be simple and classic. A ring may be worn on any finger except the thumb. Gold chains are not acceptable for men. Women may

wear a thin, short delicate silver necklace. Ankle bracelets are unacceptable. Dressy (e.g., gold-banded or diamond) watches are also unacceptable; watches should be understated and cool (e.g., leather straps or stain-
less steel). No more than two earrings in each ear can be worn at a time
for women. Only one in one ear for men. Earrings should be no larger
than a dime, and large dangling or large hoop earrings are unacceptable.
. . . No other pierced jewelry is appropriate (e.g., nose rings, pierced lips,
etc.)

Thumb rings signify alternative lifestyles at best and queer at worst. No gold
chains for men? Who has been overidentified or even stereotyped with these
in the popular imagination more than black men—from Mr. T to any number of rap artists, and "ballers" more generally? In either case, the signifier
"gold chain" demarcates potential employees of A&F in coded ways along
race and class lines. A similar case can be made with regard to the reference
to "large dangling or large hoop earrings." Here, too, Abercrombie codes for
race and class without actually having to name it.

Still, of all of the dress code rules, the most amusing one to me has to
be the following: "Brand Representatives are required to wear appropriate
undergarments at all times." Is Abercrombie afraid that their brand representatives might actually be sexualized? The image of male genitalia flop-
ping about in cargo shorts or, alternatively, of an 18–22-year-old version
of the now infamous Sharon Stone leg-crossing scene in the film *Basic Instinct* (1992) comes to mind. Call me crazy, but there is just something
about a company that flies in the face of such propriety in the pages of the
A&F Quarterly—wherein no one seems to wear underwear or much else for
that matter—being concerned about the appropriateness of the undergarments of its employees that strikes me as the height of hilarity and
hypocrisy.

If the frequent use of such coded monikers in the *Look Book* were not
enough to convince us that the A&F look is styled on a celebration of
racial and cultural whiteness, consider that the *A&F Quarterly* is chock full

of images of young white men and women (mostly men) with very little in the way of representation of people of color. Consider that criticism of Abercrombie's chosen photographer, Bruce Weber, draws him as (in)famous for his unabashed celebration of the white male nude. Recall the release by A&F in April 2003 of that inflammatory line of "Asian" themed T-shirts, which were hotly protested by the Asian American community among others. One of the shirts featured two stereotypical Chinese men drawn with exaggeratedly slanted eyes, donning pointed hats, and holding a banner between them that read: "Two Wongs Can Make It White." A spokesperson for A&F, when asked to respond to the controversy raised by the T-shirts, said, "We thought it would add humor." The line was pulled by the company soon after they were released. Consider also the variety of social engineering that goes into producing a virtually all-white sales staff in A&F stores. As one former assistant manager of one of Abercrombie's larger stores in the Midwest informed me, all the brand reps in his store were white, and all of the people who worked in the stockroom were black. Stockroom employees (in the larger stores where they employ such staff separately from brand reps) are less visible and are often assigned to work overnight shifts restocking the store.

Many people have asked me while I was working on this project—no doubt many will continue to do so—what's the big deal? Why pick on Abercrombie? They are doing no more or no less than Ralph Lauren or Banana Republic. I have said to those people and continue to say that such a simple equation is not only untrue, but denies the specificity of the particular brand of evil that Abercrombie is involved in capitalizing on. Ralph Lauren does, to be sure, commodify a particular upper-class American lifestyle. Banana Republic has a history of a similar marketing scheme. However, A&F successfully crystallizes a racism that is only rumbling beneath the surface of other stores' advertising. Also, Ralph Lauren attempts to market and sell that lifestyle to everyone equally. That is, the underlying ethos of Ralph Lauren is not unlike the ideology of the American dream itself: you, too, can have this if you work for it.

Ralph Lauren "diversified" its ad campaigns in the 1990s. To demonstrate that fact, among other things, Ralph Lauren in 1993 took on Tyson Beckford, a black model of Jamaican and Chinese parentage, to represent its Polo Sport line exclusively. True, this diversity was of the variety of CNN diversity: news is read by white and Asian reporters, while black reporters do sports and entertainment and occasionally "substitute" for white news reporters. In the same vein, Beckford was engaged to model for Ralph Lauren's "sport" line and not its "blue label" (i.e., blue blood) line of suits, formal wear, and elegant apparel. Still, Beckford's own rags-to-riches story made for good press for a company clearly working its own variety of the diversity angle, which was a popular marketing strategy among hip retailers in the 1990s. Beckford represents perhaps the most notable example of this. He grew up in Jamaica and in Rochester, New York. As a youth he was involved in gangs, drugs, and was on his way down the road toward a life of crime, when an editor of the hip-hop magazine the *Source* discovered him. Not long thereafter, it would be Bruce Weber who would introduce Beckford to Ralph Lauren—whose signing of Beckford sent his modeling career into the stratosphere. Beckford himself has recognized that he would likely be dead or in jail had he not been taken up by that editor from the *Source*. There has been speculation about the veracity of Beckford's narrative of class ascension. Regardless, its construction generated good press for Ralph Lauren.

I should note, too, that neither Banana Republic nor Ralph Lauren participate in the kind of social engineering in terms of their store employees that A&F does. The employees of Banana Republic represent diverse racial backgrounds, while the sales associates at Ralph Lauren tend to represent an older model of the suit-wearing salesman in an upscale shop. The latter, in addition to the Polo stores, also sells its line in fine department stores, where they have no direct control over choosing sales associates to represent the line. An added bit of anecdotal information with regard to Banana Republic also comes in the form of the person of Eduardo Gonzalez—one of the named litigants in the pending class action employment discrimination lawsuit against A&F. The class action complaint notes that Gonzalez, who was not hired as a brand representative at Abercrombie, was offered a job at Banana Republic:

> Indeed, immediately following his Abercrombie interview, he crossed the hall within the same mall to apply for a job at Banana Republic, a similar retail clothing store that competes directly with Abercrombie for customers and employees. An employee of Banana Republic asked Mr. Gonzalez if he was interested in applying to work as a manager. He applied to work as a sales associate, and is still employed by Banana Republic in that capacity.

If, as I suggest in chapter 6, images tend more often to follow and demonstrate where we are as a society rather than play the role of leading us to new places, then the particular brand of a socially engineered whitewashed world being advertised, branded, and sold to U.S. consumers by Abercrombie should give us pause. Movie lovers may recall the song "Tomorrow Belongs to Me" from the film version of *Cabaret*. The song begins, like the lyrics, in a pastoral mode. The camera is tight on the face of the beautiful, young, blond, boy soprano. The scene is comforting, indeed beautiful. With each successive verse, however, the camera begins to pull back and to show more and more and more of the boy's body . . . donning a Hitler-youth uniform. His face becomes increasingly emphatic and angry. By the time we get to the fourth verse of the tune, the others in the crowd have joined in the song with a seriousness of purpose that can only be described as frightening:

> *The sun on the meadow is summery warm*
> *The stag in the forest runs free*
> *But gathered together to greet the storm*
> *Tomorrow belongs to me*
>
> *The branch on the linden is leafy and green*
> *The Rhine gives its gold to the sea*

But somewhere a glory awaits unseen
Tomorrow belongs to me

The babe in his cradle is closing his eyes
The blossom embraces the bee
But soon says the whisper, arise, arise
Tomorrow belongs to me

Now Fatherland, Fatherland, show us the sign
Your children have waited to see
The morning will come
When the world is mine
Tomorrow belongs to me
Tomorrow belongs to me
Tomorrow belongs to me

The number concludes with the final verse above being repeated twice more in a chilling, thunderous unity, as the crowd of townspeople gathered at the picnic joins in.

Some may call a comparison such as the one I am drawing here hyperbole. Others might say that I am overstating Abercrombie's case and undervaluing the realities of the Holocaust. Neither is my intention. I do, however, believe fervently in what Hannah Arendt in *Eichmann in Jerusalem* once called "the banality of evil." I am convinced that a version of it is what is at work in the politics of race in U.S. society today, and that Abercrombie's marketing and branding practices represent only a symptom of that larger concern. Indeed, according to Edward Herman, "Arendt's thesis [in *Eichmann in Jerusalem*] was that people who carry out unspeakable crimes, like Eichmann, a top administrator in the machinery of the Nazi death camps, may not be crazy fanatics at all, but rather ordinary individuals who simply accept the premises of their state and participate in any ongoing enterprise with the energy of good bureaucrats." In the words of another philosopher-commentator on the "banality of evil": "Clichés, stock phrases, adherence to conventional, standardized codes of expression and conduct have the socially recognized function of protecting us against reality." This statement well describes the corporate culture of Abercrombie and the quasi-cultish devotion they seem to inspire.

There are those, no doubt, reading these pages who will find that it takes far too much of a liberal leap of faith to appreciate the argument I pose here against Abercrombie & Fitch. There are those who will not grasp, or who will feign confusion about grasping, the coded nature of the whiteness that A&F so clearly employs. It is for those readers that I include the more practical, everyday, anecdotal evidence that follows. The purview of such hard-boiled evidence (that which is usually associated with the "simple truth," a term whose discussion began this book) can usually be found in the area of the law.

As a system, the law deals in bodies, experience (rendered through testimony), and revels in the making of distinctions. The law is no place for nuances, ambiguities, subtleties, and, even at times, the vagaries so often associated with theoretical, academic discussion—and with the humanities in general. The law represents yet another realm in which the "simple truth" carries the day. Indeed, before the law, human complexity, the complexity of identities, the complexities of sexuality and desire, the complexities of social and economic circumstances, the complexities of institutional and corporate cultures and the unspoken codes by which they operate, the complexities of deep-seated racism, sexism, heterosexism, elitism, and so much more, all become flattened, cognizable, weighable, and therefore able to be adjudicated. I suppose this is why my sentiments about the law have always been conflicted. On the one hand, I have long admired the law's simplicity and the definitive clarity with which it makes claims and decides cases; on the other, I have bemoaned the law's inability to address concerns of specificity, to deal compassionately with human frailty, and to account in its judgment for the ambiguity and complexity of circumstances. Like most systems, the law is, of course, not simple. Its ways have evolved through crooks and turns—and not always ones that we would associate with justice and the good—that have brought it to this place in its history and development. It did not spring fully formed and perfect as if from the head of Zeus. As such, the law has evolved its own biases for what constitutes evidence, how evidence can and should be presented, what cases can come before the law, and how precedent drives the law's machinery. So even though I personally do not hold the truth of the law above other ways of creating and recognizing truth, I present the following here because I know that among the readers of this book will be those who do.

On June 17, 2003, a class action lawsuit was filed against Abercrombie & Fitch in the United Stated District Court of San Francisco, California, alleging discrimination in its hiring practices. Specifically, the complaint alleges that A&F discriminates against people of color, including Latinos, Asian Americans, and African Americans, in the hiring, job assignment, compensation, termination, and other terms and conditions of employment. There are nine named litigants in the complaint who filed on behalf of the class they represent: Eduardo Gonzalez, Anthony Ocampo, Encarnacion Gutierrez, Johan Montoya, Juancarlos Gomez-Montejano, Jennifer Lu, Austin Chu, Ivy Nguyen, and Angeline Wu. These litigants are represented by counsel from the Mexican American Legal Defense and Educational Fund; the Asian Pacific American Legal Center; the NAACP Legal Defense and Educational Fund; and the law firm of Lieff, Cabraser, Heimann & Bernstein. In August 2003 I had the privilege of meeting Anthony Ocampo, one of the named litigants in the lawsuit, over dinner in Chicago. Though I am not at liberty to discuss the particulars related to our dinner conversation that evening about the pending case, I do want to say what an impressive, brave, and astute— even if a bit shy—young man Ocampo is. With that, let me share some thoughts about the complaint itself (as a matter of public record), which I think further illuminates much of what I have been presenting up to this point about Abercrombie & Fitch.

What follows first are some representative points from the "Introductory Statement" portion of the complaint:

- Defendant Abercrombie & Fitch . . . is a national retail clothing seller that discriminates against minority individuals, including Latinos, Asian Americans, and African Americans . . . on the basis of race, color, and/or national origin, with respect to hiring, firing, job assignment, compensation and other terms and conditions of employment by enforcing a nationwide corporate policy of preferring white employees for sales positions, desirable job assignments, and favorable work scheduled in its stores throughout the United States.

- Abercrombie implements its discriminatory employment policies and practices in part through a detailed and rigorous "Appearance Policy," which requires that all Brand Representatives must exhibit the "A&F Look." The "A&F Look" is a virtually all-white image that Abercrombie uses not only to market its clothing, but also to implement its discriminatory employment policies and practices.

- When people who do not fit the "A&F Look" inquire about employment, managers sometimes tell them that the store is not hiring, or may provide them with applications even though they have no intention of considering them for employment. If applicants who do not fit the "A&F Look" submit applications, managers and/or Brand Representatives acting at their direction sometimes throw them away without reviewing them.

- Abercrombie publishes and distributes to its employees a "Look Book" that explains the importance of the Appearance Policy and the "A&F Look," and that closely regulates the Brand Representatives' appearance. The Company requires its managers to hire and continue to employ only Brand Representatives who fit within the narrow confines of the "Look Book," resulting in a disproportionately white Brand Representative workforce.

- . . . Each store prominently posts large photographs of models—virtually all of whom are white. In addition, the Company publishes and sells *A&F Quarterly*, a magazine/catalog featuring almost exclusively white models . . .

- The Company rigorously maintains the "A&F Look" by careful scrutiny and monitoring of its stores by regional and district managers and corporate representatives. These managers and corporate representatives visit stores frequently to ensure, among other things, that the store is properly implementing the Company's discriminatory employment policies and practices. These visits are referred to as "blitzes." When managers or corporate representatives discover that minority Brand Representatives have been hired, they have directed that these Brand Representatives be fired, moved to the stock room or overnight shift, or have their hours "zeroed out," which is the equivalent of termination.

- The Company also scrutinizes and enforces compliance with the "A&F Look" by requiring all stores to submit a picture of roughly 10 of their Brand Representatives who "fit the 'Look' to headquarters each quarter. The corporate officials then select roughly 15 stores' pictures as exemplary models that perpetuate the Company's discriminatory employment practices. They then disseminate these pictures to the over 600 A&F stores. The Brand Representatives in the pictures are almost invariably white. This practice and policy, like the others described above, constitutes an official directive to give preference to white Brand Representatives and applicants, and to discriminate against minority Brand Representatives and applicants.

- The A&F image is not limited to appearance; the Company accomplishes its discriminatory employment policies or practices by defining its desired "classic" and "cool" workforce as exclusively white . . . Abercrombie also encourages the recruitment and hiring of members of specified overwhelmingly white intercollegiate sports. However, the Company does not encourage recruitment from fraternities, sororities, or sports teams with significant minority populations.

It will surely come as no surprise that my sympathies where Abercrombie is concerned are very much in line with those of this lawsuit. When I first started thinking about this work more than two years ago now, the more I discovered about the company and its marketing and employment practices, the more surprised I was that a suit had not been brought against them sooner. Such naiveté on my part underestimated the resourcefulness of A&F's ingenuity and, indeed, the ingenuity of racist discourse in our time to mask itself in the form of coded language. Some of this language I have been discussing, and some is attested to in the excerpts from the legal complaint that I have presented. The creation of an "A&F Look," which almost invariably functions to produce an exclusively white staff of brand representatives in Abercrombie's stores, might be understood as an elaborately devised method by the company of forestalling the potential legal exposure of such an exclusionary employment policy. The formal workings of what we might call the "corporate culture" of A&F provide the infrastructure for maintaining and reproducing the discriminatory, virtually all-white A&F look.

The A&F former store managers, former assistant managers, and former and current brand representatives with whom I have spoken over the course of this project all tell eerily similar stories. All of the personnel with whom I had occasion to speak have been white men. They ranged in age from nineteen to twenty-six and were either in college or were college educated. Some were gay, some straight. All of them, almost without exception, expressed how they enjoyed working at the company when they first started there. They also expressed their discomfort with some of the "unspoken" rules of the company, which they cited as their reason for ultimately leaving the employ of A&F. The allure of the experience seemed to hold sway over these men even after they had left the company. The men with whom I conducted formal interviews all cited fond memories from the experience, even as they all were convinced that something about it never felt quite right to them.

Chance (not his actual name), a straight white man in his early twenties, spoke with me about his experience at one of the larger stores on the West Coast, where he was a brand representative. He would later move on to manage a store on the East Coast. On the matter of employment practices he said, "The hiring policy is insane." He went on to suggest that it was the common practice of the general manager (GM) at the store—who Chance describes as "Abercrombied out"—to say that he was not in the business of hiring "ugly people." Informal games between the men in the stores were encouraged by management, in which they would have contests to see who could get the most "hot high school girls' [phone] numbers." Chance related to me that on the day when the store picture that would be sent to A&F headquarters was to be taken, Leo (not his real name), "the only black guy in the store," was asked by the GM to "watch the front" while they were taking the picture.

David (not his real name), a white gay man in his early twenties, spoke with me about his experience at a smaller store in the Northeast, where he worked during his college years. He would go on to become a manager in training (MIT) and an assistant manager (AM) at a large store in another region of the country. David told me about the corporate practice of tying a "target school" (college or university) to all the stores. One of the things he started to notice when he became an MIT and later an AM was that the brand representatives in his store were almost exclusively white and that "everybody who worked in the stockroom was black." He tells the story of the one African American male employee that he had in his store when he became an AM. He said he was a good employee with a really positive attitude, but the district manager (DM) wanted us (David and the store manager) to get rid of him because he "did not fit the look." "He's not Abercrombie," the DM said to David and the store manager. The DM went on to say to them that "this person cannot be on the schedule anymore." David said that "not having the look" is reason enough to be fired or not hired in the first place. "Race as an issue is implied," David told me. He always understood that to be the case, even though it was unspoken. When I asked him what happened to the guy, David replied, rather matter-of-factly, that he was essentially fired by the manager. The process began with the employee first being "zeroed out" in terms of the hours he was scheduled to work; eventually he was fired. David said that this was a common practice. Instead of actually terminating people, you just stop scheduling them (or "zero them out") until they inevitably get the picture. I asked David why he left the company. He said that he got tired of the antagonistic relationships that sometimes exist between DMs and store-level management, where he was always hearing: "you can't schedule him . . ." or (in fits of frustration or anger) "your staff is ugly." "I got sick of judging people like that," he said. "I'm going to be a teacher. . . . It's just not right." He told me that before leaving his job at A&F, he once expressed his discomfort with some of these company practices to his GM (a white woman). According to David, her reply was: "You'll eventually get over it. You'll learn to let go of your feelings and get over it." David said he still could not believe that a store manager told him that. It was then that he knew his days with the company were numbered.

Randy is a white gay man in his early twenties as well. He started out as a brand representative at a store in the South while he was in college. Later he became an AM in another region of the country. He shared with me some of his observations in those positions. He spoke with alarming candor. At first there appeared to me to be a manner of innocence about his way of reporting this information that seemed almost unconscious of the profound implications of his statements. The more I spoke with him, however, the more I came to see that this was in part his affect and was not a statement on his level of recognition of the gravity of what he was relating.

When Randy began with the company, he had not yet come out as a gay man. The store where he started working had an all-white staff. He recalls that the managers were "really cool," a fact he came to appreciate later when he would learn that this was not the case with most GMs and DMs in the company. He reports that, in the stores, employees were encouraged to "look Abercrombie" and to "speak Abercrombie or Crombie." When they recruited new brand reps, which they all were involved in doing, Randy said that they were very clear on what they were looking for: "all-American," in "good shape," "no facial or skin problems," "clean shaven," "not a lot of makeup for girls . . . natural," "fraternity or football player–looking guys." He went on to say that it used to be "a big deal to look for white people." He added that African Americans and Asian Americans "can be A&F if they act white, have white friends, and are very assimilated." Randy reports feeling pressure to hire people who looked A&F. Employees who recruited the wrong sort knew they would run the risk of reprisal from the GM or the DM. I asked him what happened to people who were "not Abercrombie" who came in to apply for jobs. He said they were never called. He reports one case that occurred when he was an AM in which a qualified fifty-year-old woman applied for a GM position. Her application was never given to the DM because the DM "would be pissed off at us for wasting his time." He reported another case of an MIT he worked with once who "wasn't very attractive." The regional manager (RM) informed the DM that she needed to go. Randy said that while she wasn't great at her job, had she been "nice-looking she would still have gotten promoted." He cited the case of another girl who had been an A&F model who came to work in the same store. She was, according to Randy, "horrible at her job and still got promoted." She was even eventually sent to the home office.

It was Randy who first informed me about the practice of grading at A&F. The DM would review the work schedules, every name on the schedules had to have a grade (A through F) next to it, which reflected how "good-looking" the employee was. When upper management (especially Michael Jeffries or David Lieno, directors of stores) would come to town for a "blitz" (a word whose associations with Nazi Germany one cannot help noticing), people who were not A's were asked to leave the store. A preponderance of B's or worse in a schedule could be grounds for dismissal of a GM. Brand representatives were never informed of the grade they had been assigned and remained, in most cases, unfamiliar with the practice, according to Randy. When I asked him why he left the company, he said he left "because they were bad to me." He added that they treat management horribly and don't compensate them well, paying them halftime for overtime worked, with base salaries for AMs in the mid-twenty-thousand-dollar range. Even so, they want you to "look like you have money . . . come from a good family."

Ultimately, I suppose my reasons for hating Abercrombie & Fitch are not so different from the reasons that I have no truck with gay Republicans. It is not surprising when one observes that the attitudes of those sporting Abercrombie often seem to have a great deal in common with political conservatives as well. In both cases, you have a group of mostly whites (many of them social and economic climbers themselves—less often are they those who were actually born with money), who are desperate to belong to a fraternity that guarantees all the benefits and liberties of white privilege. Recall the earlier discussion in the introduction to this book about vacationing and "getting away from it all." In the case of gay Republicans, we are often dealing with a group of people who understand themselves—but for this critical difference that their sexuality makes—as in line to be the beneficiaries of their white birthright in the United States: to be and receive the mantle of whiteness and all the privileges it entails. Were it not but for their sexuality, they too could enjoy the same kind of mobility, belonging, non-discrimination, social respect and respectability, wider economic entrepreneurial opportunity, and, indeed, the right to discriminate against all those others who do not belong. After all, to borrow a well-known slogan from a surprisingly appropriate context, "membership has its privileges." This is seen most readily in the fiscal conservatism of many gay Republicans, who are typically not supporters of affirmative action, welfare, or any other variety of social programs designed to support the poor and people of color in the United States. And when one looks at the disproportionate numbers of blacks and Latinos who make up the poor in the United States, the poor and people of color are populations that in public discussion don't always require a great deal of delineation.

In my critique of white gay Republicans, I do not mean to suggest that the distinctions between them and white gay liberals are so vast as to avoid mentioning this latter group here as well. Indeed, when it comes to addressing questions about who has access to be able to make the rational choice of a mate in the gay marketplace of desire, the similarities between the two become much clearer, as I will discuss in the next chapter. But even at the philosophical and political levels, Republicanism and liberalism have far more in common than might at first meet the eye. In this regard, gay liberalism and gay Republicanism are no exception. Consider the recent June 2003 Supreme

Court ruling in the Texas sodomy case. What many in the LGBT community have embraced as a radical step forward by a conservative court really represents a new challenge in the struggle for queer liberation. The decision of the High Court effectively protected gay sexuality by privatizing it. After all, the majority opinion is based on arguments centering on privacy rights. The effect of this move is that civil expressions of gayness may at the very least be in for some hard political times ahead, and at the very worst become effectively outlawed. For privatizing gayness does not necessarily pave the way to gay "marriage" or civil unions, open expression of one's sexual identity in the military, or any number of other radical potentials with which the court's decision is presently being endowed. The extent to which the decision has a "liberal" look to it, while simultaneously retaining the potential for stultifying conservative Republican ramifications, is the extent to which gay liberalism and gay Republicanism may not be so different from one another in terms of their radical potentialities.

Still, just as much as gay Republicans are desperate to belong to a tribe of privilege and cultural and social dominance, so are those who are a part of the cult of Abercrombie. The cultish ideology that drives the engine of Abercrombie is not unlike the ideology that led Disney's Little Mermaid, Ariel, after falling in love with the beautiful white prince, to give up her birth identity (even as a princess of the Mer-people) in exchange for her legs (and more importantly her vagina, not to put too fine a point on the matter), so that she can, in the words of her principle number in the movie-musical, be "part of that world" (the world of people). Abercrombie, through its strategy of marketing "the good white life" in what is already a deeply racist society, has convinced a U.S. public—whites (some young and some not so young), some people of color, and gay men—that if we buy their label, we are really buying membership into a privileged fraternity that has eluded us all for so long, even if for such vastly different reasons. In order for such a marketing strategy to work, in all of the diverse ways that this one clearly does, the consumer must necessarily bring to his or her understanding of A&F, and what association with the brand offers him or her, a fundamentally racist belief

85

that this lifestyle—this young, white, natural, all-American, upper-class lifestyle—being offered by the label is what we all either are, aspire to be, or are hopelessly alienated from ever being. Only when such a perspective as this is brought to the consumer's viewing of the *A&F Quarterly*, to the stores and the special brand of social engineering that takes place by the company to make them "good looking" (and by definition white), and to the very dull and uninspiring clothes themselves (absent the label), does any of this literally cohere or "make sense." The very sense-making, the deciphering of the codes that allow one to appreciate what it is that "Abercrombie" stands for and means in our culture, can only be accomplished when we bring a variety of racialist thinking to the experience.

Either way, when you evolve a way to commodify and market the fundamental tenets of racist thinking that have held sway in the United States from the earliest moments of its inception as a republic (a feat Abercrombie seems successfully to have achieved), this example shows us that you can attach the label (whatever it may be) to even the most uninspiring products (in this case clothes), and they will sell in legion. Surely we know that people are not buying "Abercrombie" for the clothes. The catalog itself isn't even about featuring those, after all. People buy "Abercrombie" to purchase membership into a lifestyle. Lisa Marsh, the fashion business writer for the *New York Post*, said that Abercrombie's "aggressive lifestyle marketing makes you feel like you're buying a polo shirt and getting the horse and summer house on Martha's Vineyard with it."

Were that the extent of what they were selling, I might have less of a problem with Abercrombie. But to brazenly evolve a way of playing on consumers' worst racially based fears and inadequacies born of a racist structure that defines everything from standards of beauty to access to having the house on Martha's Vineyard, goes beyond mere "lifestyle marketing." In my judgment, that crosses the line into a kind of racism whose desire—played out to its logical conclusion—is not unlike a variety of ethnic cleansing. Its desire to produce and play on the consumer's desire for a white, "good-looking" world where one can "get away from it all," and to sell that idea as the "good life" in the context of a racist society, only redeploys and rein-scribes the fundamental logic of white supremacy which, at bottom, makes such a marketing strategy possible and even appealing in the first place. This says a great deal, perhaps, about the status of "race relations" in the United States. It says even more about the deep and abiding contradictions that can be accommodated in our public thinking about race today that would scarcely have been possible to imagine even in the late 1960s or 1970s. Another failing of the radicality of liberalism? Perhaps. In any case, the same reasoning that makes Abercrombie palatable to a U.S. public, is the same reasoning that makes claims of "reverse discrimination" palatable and possible in our society. And that, in the end, is why I hate Abercrombie and Fitch.

3 It's a White Man's World

Race in the Gay Marketplace of Desire

> These bodies [gay male gym bodies] outwardly represent a kind of
> wealth, a fullness in which a person has the means, discipline, the work
> ethic—and the leisure time—to perfect his body. It is a clean-cut, middle
> class body, symbolizing the final embourgeoisement of the gay commu-
> nity and its related aspirations. The values of the marketplace rule the
> central circles of gay life, perhaps to a disturbing degree, where the body
> is advertising and "knowing the price of everything" is a main principle
> of doing business.   —John DiCarlo, "The Gym Body and Heroic Myth"

In many ways this is the most difficult chapter of this book to write. It means
having to be honest about and to face some of the private demons that gay
men of color (and others on the periphery of the gay marketplace of desire)
confront on a regular basis. It means articulating painful lessons learned
about your value—or lack thereof—in the dominant logics that fuel that
same marketplace. It means speaking about the ways in which the variables
that constitute value in this marketplace—those variables of race, gender affect ("butch"/"femme"), body type (muscle queen, gym bunny, swimmer's
build, fat, slim), age, penis size, style (leather, preppy, corporate, pseudo alternative, A&F all-American, boy, bear, homo thug)—all work to construct
and constitute what we come to accept, and in some cases to celebrate, as our
value. To speak about the gay marketplace of desire and the terms under
which it produces value means having to speak about related issues around
which we are taught to observe and endure a code of silence or shame. For to
get to the bottom of such variables and how they work means visiting the
places of fetish, pornography, gay personals ads, bath houses and sex clubs,

the circuit scene, and, perhaps most frightening of all, the recesses of our own minds where we conceal some of the most passionate, important, and vulnerable parts of our humanity: the various expressions of our sexuality.

Such work is not easy. There is no road map, no on-board navigation system directing us when to make the next turn, or saying, "no, not that way but this." And whenever we enter uncharted territory, our first inclination is either to turn back from embarking upon such a journey in frustrated resignation, or to forge ahead, running the risk of getting lost. While working on a final draft of this chapter, I had a dream that, as will be readily apparent, was clearly related to my work and thinking here. I was lost in D.C., the nation's capital, trying desperately to get home to Chicago. My mode of transportation was a motorcycle. For anyone who knows me, this detail would immediately strike them as decidedly out of character. I was circling in one of the countless traffic rotaries in the city, trying to decide, with great difficulty, which road to take, when I noticed a very attractive, young African American man standing on the edge of the circle between two of my possible destinations. He was smiling. I stopped to ask directions on how to get to the freeway that would take me home to Chicago. My reasons for stopping were not entirely pragmatic. I stopped in part because he was attractive, in part because I was lost and needed help, and in part because his smile seemed more than friendly—it felt solicitous. He greeted me warmly and with great care gave me the following directions, as he pointed to the road to his immediate right:

> Take this road. You will travel on it across a bridge that will carry you over a body of water. Above you will be another road that will eventually turn off in a different direction. When you reach the other side of the bridge, continue on this road until you come to a point where the road will become smaller, dirt covered, and will appear to end where it meets the edge of a small mountain on the left and the body of water on your right. Don't be alarmed. You should get off the motorcycle at this point and walk it around the mountain along a path between the mountain's edge

and the water. This will eventually lead you to the freeway that will take you home.

His words sounded as curious and strange to me in the dream as they do now as I write them. Still, having no better course of action, I decided to follow his directions.

After thanking the young man, I proceeded along the road and found everything as he had described it. I crossed the bridge with another road above me and the water below. I came to the point where the road turned into a dirt road and then appeared to end as he had said. I got off the motorcycle and began walking around the side of the mountain, following the path as best I could. It was more treacherous than I had imagined; indeed, the path was barely visible in places. I began to suspect foul play or to conclude that this way was not the one that was right for me to be taking. It felt unsafe and more than a bit frightening. Then, something unexpected happened. I heard the voices of a man and a woman talking from the other side of the mountain. I intuitively knew in the dream that these were the voices of people that I should be afraid of. So I stopped and hid with my motorcycle in the woods along the path as I continued to listen undetected to their conversation. The man, I came to discover, was a white fundamentalist preacher whose life work was to root out homosexuality in the land. He and his white wife, the voice belonging to the woman I had heard, were planning their next trip into D.C., where they would be doing their work of preaching and advocating against gays and lesbians. I listened to them talk for a while until they made ready to leave and finally departed for the city. When I was sure they were gone, I came out of my hiding place with my motorcycle and decided that I was not going to continue on this path, but rather that I would return the way I had come and find my own way as best I could. I returned along the path, to the road, over the bridge, and back to the traffic rotary where the smiling, young African American man was still standing. This time as I circled, I was determined to ask no directions, to seek no further help. Instead, I would choose a road and find my way back home to Chicago on my own. This dream had such an impact on me that I shared it with the friend in my life who has had the longest and best history of helping me to make sense of my dreams. He and I marveled at the details of this one and eventually came up with the following possibilities.

Clearly the dream relates to the thinking I have been engaged in with this book. And that thinking is not unrelated to the politically troubling times that have characterized the ·federal government since the "election" of George W. Bush to the presidency. Hence, it seems appropriate that I, in my mind, should be "lost" in the nation's capital, the seat of power, the locus and center of possibility for political change. That I am riding a motorcycle further signals, perhaps, the unusual nature of the times in which we find ourselves involved at this moment in history. We literally have to think differently, not only about where we travel, but about how we travel, maneuver, and navigate this new terrain. We went on in this way, interpreting the details of the dream. We concluded finally that the young African American man, who represents an earlier version of myself, was telling me the way— the approved way—that he knew to get me home. It may have been the way represented by the wisdom of the ages of African American history, experience, and political strategy. His way was not wrong, but it was not necessarily appropriate to the new political and social terrain that we find ourselves having to chart as black people, and especially black gay and lesbian people. Once I began down that path toward home, overhearing the conversation between the fundamentalist preacher and his wife reminded me that thinking about "race" for me is never possible without also thinking about sexuality. This approved way home might have worked for heterosexual African Americans in the past, but it did not hold the same sense of salvation or comfort for a black gay man in his search for home. Along this road, there are for the heterosexual traveler possible conservative, "respectable" modes of identification with homophobia (represented by the white fundamentalist preacher and his wife). These identificatory possibilities do not work in the same ways for me or for others like me. Indeed, my own experience, formed as it is from that oft-unappreciated nexus of race and sexuality, represents the truth to which I must ever be responsible in my thinking, my analysis, my course and direction, my truth-telling, and even my dreams.

So here we are on this new road, finding a new, uncharted way home. Where it will lead, where it may actually take us, time will judge. For now, however, all I know with absolute confidence is that this is the way I must go, and that I am glad that I do not have to travel alone.

When one makes the journey of openly discussing—some might say of exposing—the inner workings of the logic of the gay marketplace of desire, there is still a worse fear than that of getting lost. That fear is that when you do make the journey and return to bear witness to what you have found, you will be shunned as a traitor by the others who have made this most private of journeys and maintained a code of silence about it; or you will be scorned by those on the outside (the enemies of public sex treated by Michael Warner in his book *The Trouble with Normal*), who know little to nothing of such a journey, as further proof of the "depravity" of gay male sexuality. Both of these views would be wrong. In the first case, there is no better place to come to understand and to appreciate the ways in which the legacy of U.S. society's profound primal experiences with race have permeated all aspects of life in this country, right down to and including our sexual desires, than to examine our behaviors in our most "unscripted" or personal of moments. Such would inevitably include an examination of pornography, personals ads, and the like, in order to see how people express and characterize their desires under cover of privacy or anonymity—when they can be sure no one is watching, no judging PC eye is there observing. In the latter case of viewing this as evidence of gay male depravity, I offer this caveat. While it is not my intention here to address the heterosexual marketplace of desire, I would be willing to assume that there are marketplace rules (with different norms complicated by gender difference) governing those desires as well. So while I am interested here in speaking to and about the gay marketplace of desire, some of the lessons we might glean from such an analysis will likely have broader applicability and appeal than first meets the eye.

I come not to this work as a fearless explorer, outfitted to take on the rough, uncharted terrain of which I speak. No, I am a rather reluctant traveler—made even more nervous by the new brand of racial profiling that has become common fare at airport security checkpoints—who even at this very moment is not certain that this work is mine to do, this journey mine to report on or bear witness to. I am afraid of the ramifications. I am afraid of the amount of personal information that this necessitates sharing. I am afraid that people will not understand. And I am afraid that I may not be up to the task of seeing this through to an end. I am afraid of the voices of propriety and respectability in my own head, which, even as I write, have to be quelled in order for any of this to be possible. In such times of fear, I take great comfort in two quotes from Audre Lorde, who I turn to when I need to be reassured of the importance of speaking my truth. The first is perhaps the most famous of all quotes from Lorde: "When I dare to be powerful, to use my strength in the service of my vision, it becomes less and less important whether I am afraid." The second provides equal solace: "I have come to believe over and over again that what is most important to me must be spoken, made verbal and shared, even at the risk of having it bruised or misunderstood." Ultimately Lorde is right in both instances, because we do not bear witness or speak our truth for ourselves alone. For when we do so, Lorde has taught us so well, we empower and liberate the tongues of the many others who share in some way or another our experience, our truth, to speak as well. After all, power of a variety of sorts—whether corporate power, institutional or governmental power, intellectual or epistemological power, or the force and power of identity politics—depends upon the maintenance of codes of silence for its very vitality.

I can recall the first time I read the introduction to Robert Reid-Pharr's *Black Gay Man,* where in demonstrating his insistence upon the inseparability of the realm of intellectual work and the realm of pleasure, he discusses in rather graphic detail (for an academic audience at least) an encounter with one of his "favorite sex partners, Rick, an ugly, poor, white-trash southerner, with a scandalously thick Kentucky accent." He describes both Rick and the scene thus:

> The image of Rick is infinitely disruptive. He knows that he is ugly, wears his knowledge like one of the fancy-dress uniforms left over from his days in the army. He loves sex, loves men's bodies, loves the sight of my face, loves to masturbate and moon over how beautiful I am, how fucking beautiful I am. When he comes, usually standing over me, jerking hard at his dick and making those strange moon faces, the liquid spills out almost like an accident. He drawls, "Goddamn, Goddamn," as the goo hits my skin. He then talks about Kentucky and poverty, about a mother with arthritis, about old boyfriends and the army, about no-good relatives and abandoned children, about dreams for tomorrow, about me. (9–10)

When I finished reading this passage for the very first time I had to put the book down and phone a friend. It was not that I could not believe that Reid-Pharr had "gone there"; I was just caught way off guard that he had done so in print. At the same time that something lodged deep inside me reviled him in this moment, I also revered his courage to speak so candidly and eloquently from experience about the complications that animate our sexual and intimate lives.

I had a similar reaction when I first read Gary Fisher's *Gary in Your Pocket*. Published by literary theorist Eve Kosofsky Sedgewick (a teacher and friend of Fisher's) after Fisher's death from AIDS in 1993, the volume is filled with poems, stories, narrative fragments, and excerpts from his journal. They do not fit easily into any pre-packaged, normativizing, easily respectable understanding of black identity, of black life, or even of black gay life. His honesty — his at times deep commitment to that, above all other considerations—is enough to leave any variety of readers both vexed yet profoundly fascinated:

D-Day! Saturday, August 18, 1979 [the day before Fisher left for college]

—Actually it's 1:00 in the morning and I'm about to sleep in this bed one last time. Today's been hectic. I went on a shopping spree to end all others and then rushed home and packed it. I'm frightened, yet anxious to be there. God, say a little prayer for me. You've brought me so very far. I don't want to make it alone. I don't, but . . . It's so confusing, so very new to me. Guide me. See me through. I really love this place. These people, the past events. Don't make change too dramatic.

Wednesday, November 7, 1979 [Chapel Hill]

—. . . With all these white friends I think in many ways I am white or not the black stereotype that blacks and whites alike have of blacks. I like it, that's all that matters. I'd really like a girlfriend though.

—Good God Rosa's beautiful!

Saturday, November 10, 1979

—A major note. I was in a bathroom (2nd floor) of the Wilson Library and found a note on the wall saying "Want to Blow Me." I replied and I will get my first crack at it Monday. I pray it's good.

—Good weekend so far.

Wednesday, November 25, 1979

—. . . I'm beginning to like Jean more and more. Seems the girl is fairly wealthy and isn't just an ordinary nigger (is that my prejudice showing) . . .

2/1 [1987]

—I don't know that I would be so stirred by Billy Budd [the title character of a Herman Melville novel] if he were black. Maybe it's something lodged in the language now?—not that the asinine religious fictions that I'm talking about aren't sublimated in the sexual tensions that I'm not talking about. Maybe I would like to *be* Billy Budd . . . I used to fantasize that being young, strong yet vulnerable, and white would be more attractive to girls, and to guys who had girls; but my fantasy preceded thoughts (and occasionally ritual) so intense that fantasy became nightmare, a knot of young S and M that I could hardly admit to myself let alone my pillows, let well alone anyone who could tell me what it was I wanted. So it is the spiritual purity of the white Billy that pulls me and the desire to both protect and ravage him; to be protected by him and to be ravaged by him; to be him as he's protected, and as he's ravaged. It is the mythical power (physical, and potentially sexual) that intrigues me about the black man on whom Billy is based. Oh, but having to live up to that myth, the myth as it comes down from your father, as it comes down from the cautious glances of white girls on a dim street, as the white boys in gym class give it to you for emasculating them (their weapons backfiring somewhere between the mid-1800s and the present).

So I don't want to be someone else's fiction, I want to be someone else, or at least that's my approach to "Billy Budd."

There is much about Fisher's private, brave, unconventional humanity that comes across in the pages of his journals. Little of it is easily assimilated to approved versions of what black life, or even black gay life, should look like, how it should be publicly performed, or what it should represent in a white racist and heterosexist society such as ours. There are times reading Fisher that we cringe. At times it is the cringe of disbelief (the "I can't believe he went there" cringe); at others it feels something more like the cringe of recognition. Indeed, were the private journals (or the internal journals which will never be written or published) of more black people made public, what might be revealed shares far more commonality with Fisher than any of us may willingly want to admit: the pervasive residue of racism that comes in the form of what is too easily and uncomfortably labeled "self-hatred" or "low self-esteem" (both terms that have always made me uneasy); the struggle to understand one's sexuality in the context of a racist and heterosexist society which has according to its own logic and investments so thoroughly overdetermined the travesty of sex that black sexuality is or can be; or the

struggle to integrate the "blackness" of the cultures and homes which produced us with the "whiteness" of the world of capital in which we are forced
to survive in some form or another. In fact, one could say, as a nodal point
of comparison, that hip-hop culture—with its celebration of bling bling and
capitalism—has been about little else if not about some of these same tensions.

None of this is to suggest that Reid-Pharr and Fisher are the same. They
clearly are not. Still, anyone who has read Fisher's book, particularly the autobiographical journal entries, will immediately understand my meaning.
Fisher is shocking on many levels. He, in the words of Walt Whitman, "confront[s] peace, security, and all the settled laws, to unsettle them." At times,
his writing tries the comfort level of even the most progressive of readers.
Reid-Pharr himself has comments on Fisher's contribution to American and
African American letters in chapter 6 of *Black Gay Man,* "The Shock of Gary
Fisher." Reid-Pharr offers the following by way of presenting the significance
of Fisher's work:

> The shock of Gary Fisher turns squarely on his fierce articulation of what
> lies just beneath the surface of polite, "civil" American race talk. The life
> of the nigger is so caught up in the debauchery of the white master that
> even when "nigger" is translated to "black" it is still possible to sense the
> faintest hint of the raw milk smell of cum on the breath.
>
> . . . I have been struck by how difficult the text seems to have been for
> those people—white, black, and otherwise—who have encountered it.
> Indeed responses have ranged from righteous indignation toward the
> text and its editor, Eve Sedgewick, to a rather maddening inarticulate-
> ness, a sort of collective shrug at a document that demonstrates some of
> the ugly intricacies of what is often saddled with the euphemistic label
> "queer." . . . Fisher neither established the fairy tale black, white, red, yel-
> low, brown beloved community so feebly articulated by innumerable
> rainbow flags; nor does he signal a separate, resistant black (gay) identity.
> What Fisher tells us is much more difficult, more shocking than any of

this. Fisher goes beyond demonstrating that black/white intimacy is necessary and inevitable. Instead, he insists that if we are to maintain the clear distinction between the black and the white, this intimacy will never move beyond the ugly display of the master's dominance over the slave and the ugly scene of the slave's yielding to the same. There is no way to say "black" without hearing "nigger" as its echo. Fisher allows none of us to remain innocent. That is his challenge and his promise.

I realize now that the experience of reading both this section of *Black Gay Man* and *Gary in Your Pocket* was shocking for me only because I allowed my reading and critical self to fall easily into playing the role of the respectable reader with high regard for propriety. Nothing that Reid-Pharr or Fisher had said in either instance was news to me. Nothing that they had described was alien to me. That is, both openly discuss aspects of black gay life that I have thought of, lived, or talked about openly with close gay friends and confidants. I allowed myself to be shocked by the public nature of these declarations, the fact that they were out there in the world. They did not ascribe to the "positive" representation of black life, or of black gay life, that we have been so thoroughly programmed to respect, revere, and, as critics and commentators, to produce. Reid-Pharr addresses this impulse to respectable representation head-on by discussing what gets silenced by it:

> Even as we express the most positive articulations of black and gay identity, we are nonetheless referencing the ugly historical and ideological realities out of which those identities have been formed. Fisher thus insists that within the process of creating (black) identity one necessarily traffics in the *re*articulation of the very assumptions embedded within Jefferson and Hegel. There is no black subjectivity in the absence of the white master, no articulation in the absence of degradation, no way of saying "black" without hearing "nigger" in its echo. The import of reading Fisher, then, is that by frankly bringing this reality into public discourse

he gives us the opportunity to imagine new ways of articulating self and other, black and white. . . .

. . . The slave is literally kept from speaking so that the master might maintain his fantasy of dominance, his fantasy of having created the nigger in his own image.

The lurking fear that I experienced upon first reading Fisher is, perhaps, not unlike the fear that many heterosexual black race men and race women share about too much of a focus being placed on black gay and lesbian sexuality. They think that somehow this will dilute, or worse, sully the respectable nature of the political work of black liberation or the righteousness of the intellectual work that has congress under the label of "black studies." Witness the extraordinary case of the gay civil rights activist Bayard Rustin and his role in and relationship to the political establishment of the civil rights movement chronicled in the recent biography of his life (*Lost Prophet: The Life and Times of Bayard Rustin*) by gay historian John D'Emilio. Strict adherence to approved representations of identities invest us not so much in truth-telling as they do in preserving the respectability of our reigning de facto intellectual and political regimes. In the same way that I have railed against such propriety and the complexity it ignores in the black community, and the silences it preserves about the nature of black life, I must not allow myself to become comfortable with another form of black queer respectability and conservatism simply because in this case mine may happen to be more radical than someone else's. So I am thankful to Reid-Pharr, to Fisher, and to the many others that I may not yet know about who have pushed the envelope of respectability in ways that have forced us, if we take them seriously and are open to their lessons, to think beyond our comfort zones. In so many ways, the likes of them make possible the journey I try to bear witness to in the following pages.

In the recent U.S. Supreme Court ruling on the affirmative action policies of the University of Michigan, the university argued that race was one among many factors in evaluating the applications of its potential students. Unlike Michigan, I want to argue that in the context of the gay marketplace of desire race is a salient factor fueling that engine. To put it plainly, the argument sketched briefly would go something like this:

1. The particular and prevalent experience of American racism (with its deep roots in the institution of American slavery) permeates virtually all aspects of American life and culture.
2. Because of this legacy of white supremacy and its persistence in the form of white American racism, the notions we have evolved of what stands as beautiful and desirable are thoroughly racialized. Indeed, even our ideas about aesthetics in the broadest sense are shot through with racial considerations that render attempts at depoliticizing them impossible. This has not prevented, however, the likes of Harvard professor and literary critic Elaine Scarry from defending beauty and aesthetics from the likes of more political cultural critics such as myself when she writes:

   The banishing of beauty from the humanities in the last two decades has been carried out by a set of political complaints against it. But, as I will try to suggest, these political complaints against beauty are themselves incoherent.

   Time will, of course, decide who finally gets to lay claim to "coherency." Meanwhile, the rhetorical and political skirmishes continue.
3. By showing that race permeates the sanctity even of desire, we demonstrate, once more, race's saliency in American life and culture.

That is to say that if race is a salient variable in the sex-object choices we make in the gay marketplace of desire (an idea that has long been resisted in favor of an investment in the serendipity of desire and its companion notion of romantic love), then those who benefit unduly under such a system (whites) have a great deal invested in depoliticizing desire. Indeed, such an investment would be akin to the stakes being invested in defeating affirmative action by those who benefit unduly from white privilege. This has been one of the places where I have often parted ways with queer theory. One of the dominant claims of that discourse is that attempts such as mine to politicize desire are tantamount to policing desire. Indeed, the realm of desire for queer theorists seems ever to represent the possibility for a kind of idealized freedom and liberality. While this sentiment is one with which I have some sympathy in its efforts to resist the rhetoric of sexual moralism run rampant in the United States, if we examine the ways in which race functions as a variable in the gay marketplace of desire, throwing out the question of politics would have the same result in this discussion that throwing out racial classification (defeated in 2003 by the people of California in Proposition 54) would have for future national and regional discussions of racial inequality. Indeed, rarely is the experience or the expression of desire always equally liberating for everyone, even (or perhaps especially) in the gay marketplace of desire. With that said, it is now possible to consider some cultural sites that may bring us closer to laying bare the function and status of race in the gay marketplace of desire.

Just about everything you ever wanted to know about the mores or variables regulating the gay marketplace of desire and how it works can be gleaned from a casual stroll through the gay pornography section at your local video store. I do not speak here, of course, of the "family" variety of video emporium of the likes of Blockbuster or Hollywood Video; but I should think that would be obvious. I speak instead of the usually privately held beacons of pleasure that populate our cities and even some of our rural areas in this country. I speak of those proprietors who can testify to the difficulties of running a pleasure industry business in a country with a public puritanical streak as wide as the Mississippi River. Indeed, if your "thing" is black men, you need look no further, on our imaginary stroll, than the "B" section (under an alphabetically organized system): since the word "black" is the majority of the time the leading title word of such films. This fact, as I will later argue, is a telling indicator of the rules that govern the gay marketplace of desire.

What can we expect to find on our imaginary leisurely stroll through the "B" section of our porn store? A sampling of titles might likely include such staples as: *Black Cowboys and Studs, Black Gomorrah, Black and Horny, Black Workout* (1 & 2), *Black Raven Gang Bang* (1 & 2), *Black Ballers* (1 & 2), *Black Muscle Machine* (1 & 2), *Blatino Gang Bang* (for a bit of deviation), *Black Men in Black* (such spoofs are quite commonplace in this genre), *Black Balled* (1 & 2), *Black Jaw Breakers* (1 & 2), *Black Jacks* (1 & 2), *Black Drills & White Holes, Black Sex Pack, Black & White, Black Brooklyn Beef, Black Jocks and Spanish Cocks, Black Hot Rods, Blacker the Berry Sweeter the Juice, Black Patrol, Black Heat, Black Street Fever,* and *Black Power White Surge.* And trust me when I say the list does go on.

The appearance of black men in gay pornography takes place almost exclusively in three distinguishable subgenres of porn flicks: the all-black genre (self-explanatory), the blatino genre (films featuring black and Latino performers), and the interracial genre (films that feature black and white performers together). If the genres themselves instruct us in the fetishistic nature of the desire of the consumers to whom the porn industry markets such films, the general rules governing each of these genres have even more to teach us about the nature and deployment of the idea of blackness in each case.

Generally speaking, in the all-black genre and in the blatino genre, black men are represented as "trade": men with hard bodies and hard personalities to match them, men from or tied to ghetto or street life in one way or another, men possessing exceptionally large penises (with few exceptions for the rare black bottom man—the passive sexual partner in sexual intercourse), and, more often than not, men as sexual predators or aggressors. Both the all-black genre and the blatino genre provide prurient consumers a glimpse into the fetishistic world of racial blackness. Operating on many of the most readily imaginable stereotypes about black masculinity, these films do not disappoint viewers who bring to them a desire for a variety of black manhood closely associated with the brutish, the socially and economically disempowered (though never physically or sexually), the violent, and a fantastic insatiable animal sexuality that will fuck you tirelessly and still be ready for more. The consumer logic at work here assumes a differential relationship between the viewer and the viewed that is based on class and on race. Sometimes one or the other, many times both. Such filmic representations of black masculinity as the ones I am describing presume a viewer who is other to the experience of the men represented in the films. The viewer is in a position to fantasize about the object of his fetish (in this case an overdetermined blackness that is stereotypical and prêt-à-porter or at the very least prêt-à-regarder, i.e., ready to watch). Here in the form of typical images of black men in the mediated context of black gay porn, the viewer can enjoy fantasies about his sexual relationship to blackness without having to account for the possibly troublesome dimensions of the brand of thinking about race that he must necessarily bring to these images for them to work their magic, so to speak. Whoever the viewers are in this case— white gay men, middle-class black gay men, any number of other viewers who might find pleasure in these images—what we do know about him is that the images he consumes, or indeed wants to consume in such cases, are not of the black or black gay respectable variety. Indeed, to return to a question I posed in the introduction to this book, which we might ask again here with a different valence: where is the middle-class gay black man in these images? If there is virtually no place for the articulate, educated black gay man in the porno market (one site in which the dominant logics of the gay marketplace of desire are laid bare), can there be much hope for him as a valuable commodity in the marketplace more generally? Fitting not even one of the prescribed stereotypes, stereotypes that confer currency onto black gay men, he is relegated to the margins of commerce in the gay marketplace of desire.

The genre that has the most to teach us, for our purposes, is interracial gay porn. Nowhere are the differential logics separating the viewer from the viewed that I have been discussing more clearly articulated than when we turn our attention to the typical roles assigned to white men and black men in the interracial genre of gay porn films. The black men featured there are not substantively different from those of the all-black or blatino genre. They are endowed with the same kind of aggressive black male sexuality I have been describing. The difference is that they are portrayed as having sex almost exclusively with white men as opposed to being in a film that is for the ocular pleasure of fetishists, as in the blatino or all-black genre. In the interracial genre, black men are portrayed in consensual sex scenes with white men, and more often in rape or gang bang scenes in which the white man plays the passive role in relationship to the black men in the film. This further testifies to the type of sex imaginable in the realm of fantasy between white and black men and tells us a great deal about the currency of black male bodies in the gay marketplace of desire. Black men, once again, are presented as fetish objects for the "white" gaze (i.e., the racially inflected demands and expectations consumers of these images—regardless of biological race—bring to them).

Cultural critic and poet Elizabeth Alexander comments on the currency of the black male body in a different but surprisingly related context when she says:

> . . . there is also the spectacle of black male bodies in splendor, in glory, a gladiatorial history of black male performance that has always been the grandest of American spectacles. However, the containment of the image and its means of production are necessary in order that white male desire—specifically, as I am arguing here, for black men—can be contained and have a safety valve for self-protection from the unfettered power of black male sexuality. Perhaps this sexuality is no grander or more glorious in and of itself than any other, but it is made magnificent by its sequestering and fetishization. There is the apocryphal tale of U.S. Senator Jesse Helms carrying around one of Robert Mapplethorpe's black male nudes folded up in his back pocket and obsessively unfolding and displaying it to prove his point about the necessity to ban such "obscene" images, which illustrates my point about the interrelationship of power, desire, containment, and domination.

It is precisely this knotty interrelationship of power, desire, containment, and domination that is so well thematized in the function of black male bodies in gay porn. Virtual, mediated, contained black maleness can be sexy, arousing, spectacular, and even worthy of imitation (witness the pervasiveness of the style of dress associated most readily with hip-hop culture and its popularity among white youth).

I am reminded of a trip that a close African American gay friend and I took while in graduate school at UCLA to a conference just up the coast at UC Santa Barbara. The first evening we spent in Santa Barbara, we decided to go out to a gay establishment to check out the local nightlife. We found ourselves at a bar (the name of which escapes me now) with thirty-five to forty men—all of them white except the two of us. We had a cocktail, enjoyed each other's company, traded comments about the obvious stares we were receiving (trying to determine whether this was because we were new meat or because we were black). Finally, my friend pointed out to me that practically every video that had been played on the large screen television at the bar since we had arrived had been of black performers. After making this observation, he quipped, "I guess virtual blackness is okay, even unremarkable for white folks in a context like this, while our presence is an entirely different story." We laughed it off and continued drinking. His words ring for me now with a resonance I would not allow at the time because I just wanted to enjoy being out and having a drink with my friend. Virtual blackness, contained blackness, is always there in different forms—including gay porn, as I have been discussing—for the taking, the watching, the pleasuring when one wants it. But because it is contained and virtual, there is no danger of it speaking back, objecting, calling you out, making demands, or not giving you exactly what you have come to expect from it—your fetishistic fulfillment.

None of this is to say that I am opposed to pornography. Quite the contrary, pornography has a place in my version of a liberal society. An honest place. Indeed, I see no reason that pornography representing sex that is consensual and takes place between adults should not be enjoyed by whomever chooses to partake. Like it or not, that is already the case in the United States. Some conservative estimates put worldwide revenues in the pornography industry at $57 billion, with estimates of U.S. revenues coming in at $12 billion. There are 4.2 million pornographic Web sites on the Internet; this accounts for 12 percent of all Web sites. Some 68 million daily pornographic searches are initiated on various search engines; this accounts for 25 percent of all daily searches. One source even estimated that 53 percent of Promise Keeper men (a national group dedicated to uniting men to be passionate followers of Jesus Christ) admit to having viewed pornography. This paints quite a radically different picture of U.S. society than the puritanical one so many seem hell-bent on maintaining. Such silences, such investments in public respectability, of course, have their own costs, which I don't address here. It does suggest, however, as I will discuss in regard to personal ads below, that Internet-based porn consumption, with its increased emphasis on privacy (if you can't see it online you can certainly order it there), makes it possible for the U.S. citizenry to consume images and products of which they have learned in the name of "decency" to be publicly ashamed. Because, after all, good people don't watch porn, and they engage in sex only for procreative reasons, right?

But to return to the interracial genre, there is one porn film that stands out in my mind. It is exemplary of the conventions of the genre, which is why I suppose it made such an impression on me. The film is *White Movers Black Shakers* (All Worlds Video 1997). The director of the film is among the most highly reputed in the genre, Peter Goesinya. "Goes-in-ya," clearly a porn pseudonym, has directed such generic standards as *Fantasies of White and Black, Black Drills & White Holes, Black Tricks White Treats,* and the *Black Balled* series. Indeed, few possess as much experience in this genre as does Goesinya. In this way, this film is produced by a director not only familiar with the conventions of the interracial genre, but who might be described as one of its masters.

White Movers Black Shakers takes place inside an unspecified corporate entity. We don't know what it is this corporation produces; it is important to the plot only that we are in a corporate culture in which the players wear coat and tie, and where questions of who holds power and the racial lines along which power operates are central to the engine driving the plot machine of the film (rarely this complex in the genre). In the first scene, a white manager, Mr. Williams, reprimands two black subordinates from accounting who he has caught earlier having sex together in the basement stockroom. During the course of his interview with them, he orders them—if they want to keep their jobs—to show him exactly what they were doing together in the stockroom. The scene ends, of course, with the two black men both having sex with Mr. Williams, with the manager playing the submissive role. The next scene is one in which a black manager is instructing a white subordinate about the use of a new accounting system. The white employee is staring at the manager's crotch the entire time and slips into a reverie in which he plays passive sexual partner to the black manager. The penultimate scene is one in which Mr. Williams's secretary, Eric, impersonates Mr. Williams (who has since left the office for the airport) in an interview in the corporate penthouse with a potential black Latino employee. The Latino man, who at the point when Eric (as Williams) asks him to take off his clothes, tells us "he needs this job," plays aggressive sexual partner to Eric in the penthouse suite.

The film's final scene opens with another white secretary in the company (the one who initially sent the Latino man up to meet Eric playing Williams) telephoning the Williams impersonator in the penthouse in a joke to say that Mr. Williams is unexpectedly on his way back to the penthouse and he had better get out of there. As he hangs up the phone the secretary begins to laugh as the camera pulls back revealing him in his underwear on a sofa in an apartment with his black lover, J.C. They both are in on the joke. We learn as the scene unfolds that J.C. is the CEO of the company, when he delivers the following line: "Eric is just like Williams, fucking with all the employees. I'm going to fire both of them tomorrow, and I'm going to put you in charge. How does that sound, baby?" To which the secretary replies, "That sounds terrific. You know that's what I've been waiting for all along J.C., ever since I met you. Now just you and me can run the company." This is the only scene in the film in which a black man plays the passive sex role (a rare occurrence in the interracial genre in general). In the end, we come to discover, Eric is literally fucking J.C. for his company. After their postcoital moment, J.C. excuses himself to clean up. No sooner is he out of the room than Eric returns to the sofa and phones an unidentified person, who we assume to be his real lover, and says: "Hey, it's me. I finally got him to give me the company. We'll get rid of him soon. I miss you too, babe. I gotta have sex with him again. All in a day's work. I'll talk to you soon. Bye-bye."

This film fascinates me for at least a couple of reasons. First, it well exemplifies the conventions of the interracial genre. Black men fuck white men in the most literal sense of the word. In all of these cases, corporate power (real or feigned) fuels the engine of desire that makes possible the sex that happens across racial lines. Indeed, it is the one common denominator that makes all the sex in this film possible. This is interesting in terms of the larger genre since there always has to be a reason that white men want to or are required to have sex with black men: as a means of either control or retribution. Two other examples from the interracial genre come to mind in this regard. The first is *Black Raven Gang Bang* (XTC Studios 1997). In the original film in this series, the only storyline we have is of a white man who swipes the wallet of a black man who is walking down the street with another black man. He is chased by the two men into a bar in which he thinks, at first, he has escaped. The men find him there and proceed to initiate what becomes a gang bang involving other black men in the bar as retribution for his thievery. The other is the original film in the *Black Balled* series (All Worlds Videos 1995), provocatively described by one online advertiser as "an all-out orgy with 10 hot Black guys and one blond pussy-boy. These Black studs all get a piece of young, smooth white ass." Here there is very little in the way of plot. A white man driving a little red t-top is having car trouble. A black man walking down the street sees him and helps him to push the car to a nearby auto mechanic shop belonging to the black man's friend. Inside, the black auto mechanic looks under the hood to assess the damage to the car. He concludes very quickly that this will be a major expense, a couple of thousand dollars maybe. The white guy tells him that he does not have that kind of money and asks (understanding his "value" in this situation) whether they might be able to work something out. The two black men initiate a gang-bang on the white man that takes place atop the hood of the red car. Other black men continue to arrive until there are nearly a dozen of them taking turns playing the aggressive sex role with the white man and various sex roles with each other on the periphery of the scene. At the end of the film we learn that the repair was actually minor when the mechanic gets the car running in less than a minute. The white guy is left with a desperate look of hurt and anger on his face because he has "been had." The black men leave him alone in the film's final frame as one of them utters to him before exiting, "It's all good." The ideological lessons taught and propagated by these films are that white men have sex with black men for reasons having to do with master fantasies and power, retributive sex for having done something they have no choice but to pay for, or to trade on their value as currency in the gay marketplace of desire.

The second reason this film interests me is that, just when we think, in the final scene of *White Movers Black Shakers,* that their sex might actually be about something more, we learn in a twist that the professional, upper-class black man is literally being fucked by the white secretary for his company. Like the sex in *Black Balled* and *Black Raven Gang Bang,* this sex too, is just "all in a day's work." It finally has to come down to a matter of labor and not simply one of pleasure, a distinction Robin D. G. Kelley resists in his essay "Playing for Keeps." Still, this pleasure/labor divide remains one of the ways that we can make sense of interracial sex in a marketplace logic that works so actively against classifying any such interracial couplings as normative.

The language at work in these films further speaks to the fetishistic nature of blackness deployed in them. The frequency, for example, with which language approximating "give me that big black dick" occurs in these films rises to such a level as to make it a hallmark of the genre. Indeed, this racialized, sexualized language is only possible in one racial direction in reference to the penis. It is virtually unimaginable that one might hear in such a film "give me that big *white* dick." The nomenclature of size is so integrated with blackness when it comes to the pornographic idea of the penis in the imaginary, it is nearly impossible to think of disaggregating the two. This linguistic point could be related to the nodal visual example of the blackness of black dildos. Until recently, black dildos were rarely flesh toned. Rather, their color existed in an entirely fetishistic realm, bearing little to no resemblance to actual phenotypical blackness. Once again, black male sexuality seems to be ever in the process of being both reduced and exaggerated to its central signifier—the big black phallus.

Another cultural site that has fascinated me in my investigation of the gay marketplace of desire is that of gay male personal ads. Since the late 1980s to the present day, they made the incredible transition from phone-based ads and print ads to the electronic, online format. That transition was itself important in at least two signal ways: the advent and use of photos in ads and the simplifying and privatizing of the placing of ads. That is, ad placing became less cumbersome and even more anonymous, which opened up the possibility of doing so to an entire group of men who might not have otherwise considered the prospect (including, among others, men on the so called "down low" or the DL, and men who identify as "bi-curious"). With print ads, one had to commit far enough to the idea of placing an ad to at least complete the necessary paper work and post it to the newspaper or magazine where it was being placed, or call it in over the telephone (not a very appealing prospect for the nervous anonymity seeker). With the advent of online ads, this not only further privatized the act of placing an ad, but also made the mechanics of it so simple that even those who may not be entirely committed to the idea of ad placing could experiment with the possibility without much difficulty. This both broadened the base of potential ad placers and increased the revenue flow in that industry, resulting in what is now a proliferation of Web sites where gay men can place and read such ads for a nominal fee.

Some Web sites have evolved to include the more sophisticated technology of chat rooms, where men can talk to potential dates, mates, hook-ups, or sex partners in real time. AOL (America Online) is the most likely household name in this regard among gay men. Daniel Mendelsohn provides an elaborate and somewhat illuminating discussion of AOL in this regard in his book *The Elusive Embrace: Desire and the Riddle of Identity.* Most sites these days also include pictures along with your self-styled profile that may be viewed by other users on the system. One of the sites with which I experimented while working on this book, M4M4SEX (http://m4m4sex.com), not only breaks down its database so that you can search men by city, but also allows its users to place public and private pictures on the web. The public picture is the one that appears with your ad/profile and may be viewed by anyone who visits the site (the thumbnail public image is all you can see unless you are a member, in which case you can click onto the larger picture). The private image may only be viewed when a user on the system sends e-mail (filtered through the site so that no actual e-mail addresses have to be exchanged) to another user. At that point, the user may grant the person to whom he sends a message the right to view his private picture.

What should not go unremarked upon here are the complex levels of privacy that are clearly at work. Indeed, these sites are often constructed to maximally protect the privacy of users' personal information: real names are rarely used as your user name, messages are exchanged through the system so no actual e-mail addresses have to be exchanged, and private images are usually able to be viewed only after being granted access to them. Each of these progressive privacy levels are easily exploitable by users, as one might well imagine, to protect their anonymity, to stave off those in whom they may not be interested, and to encourage those in whom they wish to express further interest. This extra sense of privacy, along with the fact that one is dealing only in virtual bodies and does not (except by choice and mutual agreement) have to face real bodies or real embodied persons, makes it far more possible than in a gay bar, for example, to get in touch with exactly what it is we want. And, under cover of anonymity, it becomes possible to be far clearer, more honest, and unapologetically (even if at times brutally) discriminating about what it is we want. Indeed, even the desires that most of us know enough about "political correctness" and gay propriety to realize we should have some shame around can be expressed with abandon online. The Internet freed us even from the PC shackles of the gay bar, a place where we no longer even need to patronize some and pretend to others about the often exclusive and predictably hegemonic nature of our desires on the one hand, or about the problematic fetishistic nature of them on the other. For some this might be liberating, a form of ultimate sexual liberation, perhaps. But is that equally so for all of us?

I am concerned throughout this book, in one form or another, with truth telling; that is also the case here in this chapter. As a witness for my truth, I am not always or even primarily interested in questions about the intentions of others. Indeed, in this way I follow the lead taken by the discipline of my intellectual training, English studies. Not since the advent of the New Criticism in the early twentieth century have literary and cultural critics been focused on questions of intentionality. Instead, we have moved to a place where we are routinely far more interested in how a text functions or makes meaning in the world. I would argue that African Americans generally spend a lot of time excusing away the racist behaviors of others; gays and lesbians spend far too much time looking to make allowances for what straight people's intentions are when they yet again injure us; and the poor make great allowances for the wealthy when by word or deed the rich make them feel small or patronized. The intent of the hegemonic and injuring other, it seems to me, is not a category that need unduly interest the truth teller. She is interested instead in the effect or impact that the other's actions have on her. Bearing witness to that impact is precisely a truth that she and she alone can bear witness to, the unique contribution to discourse that only she can offer the discursive world.

Having said that, it remains to review a sampling of ads I collected just under two years ago from the M4M4SEX Web site. These ads are all from

Chicago-based customers. No names are used, as is the case on the Web site. Each of the ads appeared on the site below a matching thumbnail photograph, which we of course cannot reproduce here. Just beneath each photograph (before the ad appears) is a coded user name. Each ad begins with a headline followed by the ad itself. I have added in brackets a brief description of the photos, the writing of which poses its own difficulties of visual assessment, which I do not address here. Let me state up front that I do not here take on the obvious references to bare backing and HIV brought up by these ads. Though related, I might argue, such a full discussion lies beyond the scope of this current project. There are many abbreviations used which are unique to this genre of gay online commerce. Where relevant, I translate them:

Chrischicago [close-cropped shot of a brown penis only]
Looking for hot oral and more . . .
Hey guys, I'm 30, mixed black & scottish, 5'9, 175 lbs, masc., 7" cut. I'm in Chicago regularly, and looking to have some fun with hot white guys while I'm here. I love oral, body contact, nipple sucking, being rimmed, and fucking.

Edgewsxyguy [torso shot of a toned white body with perfect abs, cropped just above the lips and just below where trimmed pubic hairs begin]
Hot Euroguy looking . . .
29/5'11"/160/ slim—defined / abs / great shape / gdlkng and masculine, uncut :-) Looking for a hottie for safe play, possible LTR. Caucasians only, be D/D free and in shape, no fems pls . . .

Hotlover4you [handsome face (framed by short cropped hair) and toned pectorals of a smiling, square-jawed, handsome white man]
Hot stud for hot latinos
5'9,165pnds,brn/brn,musc,tan,smooth. Looking for hot latin guys who love to fuck! very oral and mostly bottom. must be clean and safe

Mascvgltop [toned torso of a hairy-chested white man in khakis; one arm is curled up to show off his biceps while the other hand holds a camera]
Muscular guy seeking same, your place
Early 40's, VGL, Lean and Defined, Hairy chest, 5'9, 170, 31w, 42c, 15a. 8.5c, Sorry, built white guys only, 25 to 50

Muchmore [nearly full-body shot including face of a white body builder in a Speedo worn to accentuating his ample penis, chest out, not smiling but smirking]
Chicago Muscle Jock
Looking for hot bubbled bottoms or big dicked tops. I'm into white guys or light skinned latin men who are NOT fat or sloppy look'n. Be sexy. Be in good shape. NO heifers, NO pnp, No poppers, No cologne—Yuk!

VGLjock4u [full-body shot absent the head/face, posing arms by his side, standing in a near plié position to accentuate the size of his calves, donning boxers]
Looking for a hot guy
6'3", 210lbs, muscular, masculine, looking for the same. 25–40wht. Lets see where it goes.

Rpd3 [full-body professional photo of a smiling, white man with a receding hairline (though he refers to himself as "boy"), late 30s to early 40s, in a dated double-breasted formal suit]
CUTE WHITE BOY FOR BLK DUDE
Slim proportionate body, 5'8", 145lbs, 30W, 8"cut-piece

ChoWrslBear [head shot of a late 30s–early 40s smiling white man in formal attire, full faced, large dated glasses, and dated hairstyle]
GWM with lots of interests
aggressive play to submission wrestling. top or bottom or both, open to race.

Chgoverstop33 [average-to-unattractive white man with a receding hair-line in his mid- to late 30s in a head shot, wearing a T-shirt; head turned to the side, looking grave]
Hung Top Seeks Hot Bois
GWM, 6'1",175, br/br in shape,HUNG 9x6 cut seeks hot white bois; love making out, oral, fucking, giving massages, etc; can be aggr or tender. pre-fer younger/smooth, but not required; NO BB

Bb traveler [full-body shot of a slim, big-haired white man seated nude in a rocker with one hand on the base and the other on the tip of his penis]
21yo Travelin Barebacker
21, 6'3, 180, brown, blue eyes. Loves to fuck and suck. BB always. Few limits, just ask! Sorry bois—not interested in black men.

Alwaystop [lower-body shot of a large white man lying on a bed holding his penis, wearing a white T-shirt and white athletic socks]
Total Top—
6'5" 240 blonde/blue 7.5 x 5.5 cut Looking for long, hot fuck sessions with hot bottoms. Prefer latin bottoms. Not into blacks or asians. I'm a professional massage therapist and love to give a massage in my hot tub . . . want a ride?

AnFboy4fun [self-explanatory; shirtless, toned, close-cropped white man lying on a sofa, smiling, with his belt and jeans partially opened]
Boystown . . . iso cute/inshape & 18–30 for
28 5'9 150lb 30w smooth/inshape/cute . . . looking for 18–30something . . . UB inshape/cute

Chgodd2001 [near full-body shot of an average build, attractive, close-cropped smiling white man wearing a cut off T-shirt and gym pants]
GWM FOR GBM

Looking to meet masculine gbm NOW. 36, 5-10" 160lbs, hot tight body, 8"mushroomhead dick, versatile sex pig with few limits, love trying new things, toys, ice cubes, ropes, etc.

Tallblktight [torso shot (cropped above the waist and below the face) of a toned black man with large pectorals and tight biceps]
Black man looking for real, down sexual encou
6'5", 230lbs, 33w, tight build, 8" dick, nice plump/tight azz, smooth, clean, nice to smell and taste. Looking for brothers who take care of mind body and spirit . . . all that makes the sex exceptional. Hit a bruh back if u feelin me.

Lilhiv1 [full torso shot (cropped at the mouth and the thighs) of a nude, perfectly toned black man lying down, holding the head of his penis in one hand]
I got mad dik fo ya
mad dik, I'm poz, if u poz dat is okay, i du most anyone, my dik needs sum mad attention if u ain't up fo da ride, don't hit me. if u up fo a ride, hit me up fo sum attention.

Funguylkvw [near full-body shot of a nude, toned, baseball-cap-wearing white man lying on a bed holding his penis as he stares straight and un-smiling into the camera]
Normal Guy Looking For Some Fun
If your public pic doesn't have a face . . . 50%+ of your profile is stats or you are into the "type" thing don't bother sending me a message. Look-ing for no attitude, normal guys to have some hot sex with! "A hot body does not make u attractive!"

Taken together, these ads tell us a great deal about the gay marketplace of de-sire, what constitutes value in that marketplace, and who has access to mak-ing the "rational choice" of sex or love object in that same marketplace.

These mores, clearly racialized as they are, also speak to the depth of American racism. There is no part of our lives, thinking, and experience that it does not reach.

In this world of personals where privacy and anonymity reign, black men pander to white fantasies about what white men want them to be (even to talking in black dialect); white men freely acknowledge without being condemned as hubristic that they are "very good-looking" ("VGL") since it is only an admission of the obvious logic of the marketplace of desire at work; white men apologize for not liking black guys ("sorry bois . . . not interested in black men") without the least thought of how offensive or racist such a gesture might be; indeed, it would seem that whiteness is the all-around salient variable that increases one's value in the gay marketplace of desire. A white man (in some cases, as above, a "light-skinned latin man" may suffice—that is, if he is "clean and safe"), who is "very good-looking," with "a large penis," a "hot tight body," and a masculine affect ("no fems" allowed after all), represents the ideal type, the sexy and desirable man that we should all want in the personals world.

It should not surprise us, however, that this same type abounds in the world of corporate banking and finance as well. Though I cannot be certain about the question of penis size, I have always marveled at how white, "good-looking," tight-bodied, and testosterone-laden the men are who populate the business schools at UCLA where I was a graduate student and at Northwestern where I currently teach. And it did not surprise me when I recently recalled a line from the 1997 film *Boiler Room* (a latter-day remake of the older *Wall Street*—which is referenced in the film), when the recruiter for the firm, J. T. Marlin (played by Ben Affleck), says to his young recruits: "You will be a millionaire. . . . You are the future big swinging dicks of this firm. Now, you all look money-hungry and that's good. Anybody that tells you money is the root of all evil, doesn't fucking have any. They say money can't buy happiness; look at the fucking smile on my face: ear to ear, baby." Perhaps the thing that ties these two worlds together—these worlds in which power and value of one sort or another is amassed, sold, and consumed in a thoroughly well-ordered marketplace that unfairly advantages those who have capital of one sort or another over those who do not—is the parallel between the gift of capital and the gift of whiteness. Both define the rules of the marketplace in which we all must at some level circulate. Much like capital, whiteness is seldom something one earns, but is more often a matter of birth. As such, whiteness is a valuable commodity in a fundamentally racist culture. Its value is so compelling, so complete, that it reaches even to the most intimate parts of our lives as sexual, desiring, and loving subjects. So much is this the case that Funguylkvw (i.e., fun guy in Lakeview)—a "good-looking" white guy himself—provides in his ad a not so very implied critique of the marketplace of desire recognizing its corruption. His ability to do so, however, to be able to stand above the system and critique it in the way that he does and to still full-well expect to have the "hot sex" to which he alludes in his ad, comes from his position as a good-looking white guy in the marketplace as well. The people in a position to make the "rational choice" according to the dominant racial logic fueling the gay marketplace of desire are also people who in their disavowal still benefit from it. In this way, the knowledge that makes it possible for Funguylkvw to disavow the working of the marketplace, as he does here, is the same logic that makes other white men in the marketplace apologize ("Sorry, built white guys only"), and still others congratulate black men (as I will come to discuss shortly) for being their first sexual encounter with blackness. These men make these gestures from privileged positions in the marketplace of desire. Indeed, the declaration of a black man in exercising his exclusive desire for other black men does not resonate with equal systemic weight in the gay marketplace of desire. How could it in a marketplace where the reign of the value of whiteness is so thoroughly established?

When it comes to understanding the gay marketplace of desire, no exploration of its impact would be complete without some attention paid to the impact of personal experience. What follows are some of my own stories. I have heard so many similar experiences from countless other black gay men that I feel confident in presenting them as somewhat representative of part of our collective truth as black gay men in mainstream (white) gay spaces. The first of these occurred some time ago, shortly after I came out in 1991.

I was enjoying a happy hour with a group of other gay graduate students from the English Department at UCLA and some of our other friends. This would have been late on a Friday afternoon at the Revolver, as this was something of a weekly ritual with us that year. We did happy hour together on Friday afternoons and beach volleyball on Saturdays. On one of my rounds through the bar to see who was there, and admittedly to be seen as well, my gaze was met from across the bar by this thin, young, white man. He was cruising me hard—much harder than I was accustomed to being cruised, really. I smiled at him. This smiling and looking went on for what must have been at least five minutes when he finally crossed the room to meet me. I was excited. He was cute and I was still young enough (and not suspicious enough) at the time to be excited by someone taking such strong and unambiguous interest in me. He smiled and offered his hand as he told me his name and asked mine. I gave him my hand and told him my name was Dwight. We talked for about a minute or so—the polite chitchat that people who are first becoming acquainted use. The sexual energy of our conversation, the way our eyes moved purposefully over each other's bodies, and the ease with which tactility entered our exchange, signaled that we had both done this before and there was something of appreciation on both our parts of the skill with which it was being executed. He was from Hawaii and had been living in LA for the last few years. I was in graduate school at UCLA in the English Department working on a Ph.D. He liked LA. I was ambivalent about it as a place to live. Two minutes into the conversation, which I thought was going very well, he threw me for a loop with his declaration that he and his friends were "out looking for black guys tonight."

He was smiling as he said it. There was no malicious intent on his part. The line was delivered almost as if he had said something that would make me happy. To his mind, he and his friends were out to give the gift of whiteness to a few fortunate black gay male souls. Tonight a few poor, benighted, black men would hit the whiteness jackpot with this guy and his small band of brothers and get to participate in, have access to, or be the recipients of the gift that trumps virtually all others in the gay marketplace of desire—the gift of racial whiteness. And here it was being offered so nakedly, so clearly, so easily to me. I hated him in that moment. I hated the set of assumptions that made it possible for him to imagine that this statement was something that he could say to me in this way. I hated not being able to injure him in the same way. At that moment, I wanted to be far away from him, from that place, from West Hollywood, from the gay world that had brought me such a perceived sense of liberation only a few months before when I was coming out. That same gay world was now beginning to teach me some important lessons—which it had undoubtedly taught to countless black gay men before me—about my value in that world and the ways in which race and racism would have congress in even my most intimate of negotiations within it.

The next experience of this sort would come a couple of years later. This one was with a white guy around my age. We had met at my health club. We exchanged numbers, and he eventually called and invited me out to dinner one night later in the week. A real bona fide date. The date went well. Conversation flowed easily; the restaurant was nice but not too nice for a first date; and he was a student as well (law school, I believe), which left much in common for us to talk about. At the end of the date, we went back to my place where we spent the night together. During sex, a sentence he uttered chilled me. It sounded so foreign, and demanded so much from me in the way of turning my concentration away from the physical moment I was in to my thinking about the moment instead, that I almost went limp: "Give me that big black dick!" Was that what this man who had been getting to know me only a couple of hours before over dinner thought of me? Had he reduced me to the "big black dick" in his mind, which might really have come attached to any black male body? Did the fact that the words came so easily in the throes of sexual passion mean they were more real than the conversation we had been engaged in over dinner? And why was I feeling resentful of being made to confront or think about this at all in the middle of what was an otherwise satisfying sexual experience? Wasn't this what you had to be prepared to endure as a black man if you were going to have any traffic at all with white male flesh? We finished and lay quietly for several minutes. My mind no longer on the sexual fulfillment we had both just enjoyed, but rather thinking hard now about what had just transpired and whether it was worth talking to this now near-stranger that I had only a couple of hours earlier invited into my home. In what should have been a tender pillow-talk moment after sex, he added insult to injury when he said to me (as if he somehow needed to and as if it would somehow make a difference to me): "You are the first black guy I've ever been with." I knew there would be no second date. I knew I could not, would not, allow myself to see him again. I was not angry this time as I had been with the guy at the Revolver. This time I was simply resolute. I knew that whatever were my reasons for being so resolved and whatever were his intentions in revealing my status as his first black man, I would not see him again because something about this experience, even at the time, felt not only unsettling but wrong.

Shortly after I moved to Chicago, I met a young white flight attendant at a local bar. We talked for a while and then he invited me back to his hotel where we proceeded to have a very satisfying sexual encounter. We did not talk a lot during sex, a trait I have come to appreciate more and more as I have sexually come of age in the gay community. Less risk of hearing something that will be offensive or thought-provoking (especially in a time like this when you precisely do not want to think). When it was over and we had talked for a while, I made ready to leave to go home. He had an early flight the next morning and I had a full day ahead as well. He smiled at me as I was getting dressed to leave and said, "Congratulations." I was caught off guard by this declaration. I said, "I'm sorry?" He repeated, "Congratulations," still smiling. "For what?" I asked. "You're the first black guy I've ever let do what we just did," he said, fully satisfied with the sufficiency of his response. I dressed more quickly now. When I found my bearings, still wanting to escape with my dignity intact, I simply replied in a slightly annoyed tone of voice, "Well, I'm glad I could be your first. I hope it was everything you thought it would be." He stopped smiling, as if recognizing from my perspective for the first time the possibly troubling character of his "congratulatory" remark. No numbers were exchanged even in pretense that we might meet again. Our goodbye was quick and smacked of the perfunctory.

Stories such as these are quite representative of much about the sexual and intimate experiences of black gay men navigating the terrain of mainstream gay social communities. The racialist, racist, or stereotypical dimensions of how black male value is produced in the gay marketplace of desire are fascinating. They are deeply tied up with mainstream heterosexual versions of the same stereotypes about black male sexuality. There is the Mandingo fantasy (the exceptionally well-endowed black man often, though not exclusively, associated with a brutish sexuality). There is the search for "trade" (the fantasy of a working-class man—the term is not used to connote black men exclusively) by some. Trade is not what you "marry" or "take home"—it is what you "hook-up with." There is the homo thug fantasy, which many exhibit as well. The search for thug love is undertaken by those who want or need a gangsta or thug, a hard, streetwise brother to help them to fulfill their fantasy. Then there are the names ascribed to the men who want to be almost exclusively with black men. They are known as "chocolate queens," "chocoholics," or my absolute least favorite, "dinge queens." These circulate in the marketplace alongside such companion terms as "cha-cha queen" (if you like Latinos), or "rice queen," to describe those who prefer Asians. Such language reveals the racial complexities of this marketplace. Some have taken this cue and deemed it impossible to sort out what about all of this exists in the realm of fantasy and what about it is real. Such commentators have suggested that this is all play or performance and, therefore, not to be taken with the degree of seriousness that I am employing here. To those commentators I say that in the same way black people know when they are being called "nigger" by those who intend hostility and when by those who intend play and solidarity, and the way in which gay men know when they are being called "fag" by those who intend hostility and when by those who intend play and solidarity, I know and understand the labels I have been discussing here. To borrow the words of cultural critic Tricia Rose in her discussion about black women's sexuality and intimacy in *Longing to Tell*, which I think are very useful to this case as well: "We are looking not only for reflection but also for affirmation, advice, and a space to hear our side of the story told without taking into account someone else's agenda, needs, or expectations."

These terms represent just some of the ways in which black gay men are imagined by others and, in many cases, by themselves as well. Being a black gay man or a gay man of color does not necessarily exempt one from the rules governing the gay marketplace of desire. Indeed, such terms and fantasies have currency among black gay men as well. To say, however, that they mean the same things when articulated between black men would be not only a gross oversimplification, but would also be to ignore the complicated racial histories that animate the ways in which blacks and whites have learned and continue to learn to see and imagine each other in the United States.

Still our stories do not end here. Some black gay men who find that they are committed for whatever reasons (and there are many theories about this phenomenon) to dating exclusively white men evolve ways of turning the tide of racist thinking that they know exists about them in the gay marketplace to their "advantage." Many of them talk easily and quite openly about fashioning themselves to give the white men they are interested in attracting exactly what they believe they want. So they play the racial pandering game—cultivating a certain kind of affect, dressing in a certain way, talking differently when necessary. This is one efficient way for such men to get what it is they want while giving their partners what it is they want as well. Still other black men who come of age in the gay marketplace develop early on an aversion for "snow" and choose to socialize exclusively with other black gay men, to frequent black gay clubs and bars (available in most larger cities), and to date exclusively other black gay men. This, too, is another valid response to the clear and evident racial dimensions of the gay marketplace of desire. Still others, like me, try negotiating (with varying degrees of success) a sexual and social life of navigating back and forth between these polar responses—dating or hooking up with the "rainbow coalition." Those in this group have usually evolved (educated by their experiences like the ones I discussed earlier) highly articulated conditions under which they will date white men. And the most politically attentive of this set usually have deeply principled feelings against dating choco-holics or dinge queens. We don't want to be with any white man whose desire for black dick is fetishistic. In such cases, his desire is not about or for the particular black man but for his idea of whatever the blackness of the black man signifies in his imagination. Some have said that such a position is splitting hairs, that all desire is fetishistic. The degree to which such statements are true render meaningless any number of distinctions, salient and otherwise, making one man's fetishistic desire for black men equal to another's foot fetish. Such sweeping statements do not provide much in the way of distinction and serve only to mask the operation of power in some not-so-very-subtle ways.

What I think is interesting about both labels describing men whose desire for black men is virtually exclusive and about black men's responses to the racism of the gay marketplace of desire is that all these labels or reactions take place in a marketplace that centers on "whiteness." That is, all of them are ever in the process of either defining themselves against or in relation to the norm of whiteness as racially most desirable, or the norm of white-on-white relationships as the ideal. After all, there is no label that I am aware of in the gay marketplace of desire for men who constitute the likely majority in mainstream gay communities—white men who sexually prefer other white men. And all three of the responses I discussed of black men to negotiating the racism of the gay marketplace of desire can be viewed as emerging in strong relationship to the hegemony of whiteness in the marketplace. The black gay men who embrace their ascribed position, and fashion and style themselves according to the logic of the marketplace, thereby maximizing their effectiveness in attracting white men, do so in strong affinity with the hegemony of whiteness. The black gay men who reject whiteness in favor of the virtually exclusive social and sexual company of other black men do so in strong aversion to whiteness and their prior experiences with it. And the black gay men who endeavor to navigate between these two poles do so by developing sophisticated sets of rules about what are acceptable and unacceptable forms of whiteness. This position, too, evolves from an aversion to an ever more specific brand of whiteness in the marketplace. All of this points, however, to the centrality of whiteness and of white-on-white gay male relationships as a sense-making norm that fuels the logic by which we ascribe value in the gay marketplace of desire. This is the extent to which gay white men know, and all of us who would have commerce in the marketplace know, that of all variables that circulate, none are more central and salient than "the gift" of racial whiteness. Whites know they have it, others know they will never have it, and virtually everyone wants it. This might be understood in the gay marketplace of desire as the main principle of doing business.

I have a friend, Steven (not his real name). Steven is a gay white man, in his late 30s, smart, professional, and very handsome. In fact, very handsome is an understatement. Steven is, in the logic of most any marketplace of desire, drop-dead gorgeous. Men and women both notice him when he enters a room. His beauty is remarked upon and appreciated by others openly and often even in front of if not directly to him. He is the kind of man men fawn over, cross rooms and make fools of themselves to meet. On more than one occasion Steven and I have been in a gay bar in the middle of a clearly serious conversation (or so it would be clear to any thinking individual), when we have been interrupted mid-sentence by someone simply wanting to introduce himself to "us," all the while looking at Steven. On countless occasions I have been out with Steven when men have come up to me while I was on my way to the bathroom or to the bar to get another drink, ostensibly to meet me. No sooner have I told them my name than they say something resembling the following: "Your friend is so cute! What's his name?" Talk about stating the obvious and thinking that's going to win you points. Everyone in the bar knows Steven is cute and is, indeed, at the top of the food chain in the gay marketplace of desire. And importantly, Steven knows it too. This is one of the reasons that he and I have been able to become great friends (added to the fact that he is one of the smartest and most caring people I have known). He understands how the gay marketplace of desire works and has no investment, as so many white gay men do, in denying its power and its impact. To my mind, Steven has even corrected for this fact by developing a desire that is not at all like what one would expect of someone in his position. Steven rarely dates other muscle-bound white boys. His racial tastes have been all over the map. He has no investment in being or even in appearing to be the "good boy" that is most closely associated with whiteness in the gay marketplace. Steven enjoys sex and sexual variety and is in no way a prude.

Steven and I have talked often about the marketplace of desire and I have learned a lot from him in those conversations. He has heard white people and white gay men make statements about race that I will likely never be privy to as a black man. He, along with a handful of other white gay male friends, have been native informants of sorts as I have undertaken the writing of this book, and they have been very able teachers. It was Steven and another white gay male friend of mine who lives in New York City, Mike, who first got me to think about the similarities between how whiteness and blackness function in the gay marketplace of desire. I resisted the idea at first, but the more I considered it, the more I thought they were right.

The function of both whiteness and blackness in the marketplace of desire is to dehumanize (though toward markedly different ends) the person to whom they are ascribed and to endow them with qualities that they often do not possess. Guys have often said to Mike and about him that he is blond and is very outgoing and friendly. Now, I love Mike. We have known each other for years. That said, however, he is nowhere near blond—his hair is clearly brown—and no objective jury would call his personality outgoing or overly friendly. Mike can be charming, but in social settings he is hardly the person whose personality is going to light the room on fire. Both Steven and Mike have also been described to me by others who have only just met them as "nice," "sweet," and my personal favorite, "so innocent-looking." I imagine similar things were said of Jeffrey Dahmer (and I don't, by the way, think it incidental that most of his victims were men of color), but that's an entirely different story. Also, it is not uncommon for people to meet Steven or Mike once, sleep with them, and become uncommonly attached to the point of stalking them. It seems clear to me that this kind of quick emotional overinvestment among gay men is possible only when men endow Steven and Mike with traits that they do not necessarily have and foist onto them their image of the idealized gay white man whom we are all taught to want and to desire. Indeed, to refer to my argument about Abercrombie & Fitch in the last chapter, a desire to possess or to participate in such idealized whiteness has the power not only to fuel the success of the Abercrombie line, but also to fuel the logic of the gay marketplace of desire. In this rather limited way, the kind of whiteness ascribed to Mike and Steven is similar to the kind of blackness ascribed to black gay men that endows them with superhuman-sized penises, insatiable sexual appetite, and a performative blackness associated with the homo thug or the Mandingo fantasy.

There is a linguistic dimension to this imagined blackness as well that I am reminded of often. I have a Ph.D. in English and would be an easy candidate (especially in professional circles) for over-enunciation. That means I speak standard English (though I am no stranger to code-switching in my less professional circles) and have been known on occasion to use a polysyllabic word or two. This often creates cognitive dissonance for many white people who encounter me as a speaker for the first time. The words and the accent coming out of my body don't resonate with their image of how I should sound as a speaker. At times people have reported hearing me speak with a black vernacular accent, a Jamaican accent (go figure!), and an English accent. Linguists call this a form of linguistic discrimination, when a hearer reports hearing a speaker (based on what she sees) with an accent other than what she actually hears.

Perhaps it was this tendency to endow white men with qualities that they do not necessarily possess that infuriated me when I watched my first episode of *Boy Meets Boy*, which might more accurately have been called *White Boy Meets White Boy*. James, the "boy" at the center of the show (who I found to be hopelessly dull and uninteresting) is charged with ultimately choosing the "boy" with whom he will have this dream date at the show's expense. James is an example of the whitest of white boys, total milquetoast. He is described on the official Bravo Web site for the show (http://www .bravotv.com/Boy_Meets_Boy) in this way:

> James is a 32-year-old Benefits Administrator who grew up in Oregon. Now living in Los Angeles, James spends his spare time hanging out with a small group of close friends. He's an outgoing guy who'd rather go to the theater than go clubbing. James loves to play games and can often be found playing beach volleyball on the weekends. He is very competitive and up for anything. James' taste is very refined when it comes to both men and food. He is romantic, loyal and looking to complete his life with Mr. Right. He has all the right qualities to make the perfect husband. As he puts it, "I am a sweetheart who is looking for love and willing to wait for it."

James is a wholesome, monogamous, professional, athletic gay white man. He represents the purest ideal of a gay man in the American ocular imagination. We learn all of this about James in the first episode, which begins by introducing us to him by running video footage of him with friends in his native habitat of Los Angeles (though he was raised in Oregon). His best friend, Andra, is a straight woman (not a promiscuous and possibly competitive, focus-pulling gay man), and he enjoys dinner parties and evenings at home with his friends. Indeed, he is shown at home around a dinner table playing a game with them. He is constructed in this introduction in the image of the ideal white gay man, the catch that any and all of us should want.

Then we are introduced to the cast of fifteen men vying for James's affection. All of them, save the lone African American man who is booted off on the first episode, are white. The scene looks like it could be an outdoor event at any mainstream gay bar in the middle of summer—lots of good-looking white boys with little to no representation of men of color. The African American man, a twenty-three-year-old molecular biologist from San Diego, is dismissed ostensibly because he has only recently come out. James decided he does not want to deal with a man so new to his sexuality. James retains another contestant Dan, however, who tells James that he has a boyfriend but is open to other possibilities. So much for James's commitment to monogamy.

As I watched the episode, I was troubled by several aspects of it. First, the show is billed as a "gay dating show," which it actually is not. The producers have chosen to add a twist to the mix by including among the fifteen men competing for James's affection a number of heterosexual men. The viewing public is aware of this fact, and so are the straight men (obviously). James is not aware of the twist when the show begins and is not made aware of it until weeks into the run of the show. The voice-over, which takes us to and brings us back from commercial breaks, announces this fact again and again. It is clearly meant to be the titillating hook for a mainstream viewing audience. The show in this way really becomes about trying to determine who is gay and who is not; so much so, that the two gay male friends with whom I watched this episode on Tivo (they had watched and recorded it earlier) first and foremost wanted me to see if I could pick out the straight men from the gay men. It would appear, in this way then, that in order to have a main-stream gay "dating show" on national television, it would really need to be about feeding into one of heterosexuals' chief sexual anxieties—identifying who is and who is not. Just like the rationale for a show on national televi-sion about five fabulous gay men who provide a valuable makeover service to heterosexual men (*Queer Eye for the Straight Guy*), at the show's center must be the advancement and shoring up each episode of a heterosexual relation-ship. Queerness, in this way, is good and palatable to mainstream audiences to the extent that it works in the service of advancing heteronormative rela-tionships. One white gay male colleague pointed out to me that another pos-sibility is that these straight relationships on *Queer Eye* are improved by "queering" heterosexual men, thus rendering queerness a site of radical po-tential in relationship to the show's mainstream viewing audiences. Maybe. But I think my colleague has more faith in the sophistication of the main-stream U.S. viewing public than do I.

As I watched *Boy Meets Boy,* I allowed myself to wonder what it would look like if the show's "James" had been an African American man. My mind could literally not produce an image of anything that could possibly work in this way given the reality we have learned and, indeed, come to expect from U.S. television. An African American man could not possibly be viewed as representing universal gay male experience in the way that a white man can and does. A quick perusal through the ads and photographs in any of the national gay tabloids—*Out, Genre, Advocate, Instinct*—will bear this out. Even if we could get beyond that hurdle, the idea that fifteen eligible white gay men would be competing for the affection of a black gay man is not only implausible, but unbelievable. And if the show had more black men or men of color than white men, whether the James figure was white or black, that too would not make for good television. It does not jive with the televisual image of gay life that has been manufactured, packaged, and produced by mainstream U.S. culture. So the fact that *Boy Meets Boy* has met with some degree of popularity is in my view no reason for dancing in the streets. Just as I warn, in my reflections on Ellen DeGeneres's coming out, against putting our salvation in the power of images alone, we also have to consider the clear and apparent limitations placed on such images in order to insure their popularity. Success for *Boy Meets Boy* may extend the cachet of and interest in a particular kind of mainstream gayness (white), but I dare say it does very little for the rest of us. The logic of the politics of queer representation feels strangely like that of black anti-racist politics in the 1960s. There was the popularly held belief—challenged, of course, by black feminists—that if the black man was successful in his liberation, it would follow that black women would be as well. Like my early black feminist sisters in a somewhat parallel universe, I am not convinced that my liberation is tied to the success of either white gay male images or to the liberation of the white gay male. There is very little in the way of collaborative history or the history and present of race politics in the queer community that leads me to trust my liberation solely to the hands of white gay men.

None of what I have said in the preceding pages is definitive. Even less of it is complete and totalizing. It represents my own efforts at beginning to get real and to be honest about how I, and so many others like me, experience the forces of the gay marketplace of desire, and the impact they have had on our lives. Any totalizing analysis of this lies far beyond the scope of this project, and the telling of such a complete truth will require many voices and a multipronged, multidisciplinary approach. It would require the experimental skills of a psychologist. Such a study of sexual orientation and attraction is currently underway by colleagues in psychology at Northwestern University. It would require from sociologists and political scientists attention to social formations, demographics, and possibly to income levels in this marketplace. Studies like the *Black Pride Survey,* which I referenced in the preface, represent a noteworthy start in this direction. It would take further investigations by the literary and cultural theorists who might examine the politics of narrative representations by white gay men of gay men of color and vice versa. Still, all of this would be only a beginning.

So much work remains to be done on the nature of the gay marketplace of desire, and it is important work worth doing. For I am convinced that if we are ever to crack the riddle of racism, to make a dent in our understanding of the depth of the commitments we exhibit in this country to making racial discriminations, to understand the increase in rates of HIV and AIDS among black gay men and in black communities more broadly, and to appreciate the historical reality of the specific nature of black homophobia, we must turn chiefly to the realm of sexual pleasure and the marketplace of desire for direction. So much of our humanity is laid bare there. More of ourselves and our investments are risked there and portrayed most forcefully there. So until we are able to go there and talk openly—I mean really honestly—across racial lines about such matters, about our desires, about how our particular sexualities impact not just ourselves but others with whom we are in commerce, we are likely never to be able to speak any of the whole truths that will further liberate black people, queer people, and black gay and lesbian people.

Part II Race and Sexuality on Occasion

4   On Race, Gender, and Power

The Case of Anita Hill

Rare are the occasions that so-called critical theory and politics (in a rather narrowly defined sense of the latter word) converge in illuminating and provocative ways that aid in the interpretation of popular political events. However, the controversy over the 1991 nomination of Clarence Thomas to the U.S. Supreme Court—particularly a consideration of the testimony of Anita Hill and the responses to it—provides an excellent focal point for the investigation of such a critical moment. A study of the idea of intersectionality (how different identities such as race and gender interact and marginalize) vis-à-vis this event can provide a useful understanding of intersectionality in relation to subject position (i.e., the significance of the place or social location from which we activate certain rhetoric). Such an analysis should serve to deepen our sense of how subjects at the identity intersections of our society are marginalized by what has also been called the "simultaneity of experience."

Kimberlé Williams Crenshaw, in her essay "Demarginalizing the Intersection of Race and Sex: A Black Feminist Critique of Antidiscrimination Doctrine,

Feminist Theory and Antiracist Politics," provides an appropriate point of departure for my discussion of the media dramatization of the Thomas hearings. Crenshaw aims to set forth something of the "problematic consequence of the tendency to treat race and gender as mutually exclusive categories of experience and analysis." She centers

> Black woman in this analysis in order to contrast the multidimensionality of Black woman's experience with that single-axis analysis that distorts these experiences. Not only will this juxtaposition reveal how Black women are theoretically erased, it will also illustrate how this framework imports its own theoretical limitations that undermine efforts to broaden feminist and antiracist analyses. (139)

There are any number of issues raised by the Thomas hearings, and any number of readings that are enabled by them as well: the annihilation of the essentialist black body, the dramatization of political ruptures in the feminist movement, the rehearsal of stereotypically black sexuality in black male/female relations, the instability of the political left in the United States, and the Rambo-ization of the American sensibility, or what some have called "compassion fatigue."[1] However one reads this media event, all readings seem to function in the interest of the political construction, naturalizing, and shoring up of right-wing conservatism in the United States—a powerful, mostly white, hegemonic block which seems to be successfully representing/re-presenting itself as normative. Both in the service of brevity and an inability to exhaustively explore all these possibilities here, I will focus instead on Anita Hill as a metaphor for the problematics of intersectionality and the potential pitfalls of comparative oppressions. Some might say that the Hill testimony represents a dated issue. But as recently as January 2003 one *Boston Globe Magazine* reporter rightly suggested otherwise:

> For many people, Hill remains a symbol frozen in time: a single video frame of the self-possessed woman in a turquoise suit holding her own

against a phalanx of white male senators who, as they grilled her, shifted the focus away from Thomas's fitness for the Supreme Court and, in effect, put her—a witness—on trial.

It is precisely this aspect of the hearings, this shifting of focus from Thomas to Hill as the one who is on trial, that I still find telling in our discussion of this case.

The media airings of the Thomas hearings were called by many, including the *Los Angeles Times,* a modern day "morality play," a "courtroom drama." If this is true, it remains to say a word about the characterization of the players in this hi-tech drama. It would seem that the easily identifiable cast of characters in this event are the U.S. Senate Judiciary Committee, Clarence Thomas, and Anita Hill. If, for our purposes, the Judiciary Committee represents (among other things) the law, or rather the failings of the law to understand and properly to address the complexity of Hill's experience of sexual harassment as a black woman, then Clarence Thomas (and the overwhelming public response favoring Thomas) represents how easily and summarily dismissible Hill's experience really is. In all of this, Anita Hill—a well-educated, articulate, and erstwhile credible black woman whose motivations for what Senator Arlen Specter called "perjury" are still perplexing—is rendered simultaneously (and not separately) the victim of her race and of her gender. She is at once the enabler of, or the material for, what Thomas characterizes as the "hi-tech" lynch mob (the Judiciary Committee) that is trying ostensibly to hang an "uppity black," and a symbol for the stereotypically historical black temptress (evidenced by the dismissal of her claims even with no demonstrated motive Hill might have had for lying). Indeed, had Hill been a white woman with the same credentials and credibility, not only would the dynamics of the hearings have been different, but Thomas's rhetorical move here might not have been so readily available to him or effective for him.

But for the moment, I want to reflect on how Hill's gender is involved in the dismissal of her testimony to the point of innuendoes of psychosis on her part made by committee members and witnesses. It is worth quoting at some length here from Columbia Law School professor Patricia Williams's book, *The Alchemy of Race and Rights,* which sets out (in a similar context) a framework in which to understand the collusion of forces at work in this process of dismissal:

These questions [about Williams's own reliability] question my own ability to know, to assess, to be objective. And of course, since anything that happens to me is inherently subjective, they take away my power to know what happens to me in the world. Others, by this standard, will always know better than I. And my insistence on recounting stories from my own perspective will be treated as presumption, slander, paranoid hallucination, or just plain lies.

Recently I got an urgent call from Thomas Grey of Stanford Law School. He had used this piece in a jurisprudence class, and a rumor got started that the Benetton's story wasn't true, that I had made it up, that it was a fantasy, a lie that was probably the product of a diseased mind trying to make all white people feel guilty. At this point I realized it almost didn't make any difference whether I was telling the truth or not—that the greater issue I had to face was the overwhelming weight of a disbelief that goes beyond mere disinclination to believe and becomes active suppression of anything I might have to say. The greater problem is a powerfully oppressive mechanism for denial of black self-knowledge and expression. And this denial cannot be separated from the simultaneously pathological willingness to believe certain things about blacks— not to believe them, but things about them.

When students in Grey's class believed and then claimed that I had made it all up, they put me in a position like that of Tawana Brawley. I mean that specifically: the social consequence of concluding that we are liars operates as a kind of public absolution of racism—the conclusion is not merely that we are troubled or that I am eccentric, but that we, as liars, are the norm. Therefore, the non-believers can believe, things of this sort really don't happen (even in the face of statistics to the contrary). Racism or rape is all a big fantasy concocted by troublesome minorities and women. It is interesting to recall the outcry in every national medium, from the *New York Post* to the *Times* to the major networks, in the wake of the Brawley case: "who will ever again believe a black woman who cries rape by a white man?"[2]

Williams's comments here are most instructive in the way they enable a glimpse of the larger epistemological war at work. Not only is the credibility of Anita Hill at stake, but so is the credibility of any black woman literally to "know" that she has been sexually harassed. That is, the very status of black women's epistemology is under attack. In many ways this is even more pernicious, because if black women are not credible to voice their own experiences (because of the historical hysteria of women on issues of sexual violation and the historical absurdity of the status of chastity where black women are concerned), they are, in effect, rendered voiceless in such cases, their issues unspeakable. This rhetorical silencing technique is demonstrated most clearly when Senator Orin Hatch during the hearings reads from *The Exorcist* in order to insinuate that Hill may have borrowed or, worse, fabricated, the now famous Coke-can-with-pubic-hair metaphor. His logic runs something like this. Since the metaphor appears in *The Exorcist* as well as in Hill's testimony, this may show that Hill has problems distinguishing reality from fiction. This stands as a direct attack on the status of Hill's epistemology. Furthermore, Senator Specter's claim of perjury against Hill echoes Williams's sentiments as well: "My insistence on recounting stories from my own perspective will be treated as presumption, slander, paranoid hallucination, or just plain lies." All of these are charges brought against Hill at one time or another during the course of this national tele-drama.

To complicate the matter further, with the Tawana Brawley example, Williams raises the question of the status of black women's epistemology in relation to the epistemology of white men. How are we, then, to understand the ideological shifts that take place when the parties involved are a black man and a black woman (as is the case with Thomas and Hill)? This is where the status of "race" becomes more an issue of political ideology, even "interpellation." Put another way, the question might be one of who has the readiest claim on the force of the race card. Hill's gender and race collude, it would seem, if not to silence her testimony, then to render it un-/incredible and thereby dismissible, whereas Thomas's "race" and gender are associated with that which we might call, in our dialectical political reality, the "ideologically white" and undeniably patriarchal. This, I hope to show, points to one of the fundamental irrationalities of racialized discourse, the moments when it trips and falls on the obstacles of its own unreason. Such moments of utter unreason are the cornerstones of black neoconservative politics.

Cornel West describes in some detail the political oversights involved in black neoconservatism in his essay, "Assessing Black Neoconservatism," in *Prophetic Fragments*:

I am confident that if more rational debates are held, with conservative, liberal, and left voices heard, the truth about the predicament of the black poor can be more easily ascertained—with a few valuable insights of the new black conservatives incorporated into a larger progressive perspective which utterly rejects their unwarranted conclusions and repugnant policies. I suspect such a rational dialogue would unmask the new black conservatives to be what they really are: renegades from and critics of black liberalism owing to the limits of this liberalism, yet also highly rewarded and status-hungry ideologues unwilling to interrogate the narrow limits of their own new illiberalism. This parasitic relation with their black liberal foes and patronage relation with their white illiberal friends would be a farce if enacted on stage—but given the actual roles they play in present-day America, there is too much at stake to simply be amused. (63)

Thomas's stance throughout the confirmation process was to downplay the significance of race, until Hill came forward with her charges. At that strategic moment, Thomas (as a metaphorical shifting signifier, who identifies himself as one with the very agency to be such by his ability to characterize the hearings as a lynching), in effect plays the race card. To be ideologically white is to be able to speak and to "know." It is not only the ability to speak about one's own experience and from one's own position, but also to speak for the Other (in fine colonialist fashion), since we have already established the unreliability of the Other's ways of knowing. Thomas's seizure of the status of race in these hearings is highly problematic given his subject position in this case. A brief gloss of lynching and the crime of rape demonstrates that by characterizing the hearings as a lynching, Thomas overstates his case with some dangerous mixing of metaphors that collude to erase the specificity of Hill's experience (including the impact of history) as a black woman. I hope I might be forgiven for using rape in a somewhat metaphorical fashion here, since there is no equal "historical" discourse about sexual harassment as there is about rape. Given the close associations of the two issues, however, I think that such a substitution can be borne out in the context of this argument.

The implicit role that Hill plays in this "lynching" as black woman is historically and politically suspect. Also, the idea of a black woman being used as the catalyst for such a "lynching" is suspect, given the history of rape in this country. The very suggestion that a black woman's "chastity" (a category reserved for white women in all respects) could be "violated" is itself historically ignorant. So not only does Thomas's comment have profound effects for Hill's experience, but it also denies the historical oppression of black women's bodies at the hands of white men as well as black men. What Thomas is, in effect, relying upon is not clearly a racial matter, since he and Hill should have equal access to that category for all the good it does them. Had Hill been a white woman (as problematic as that would still be), there may be more reason to be found in this rhetorical, racial move (consider public black sentiment in the O. J. Simpson case, for example). Instead, Thomas's gesture, complicated as it is, seems to rely upon his identifying with the one thing that escapes critique in this drama—right-wing, conservative ideology.

This identification seems to be enabled, in part, by the fact that Hill is a black woman. The irony of this moment, of course, is that Hill can simultaneously be the pretext for his "lynching" and silenced by the very racial interpellation that here gives Thomas voice to speak.

For me this example demonstrates that we are only just beginning to understand the intricacies of intersectionality in ways that will allow us to render and analyze the experience of black women in all its fullness and complexity. It is the marginal silence that is finally being broken by rigorous critiques like those of Crenshaw and Williams. The work is not easy, but the labor is most rewarding and necessary to any informed and truly inclusive, progressive African American political and intellectual agenda.

5 Feel the Rage

A Personal Remembrance of the 1992 Los Angeles Uprising

(I have chosen here to preserve the perspective from which this essay was originally written on May 3, 1992, just on the heels of the Los Angeles uprising, which began April 29, 1992. I was a resident of Los Angeles at that time, attending graduate school at UCLA. The piece was published a few weeks later in a small African American progressive Christian newsletter in the San Francisco Bay Area.)

Even as I begin the process of putting pen to paper, something about this project feels hopelessly anachronistic, out of sync with time. As a people, African Americans are told almost daily by the government and the media of the "progress" we have made. We are reminded on a regular basis (as if someone were trying to convince us) of how much better off we are now than we were some thirty years ago. However, the events of the several days following the announcement of the verdict in the Rodney King case tell quite a different story. These events expose such assertions of "progress" as the same dangerous rhetoric being used at this historical moment to undergird the political right's ridiculous claims of "reverse discrimination" and to dismantle important strategies for achieving equality like affirmative action.

Today (Sunday, May 3, 1992) I heard Congresswoman Maxine Waters deliver an invigorating speech at the First African Methodist Episcopal Church. In that speech, she outlined the complex of social and economic inequities leading up to the eruption of violence following the verdict. Her speech was so similar in tone, critique, and content to statements made by Dr. Martin

Luther King Jr. following the Watts "riots" of twenty-seven years ago, that for a moment I almost thought the congregation had been transported back in time. In the media, we saw some racially motivated violence (a thought that the media has been reticent to address) against whites by blacks, violence borne out of frustration. We witnessed burning and looting in the streets of Los Angeles, which when televised bore an uncanny resemblance to the earlier Watts rebellion as well. So, while we are often inclined toward progressive models for understanding history, "progress" for African Americans has always been somewhat of an illusion. The story of our history resembles more the impossible fate of the legendary king of Corinth, Sisyphus, who is doomed for eternity to roll the stone up the mountain even though it inevitably rolls back down on him. But history is not what I want to address in this essay. Rather, I want to turn our attention for a moment to the anger, rage, frustration, disenfranchisement, hopelessness, and injustice that gave rise to the violence we all witnessed at the close of April.

In the media, as in everyday discourse with people, we have heard those who participated in the LA rebellion referred to as "thugs," "hoodlums," "vandals," "freaks," "murderers," "gang-type individuals" (my personal favorite), and a host of other derogatory appellations. We have heard people say that violence and destruction are not the "right" ways to respond to the verdict. We have heard people say that they are ruining "their own neighborhoods." And, perhaps worst of all, we have heard this rebellion referred to as "random violence." Such statements dramatize the vast difference between the way that the "haves" and the "have-nots" perceive the world and their positions in it.

Let us be clear: anger *is* an appropriate response to the verdict in the Rodney King case. As a people, African Americans have never gotten their fair share in the United States, to be sure. Our homelands were looted when we were first brought to this country as slaves. Our dignity and humanity were further stolen when we were counted as three-fifths human beings by the "founding fathers" in drafting the Constitution. Our labor was looted during slavery to build the legacy of a capitalist economy that continues to be responsible for the wealth of so few and the destitution of so many in this country. A further violence was committed against African American people even after the Emancipation Proclamation, when we were violated once again by the rise of Jim and Jane Crow. We were looted of our promised forty acres and a mule, our reparations for slavery. After slavery, many of us were forced negligently into urban ghettos during the rise of industrialization, where we were untrained and, because of racism, uncompetitive in the job market. This was one way of containing and controlling urban poverty and anger. Such social conditions created much of the cycle of poverty and subsequent despair that many of us live under even to this day in the United States.

Every day we are either homeless or witness to the homelessness of our neighbors. Every day we are hungry and we watch our children go to bed hungry. Every day we are unemployed or underemployed, while there seem to be fewer and fewer job opportunities to be had. Every day we are subjected to vendors who sell products of dubious quality in our neighborhoods and charge us outrageous prices for the privilege of buying them. Every day we live in close proximity to some of the most conspicuously consumptive people and places in the world (Beverly Hills, Brentwood, Bel Air, Pacific Palisades, and so forth), while we are asked to put up with subhuman living conditions. Every day we see the government spend billions and billions of dollars abroad to fight their wars, to feed the mouths of people we have never seen, and to rebuild Europe, while we are told in no uncertain terms to pull ourselves up by the bootstraps! And you wonder why we are angry? You wonder why we are violent?

Martin Luther King Jr. (quoting Victor Hugo) wrote in 1965 following the Watts rebellion that: "If a soul is left in darkness, sins will be committed. The guilty one is not he who commits the sin, but he who causes the darkness." This well characterizes the situation of African Americans in this country. We have been too long left in the darkness. We have been left in the darkness of poverty, the darkness of neglect, the darkness of unemployment, and the darkness of a system that has lied to them again and again and again. So you see, Rodney King was not the cause of the LA rebellion. Every black person in the United States knows that there have been many Rodney Kings who have been brutalized by that long, repressive arm of the state known as the police. The difference (or so we thought this time) was that there was a video-tape for all the world to *see.* This time, we thought, they will have no choice but to serve justice. But alas, we were wrong. When presented with the choice of serving justice or serving the interest of the state and white hege-mony, the jury chose the latter. It was more than a slap in the face for those of us who witnessed this verdict. It wounded us deep down on the inside. It cut to the very core of our souls. It was a direct affront to all of the hundreds of years of suffering, patience, and cooperation that we have tried to exhibit toward this country. And this time we could not hold our peace!

If, as Dr. King also once said, "riots" represent the voices of the unheard, that is what we witnessed here in Los Angeles. White America cannot say that they did not know the gravity of the social conditions under which the urban poor live (and let us be clear that it is no coincidence that the vast ma-jority of these are people of color). Urban poverty experts, political figures like Maxine Waters and Jesse Jackson, grassroots organizers in the commu-nity, and even progressive intellectuals have been doing little else if not rais-ing these issues. So, I am convinced that it is not a question of ignorance. Rather, it is a question of a refusal and an unwillingness to hear. One the-ologian has called it "compassion fatigue." White America and its govern-ment simply got tired of hearing "those people" complain about their prob-lems, their history, and their victim status. It made white America feel bad, so they decided it was no longer important to hear. And this was the contin-uation of leaving souls in darkness. The Reagan and Bush eras, with their "bootstraps" mentality, have created a great season of darkness for the urban poor, and they have taken it until they can take no more.

Many cannot believe how those who participated in the rebellion could think that this was the "right" thing to do. We must understand that we can-not understand unless we are willing to step out of self and to try to see the world from the position of the urban poor. What does the discourse of "right and wrong" mean to someone who has no home, or no job, or no food, or no money, and no hope of ever having those things? Those of us who speak of "right and wrong," of "law and order," are people who benefit from the social contract. We get something out of lawfulness. Many of the people who participated in the LA rebellion have never known "law and order." What do such concepts mean when you barely have or lack altogether the necessities of life? So, when there are no other venues left to you, and your situation seems hopeless (as was the case for many African Americans after the Rodney King verdict), "sins will be committed."

But let us be clear: those sins could have been prevented. Since we know that to those to whom much is given, much is required, such preventative measures should have come from the White House, Congress, the state house, the well-to-do, and community leaders. And in order to prevent such uprisings in the future, we as a nation will need to rebuild the structures for honest communication. We will need to be sure that we do not become weary of doing good. We will need to be sure that we are willing to step out of self and to see the world from where others stand. We will need to find ways of rebuilding torn-down hopes. We African Americans must also (eventually) find ways of managing our rage so that it does not blind us from finding new ways (and I am convinced that we need *new* ways) to find the strength to love those who have despitefully used us.

I do not mean love in any facile, "touchy-feely" sense. On the contrary, I mean a love that gives us the strength to correct the wrongs and injustices that will be perpetrated upon us. I mean a love that empowers us in the way that it empowered our ancestors to hope against hope. I mean a love that will liberate us from an obsession with either deifying or demonizing white people. I mean a love that will give us the courage to refuse to suffer indignity and subordination at the hands of a government and a society that owes us so very, very much. This is the love with which we need to arm ourselves. I think it was the apostle Paul who said it best: "Be strong in the Lord and in the power of his might. Put on the whole armor of God, that you may be able to stand against the wiles of the devil. For we wrestle not against flesh and blood, but against principalities, against powers, against the rulers of the darkness of this world, against spiritual wickedness in high places."

In the meantime, my brothers and sisters, it is okay to be angry. It is human to feel frustrated. It is a further testament to our humanity that we could not hold our peace when we got the word about the Rodney King verdict. To suffer such indignity and brutality in silence is anything but human. So for right now, for this day, we should feel the rage. And tomorrow, because we are God's and because we are all stuck here together on this orb of dust and spit we call Earth, we will find the strength to begin to love again.

6 Ellen's Coming Out

Media and Public Hype

(I have chosen here to preserve the perspective from which this essay was originally written on April 30, 1997, in Los Angeles on the night of the airing of Ellen's coming-out episode.)

I am quite predisposed toward skepticism. Perhaps a result of being an intellectual, or a black gay man, or a confirmed urbanite whose pose, in part, is not to be in the habit of letting much wow or impress. In fact, just about anything that receives as much public attention and produces as much hype as did tonight's special episode of *Ellen* seems a prime candidate in my book for examination and interrogation. Whether we were caught up in the *Ellen*-induced frenzy or not, this phenomenon—and it was a phenomenon—undoubtedly has much to teach us about the state of the gay and lesbian community.

West Hollywood was a scene tonight! I mean, everyone sat perched in front of television sets throughout the city with friends (or in some cases with complete strangers) to watch the airing of Ellen DeGeneres's "coming out." Bars all along Santa Monica Boulevard had special showings of the episode. Countless private parties were held in homes throughout the city. Even the neighborhood health club, the Sports Connection (now 24 Hour Fitness) in West Hollywood, rented large-screen televisions and chairs for the event and opened its aerobics rooms and cafe to allow viewers to watch the show together. And certainly not to be outdone, the media was also out in full force to record the event they had created in the weeks and days leading up to it. Television and camera crews were out to gauge "the happening"—and the opinions and emotions of the gay and lesbian community—that everyone had been discussing, planning for, and waiting for weeks to see. They camped out in front of Little Frida's, a local lesbian coffee house in West Hollywood (since closed), which was featured in the episode, and all along the boulevard.

It all began for me a few weeks ago when a friend introduced me to a friend of his who, in turn, very kindly invited me to his "Ellen's Coming Out" party. Later I heard buzz about Ellen's coming out among my undergraduate students at UCLA. Finally, today, I ran into my neighbor who came out (pun not intended, unlike the show's overly cute opening scene) of his apartment to pick some of our communal roses for his house. I asked what was the occasion. He told me that he was having a few people over to watch *Ellen*. It was then that I decided I needed to go to that party I had been invited to attend. I wanted to know what this event meant to people. I wanted a better sense of what was happening "out there." And I wanted to see (with an invested audience) how the episode would deal with gay sexuality in what would have to be, as per the genre, a comedic and non-threatening way. So like a good Angeleno, I hopped into my sports utility vehicle and negotiated my way from my Los Feliz home through the urban quagmire that is Hollywood to the primary locus of gay sociality in LA, West Hollywood, my prior home of four years.

After finding parking on the periphery of the more precise destination where the party was taking place, I walked several blocks on Santa Monica Boulevard, passing the hubbub at the Palms (the one real bona fide lesbian bar in town), passing the circus that was beginning to convene at the health club (with the lines to get in stretching down the block), and passing the crowd of people beginning to assemble at Little Frida's as well (the other lesbian stronghold in town). With all of the excitement that was discernable in the air and on the faces of passers-by, one might have thought that scientists had discovered a cure for AIDS or that it was really, in the words of one enthusiastic lesbian who spoke on the evening news, "gay independence day." I soon arrived at my destination where I was joined by a host of other gay men and one heterosexual couple—all friends of our host—to celebrate the occasion with champagne and some light fare.

When the show began, the anticipation in the room was palpable. It was really as if we were all somehow thoroughly convinced that gay/lesbian liberation itself was riding on the images we would see in the next hour. What followed, instead, was to my mind not particularly revelatory, revolutionary, or progressive. The show was an hour of K. D. Lang along with a host of heterosexuals ranging from Oprah Winfrey to Billy Bob Thornton assuring American viewers that it is okay for Ellen to be a lesbian. (Oops! I am sorry. She is "gay"—or just "Ellen," as she instructs the friend who asks whether she should call her "gay" or "lesbian.") This curious marshaling of the cameos in the show was both entertaining and telling. In order to deal with lesbian sexuality on prime-time television, it is necessary to employ the authority and legitimacy of America's number one talk show host/sympathetic ear/voice of reason, Oprah Winfrey, in the role of Ellen's Yale-trained therapist whose point of identification with Ellen, as the show explicitly names, is her own experience of racial discrimination. One of the rhetorical contradictions that still amazes this viewer/reader is the way in which race, though itself a maligned category on the contemporary political scene (consider, as I have noted, the recent proposition defeating affirmative action in California as reverse discrimination), can still function to provide this kind of legitimacy to other forms of oppression when necessary.

The show definitely had far more to say to heterosexual America than to gay/lesbian America. This goes a long way toward explaining why the show was cast in the least offensive way possible. First of all, we have in Ellen herself the model of moral and social rectitude. She is the non-threatening, all-American girl-next-door with whom Americans can be comfortable, unless you are listening to Pat Robertson (who everyone knows is *really* crazy). The show goes far to demonstrate that gays and lesbians are just like heterosexuals in that they want the same entrenched American dream of the house with a picket fence and someone to love them. I think this is why the writers/producers of the show chose the term "gay" as opposed to "lesbian." The term "gay" has a kind of popular currency, perhaps even cachet, in heterosexual America that the specificity of "lesbian" does not. Additionally, the show, like the film *Philadelphia,* which made this viewer just as suspicious, showed us more man/woman intimacy (between Ellen and her old college chum) than it did woman/woman intimacy. The choice to have Laura Dern's character be involved in a relationship when she meets Ellen is a way to stave off any real sexual intimacy between the two women on-screen. So, by the end of the episode, we have an Ellen who is out, innocent of sexual intimacy with a woman, and approved of by her cohort of friends and Hollywood celebs, representing a blending of the world of the show and the real world beyond the show.

In order for this episode of *Ellen* to work as a metaphor for gay liberation, we have to believe in Ellen as a representative figure. But of course Ellen is not all gays and lesbians. She is not the amalgamation of a very complex and multifaceted community. And, of course, not all gays and lesbians want what Ellen wants. It is dangerous for us as a community to believe that images in themselves can or will liberate us. Images have never had that kind of cultural autonomy and always function in a complex relationship with the social and political mores of the day. In this sense images tend, for the most part, to follow—indicating a great deal about where our culture and society may be at present—rather than to lead to liberating possibilities.

Still, it is good that Ellen "came out." And it is good that America had a chance to see another positive, if overly anesthetized, image of gay/lesbian sexuality on prime time. But as a community of gay men and lesbians, we must not be fooled into thinking of such images as our salvation. We have to put our anger, frustration, joy, and excitement where it is most likely to matter. I can only query, for example, about why we did not see such an overwhelming response in the streets and in the bars of West Hollywood when

AB 101 (the California Assembly Bill that proposed to add "sexual orientation" as an additional basis on which discrimination is prohibited) was defeated. What *Ellen* demonstrated is that it is easier for all of us, heterosexuals
and gays/lesbians alike, to identify with a character in, and the drama of, a
situation comedy than to address the political realities of gay/lesbian life.

Don't misunderstand me. I think it is okay to be excited about *Ellen*. In
fact, if anything, the most profound cultural work that *Ellen* did was inside
the gay/lesbian community. It was the first time that I can recall a popular
event that the entire community rallied behind in this public a fashion that
dealt specifically with a lesbian and not a gay man. In a community that is
still very male-centered in its focus and its imagery, it was refreshing—and, I
hasten to add, about time—to have an event featuring a lesbian at the center of it be the cause for communal solidarity and celebration. Still, we must
be ever diligent about where we put our trust and how we expend our ener-
gies. Images alone have not the power to save us. For that we will have to rely
on the extraordinary will and character of everyday people, committed to
being out every day and to making their worlds, wherever those may be,
worlds that are safer for all people to be who they are.

7 Affirmative Action and White Rage

Affirmative action is the last topic to which I ever thought I would consent to address myself publicly. This does not mean that I don't consider affirmative action to be among the leading issues of our time, because it most certainly is. If there is any doubt on that score, we need look no further than the near-Herculean political, rhetorical, and legal efforts undertaken to bring about its very dismantling. And if one needs any further proof of its significance in our time, we need only consider the bitter and sometimes regressive and odious quality of the rhetoric that animates the debate around the issue of affirmative action. Nor is my caution about addressing this question like the trepidation Emerson records when he did finally address himself to the Fugitive Slave Law in 1854, saying: "I do not often speak to public questions. They are odious and hurtful and it seems like meddling or leaving your work."

While I certainly more than appreciate Emerson's sentiments about the odious quality of public questions—because they are not mere stylized, textbook philosophical considerations only, but have something of the difficult and irksome added quality of responsibility and real human consequences—

still, if our modern-day debates about public intellectualism in the United States have taught us anything, they have surely convinced us of the pertinence of considering and of contemplating the role of our vocation as intellectuals in the public sphere. No, my hesitation about addressing affirmative action publicly, rather, has more to do with a frustration over the state of the discussion itself. That is to say that affirmative action has achieved status as one of the great issues of our time—like abortion or the death penalty—wherein the terms of its very articulation have become so concretized and overdetermined that saying anything that will not be all too quickly and with remarkable efficiency logged into a pre-existing position in the debate is an utter impossibility. Almost immediately the speaker's racialized and gendered corporeality, along with what he or she might have to say on the issue, gets locked into the discursive echo chamber of positions that we think we already know all too well. In other words, the political right has effectively rendered affirmative action—like its first cousin, the category of "race" (discussed elsewhere in this book)—a thing about which nothing truly new can be said because everything constituting the "simple truth" about it worth saying is already known. It is this "simple truth" to which I want to return in very short order.

So, we know enough to perceive that the set of circumstances defining the terrain upon which the would-be commentator on affirmative action must tread is dicey, a war-ravaged landscape left in the wake of a minefield wherein all the explosives have fired, a veritable *terrain vague*—a wasteland. But unlike most wastelands, this ostensibly barren soil continues to produce fruit—and strange fruit, indeed. The fruits of resentment, hatred, envy, bitterness, and, even more to the point, violence. In fact, it is my deep suspicion that the quest by those on the political right to reverse—legally, rhetorically, and politically—the small gains afforded by affirmative action to women and people of color has fostered an important by-product. That by-product is nothing other than a culture of righteous anger among white men. And as we have been instructed by the words of the late filmmaker Marlon Riggs in an ironically different context: "Anger unvented becomes pain unspoken becomes rage released becomes violence . . . cha, cha, cha!" Only this time, the violence being perpetrated is by white men against people of color.

When I speak here of violence, I am not speaking simply of violent acts perpetrated against people of color by white men, like the slaying of Filipino-American U.S. postal worker Joseph Ileto (August 1999), or the two black children outside Chicago who were run over by a pickup truck driven by a self-proclaimed white supremacist, or of the killing spree that one white male went on a few summers ago, killing people of color in his wake as he moved through several states in the Midwest, or of James Byrd (a black male in Jasper, Texas) tied to the back of a truck by three white assailants in 1998 and dragged to his death . . . and the list goes on. Such images, horrific and disturbing as they are in their own right, were produced in a culture which gave legitimacy to the misplaced anger and frustration of white men who are under the pressure of having to really come to terms for the first time with what it means to live as "white" in a truly multicultural society. Perhaps this is in part what James Baldwin, of whom I have written at length in other chapters of this book, meant when he uttered these prophetic words: "As long as you think you are white, there is no hope for you. Because as long as you think you're white, I'm forced to think that I'm black." To that statement I might add only this phrase: "and *you* are forced to think that I am black as well."

Multiculturalism, like its cousin "diversity," are two race-lite terms used often in current political discussions to talk about race while glossing any mention of what Harvard Law School professor Randall Kennedy calls the fundamental "crisis of trust besetting American race relations." In a multicultural society Americans have learned to take pride in who we are and to assert our various identities as a positive attribute in that society. And in a world in which racial minorities have always been defined by their difference from whites, and in which whites have always defined themselves by the negation of racial minorities (that is, cultural whiteness as an identity is assertable only as the amalgamation of the things that it is not), whites are left wanting for a positive identity of their own to assert. This represents, at least in part, the crisis in cultural whiteness precipitated by the explosion of multiculturalism onto the U.S. educational and political scene. In a world in which victimiza-tion was a negative, the symbolic and rhetorical representation of cultural and racial pride in what shared experiences of fierce racism produced for racial minorities became a positive. This move, however, placed a high value on the status of victimhood in the political discourse around affirmative ac-tion, which developed historically right alongside the multicultural explo-sion in this country. As a result, through the logic of reverse discrimination, the political right has provided a significant number of white Americans with a language by which they have turned the tide of discrimination in their favor. Victim status has become sacred turf in the battle for "special privi-leges" that, conservatives have argued, blacks and other people of color used for their own gain. If this is true, one logical move toward dismantling it would be to show how flimsy victimhood itself is as a concept. The right ac-complished this by claiming it for their own "plight" via affirmative action, a phenomenon that has over time led to a kind of righteous indignation among white males that sanctions retaliatory violence against people of color.

The strategic appeal of this rhetoric of reverse discrimination created by the political right draws its strength from the logic of Occam's Razor: a rule in science and philosophy (named after the fourteenth-century figure William of Occam) stating that entities should not be multiplied needlessly, which is interpreted in more common parlance to mean that the simplest of two or more competing theories is preferable and that an explanation for unknown phenomena should first be attempted in terms of what is already known. That is, the American public is largely a public weaned off any tol-erance for complexity at an early age. Indeed, so much of American identity is about the maintenance of innocence. We have a deep investment in per-sonal innocence, sexual and emotional innocence, political innocence. For this we need look no further than the example of the film *Forrest Gump*. This is a movie about a mentally challenged, hapless political agent in history. Indeed, Forrest does good in the world effortlessly, without even knowing that he is "doing good," because his simplicity is good and represents the truth—the real American heart of unspoiled innocence. We have a deep need to believe this about our leaders, our political and social commentators, our clergy, and so forth. The U.S. public is infinitely capable of being shocked precisely because we want so desperately to believe in the perfectibility of people through the triumph of simple innocence. This is why the near impeachment of President Bill Clinton was such a huge issue for this country. This is why—aside from the fact that he hijacked an election—George W. Bush is in the White House today. This is why Ross Perot was not so long ago a serious contender for the U.S. presidency. This is why scandal of all kind sells like hotcakes in the United States, even though as a citizenry we stand ready to display our shock and amazement again, and again, and again.

Ours is a society in which he who generates and masters the art of the sound bite carries the day. Any explanation of an idea requiring complex thought or articulation is viewed with a great deal of suspicion by the public. The "simple truth" is what the political right sells us when they talk about God's plan for the family, the "simple truth" of the so-called errant nature of homosexuality, or the "simple truth" that affirmative action represents special rights and privileges for people of color. Never mind that such simple explanations demonstrate a flagrant disregard for history, context, or ideology. Conservative Republicanism in the United States, in terms of its rhetorical strategies, has become very much akin to a brand of religious fundamentalism. Take note of any form of fundamentalism and it will demonstrate that believers find it far easier to hold onto and to ground their beliefs in untruths or partial truths that are simple, than to encounter the complexity of thought that animates even many of the earliest statements on affirmative action, like that of President Lyndon Johnson in a speech at Howard University when he declared the following:

> Freedom is not enough. You do not wipe away the scars of centuries. You do not take a man who for years has been hobbled by chains, liberate him, bring him to the starting line of a race saying, "You are free to compete with all the others," and still justly believe you have been completely fair. Thus it is not enough to open the gates of opportunity.

Another more contemporary commentator on affirmative action echoes these thoughts—which are now easily dismissed as tired old concerns in part because they have not the simple appeal of a "we should treat everyone the same" ideology. Never mind that the trust it would take to accomplish such a thing is near unimaginable in U.S. society and would entail a degree of faith across racial lines that history has again and again proven to be untenable. Howard University law professor Frank H. Wu offers these instructive words:

> A majority probably agrees—as suggested by the conflicting surveys on affirmative action—on moderation rather than extremes. For the time being, even equality of opportunity is demonstrably not available. African Americans suffer higher infant-mortality rates, shorter life spans, diminished education opportunities—virtually every comparison that can be made along racial lines show racial disparities to the disadvantage of African Americans. Affirmative action, like much of real life, operates within a gray area. We will be able to do better than affirmative action, if we agree to avoid ideological absolutes, and instead look for principled compromises. In the end, affirmative action is only a means. It serves as a remedy, nothing more. In devising new visions of a diverse society, we may need to do more.

Comments like those of Wu and of President Johnson are in grave disfavor at present in the debate on affirmative action. The discourse has taken a turn to the right and it seems set upon a course from which it shows no visible signs of returning. The compromise represented by the recent Michigan decision of the U.S. Supreme Court (while it might certainly have been much worse) is in many ways indicative of this state of affairs.

The rhetorical, and subsequent political and legal, victories won by those on the right on this score have created a culture in which white males can understand themselves as victims and can even in extreme cases be justified in lashing out in violent ways against people of color as a result. The connection between rhetoric and violence in this case requires our attention. For, in our thoroughly racialized society, any policy, rhetoric, or law that draws white men—still a hegemonic block if ever there was one—as victims, deserves our highest scrutiny. The political work has already begun in connecting the rhetoric of hate (around questions of gay and lesbian sexuality) to real violence perpetrated against gays and lesbians. Even the Rev. Jerry Falwell once met with gay and lesbian Christians in an effort to mitigate some of the harm this connection admittedly causes. A similar move needs to be made in terms of the discourse of race and of affirmative action.

I conclude these remarks with the words of Anna Quindlen from a piece published in the January 15, 1992, issue of the *New York Times*. Her words, constructive then, continue to be so relevant today that I trust I may be forgiven for quoting her at some length:

> The new myth is that the world is full of black Americans prospering unfairly at white expense, and anecdotal evidence abounds. The stories about the incompetent black co-worker always leave out two things: the incompetent white co-workers and the talented black ones. They also leave out the tendency of so many managers to hire those who seem most like themselves.
>
> "It seems like if you're a white male you don't have a chance," said [a] . . . young man on a campus where a scant 5 percent of his classmates were black. What the kid really means is that he no longer has the edge, that the rules of a system that may have served his father will have changed. It is one of those good-old-days constructs to believe it was a system based purely on merit, but we know that's not true. It is a system that once favored him, and others like him. Now sometimes—just sometimes—it favors someone different.

To such simple and eloquent truth, I can only say in fullest agreement what the black church has taught me is the highest form of approval and solidarity in the tradition of call and response—amen.

Part III   Straight Black Talk

8 Speaking the Unspeakable

On Toni Morrison, African American Intellectuals, and the Uses of Essentialist Rhetoric

Now that Afro-American artistic presence has been "discovered" actually to exist, now that serious scholarship has moved from silencing the witness and erasing their meaningful place in and contribution to American culture, it is no longer acceptable merely to imagine us and imagine for us. We have always been imagining ourselves. We are not Isak Dinesen's "aspects of nature," nor Conrad's unspeaking. We are the subjects of our own narrative, witnesses to and participants in our own experience, and, in no way coincidentally, in the experience of those with whom we have come in contact. We are not, in fact, "other." We are choices. And to read imaginative literature by and about us is to choose to examine centers of the self and to have the opportunity to compare these centers with the "raceless" one with which we are, all of us, most familiar.

—Toni Morrison, "Unspeakable Things Unspoken"

To be a subject means to activate the network of discourse from *where one stands*. Discourse is not a circle with one center, but more like a mycelium with many mushrooms. To be a subject also means to take nourishment from more than one source, to construct a new synthesis, a new discursive ragout.

—Barbara Johnson, "'Response' to Henry Louis Gates's 'Canon-Formation and the Afro-American Tradition: From the Seen to the Told'"

In the wake of deconstruction and poststructuralism's move into the American academy, our fundamental understanding of the role of language in mediating our "reality" came to the fore. The advent of poststructuralism, then, has also meant a basic shift in the debate around such categories as race and experience. No longer are race and experience assumptions in critical discourse, but rather "race" and "experience" themselves become sites of critical contestation. To use Jacques Derrida's language, the "transcendental signified" race and experience are "under erasure." The political and rhetorical impact this move has had on African American critical discourse requires some comment. What has this critical shift meant for the authority of African American scholars doing work in African American studies in racist institutions? If not racial experience, on what grounds do they address the study of African American culture? How do they negotiate the relationship between the discourse of multiculturalism that argues the need of a culturally diversified academy, and poststructuralist discourse that makes the sign "experience" a site of contestation? Indeed, what, if not some understanding of their cultural experience, do African Americans uniquely bring to critical inquiry?

These opening observations are what I bring to this reading of Toni Morrison's "Unspeakable Things Unspoken: The Afro-American Presence in American Literature." The reason I begin my investigation of these concerns with Morrison is because she is, arguably, the most prominent artist-critic in contemporary American and African American letters, a position that uniquely qualifies her to speak to the variety of impacts that poststructuralist discussions of "race" and "experience" have had for African American artists and intellectuals. It may be precisely this dual role Morrison plays as African American intellectual and artist that allows her to see so clearly the impact of contemporary discussions of race on both imaginative work and critical work. This may explain some of the reasons Morrison took the turn into critical work to begin with. Let me say up front that I believe Morrison's essay implicitly outlines a critique of poststructuralism's treatment of the category of "race." I hope to demonstrate that the essay also enacts a rhetorical strategy African American intellectuals often use to reclaim a racial essentialism based on experience that authorizes or legitimizes their speech in some very politically important ways.

What is simultaneously interesting and difficult about Toni Morrison's "Unspeakable Things Unspoken" is that while the essay is careful to issue its anti-essentialist disclaimer, it does finally argue for, and depend upon, a variety of racial essentialism (grounded in racial experience) that has significant bearing on contemporary debates surrounding the question of essentialism in critical discourse.[1] An example of this, which I will discuss later at greater length, appears in my epigraph where Morrison invokes the first-person plural pronoun form of address. By "essentialism" here, I follow Diana Fuss's admirable treatment of the term in *Essentially Speaking: Feminism, Nature and Difference*. It may be enough for now to refer to what Fuss identifies as the most commonly understood definition of the term—that is, "a belief in the real, true essence of things, the invariable and fixed properties which define the 'whatness' of a given entity" (xi). Morrison's essay is, as I say, interesting because of the way it turns around the issue of racial essentialism. That is, she demonstrates from almost the very outset her awareness of contemporary criticism's move to complicate "race" as a category of critical investigation. The essay is also difficult because of the way it boldly enacts a carefully articulated form of racial essentialism even as it understands the critical risks involved in such a move.

For this reason it will be important to consider the rhetorical strategies Morrison uses to deploy racial essentialism as a useful means of analysis, as well as some of the implications this deployment may have for rethinking larger discussions of the status of racial "experience" (as an essentialist ground for knowledge) in poststructuralist discourse. For the purposes of this project, a consideration of both Morrison's experience (as a high-profile African American, woman, artist/author and critic) and of the worlds she creates in her fiction is crucial. In fact, it is precisely this variety of identity negotiations—self-canonization as author, critical legitimation as artist in the academy, authority to narrate African American experience as African American, and so forth—in which Morrison participates that makes her essay more than suitably representative for the kind of rhetorical analysis I wish to undertake.

My project neither takes issue with nor apologizes for Morrison. For let me admit up front that I believe Morrison's rhetorical strategies not only to be common among African American intellectuals, but politically indispensable as well. Even in the literary and cultural critiques by African Americans that are informed by much poststructuralist thought, these scholars, almost without fail (and out of political necessity), pause to genuflect before the shrine of essentialism. I will not here try to address the ostensibly unspeakable character of these essentialisms to which many African American critics seem to return.[2] Instead, I will limit my remarks to the politics of the difficult negotiations I have been outlining in which African American scholars engage, negotiations that motivate the intense and recurring return to the essentializing gesture.

"Unspeakable Things Unspoken" is a text that is highly suggestive and large in scope. It may be useful, therefore, to begin with a word on the structure of the opening section (my primary focus) to Morrison's three-part essay. First, the essay provides an overview of the stakes involved in the contemporary canon debate, with particular regard to the "race" question. This portion of the essay critically tracks the trajectory of race in intellectual discourse, attempts to define a racially formed Afro-American "culture" (as distinct from a "race"), destabilizes the notion of "taste," and identifies the most disturbing aspect of the resistance to "displacement within or expansion of the canon" in the "virulent passion that accompanies the resistance" and not in the resistance itself (4–5). Also in this section, Morrison suggests (with the example of Milan Kundera's *The Art of the Novel*) the analogous, hierarchical relationship that obtains between European and American literature and American and African American literature, while comparing Martin Bernal's project in *Black Athena* (the illustration of the process and motives of the fabrication of ancient Greece) to her own project (or rather the project of "Afro-American critical inquiry") of illuminating the process of silencing the African American presence in American literature. That is, she identifies canon-building with empire-building. The last gesture in this first portion of the essay is the recognition of the role "serious scholarship" has played in this process of "disentangling received knowledge from the apparatus of control" (8).

The two aspects of Morrison's essay that I want to elaborate on at some length are: the way she works to deconstruct the dichotomy between critic and scholar, and how this may inform our understanding of how Morrison occupies the language of the racial discourse available to her and locates her liberating possibilities from inside that discourse through her deployment of racial essentialism. Because the former informs the latter, let me begin by discussing how Morrison de-essentializes the categories of artist and critic in ways that ultimately legitimize and empower her position as artist-critic.

Morrison has a keen interest in what she calls the academy's contrived barriers between critic-scholar and artist. In fact, much of her own distinguished career as a writer, teacher, and editor—not to mention her more recent forays into criticism—throw such easy divisions into doubt. Even in the essay at hand, Morrison is invested in collapsing these barriers in statements like: "Certainly a sharp alertness as to *why* a work is or is not worthy is the legitimate occupation of the critic, the pedagogue and the artist" (5). Consider also the essay's closing paragraph:

> For an author, regarding canons, it is very simple: in fifty, a hundred or more years his or her work may be relished for its beauty or its insights or its power; or it may be condemned for its vacuousness and pretension—and junked. Or in fifty or a hundred years the critic (as canon builder) may be applauded for his or her intelligent scholarship and powers of critical inquiry. Or laughed at for ignorance and shabbily disguised assertions of power—and junked. It is possible that the reputations of both will thrive, or that both will decay. In any case, as far as the future is concerned, when one writes, as critic or as author, all necks are on the line. (33–34)

Here Morrison makes it clear that, "regarding canons," time will tell not only the story of the reception of the artist, but of the critic as well. By equating the risks of historical permanence involved for writers with the (all-too-often unspoken) risks involved for critics, Morrison issues an equalizing blow to the power of the critic in his or her relationship to writers. The final example of Morrison's deconstruction of the artist-critic dichotomy comes in her discussions of Kundera's *The Art of the Novel* and Terrence Rafferty's review of the same in the *New Yorker*. She writes:

> Kundera's views, obliterating American writers (with the exception of William Faulkner) from his own canon, are relegated to a "smugness" that Terrence Rafferty disassociates from Kundera's imaginative work and applies to the "sublime confidence" of his critical prose. The confidence of an exile who has the sentimental education of, and the choice to become, a European. (5–6)

The amalgamation of this statement with the preceding one accomplishes several things, not the least of which is that it invites us to take seriously the rhetorical strategies and subtext of Morrison's discourse. For if Rafferty can distinguish the character of Kundera's imaginative work from his critical prose, we are certainly invited to determine how to negotiate the same issue in the case of Morrison. By challenging the boundary between artist and critic, Morrison creates a legitimate place in critical literary discourse for her own voice. She resists the kind of facile distinction Rafferty makes with Kundera, and, in fact, depends upon the play between the critic-artist dichotomy for her rhetorical positionality in this essay. Nowhere is this more clearly demonstrated than in the essay's equalizing final paragraph. I argue later that Morrison is negotiating two kinds of "otherness"—the otherness of "artist" in the academy and the otherness of "race" in America. In this way, the rhetorical gesture of challenging the artist-critic dichotomy becomes a crucial move for Morrison in order to enshrine herself (as much of this essay arguably does) as a legitimate critical voice.[3]

But let me return for a moment to Morrison's discussion of Rafferty's review of Kundera, in order to concentrate on how Morrison's rhetorical strategies function in that instance. It is worth quoting at length here from Morrison's excerpt from Rafferty, as well as from Morrison herself:

Kundera's "personal 'idea of the novel,'" he [Rafferty] wrote, "is so profoundly Eurocentric that it's likely to seem exotic, even perverse, to
American readers. . . . *The Art of the Novel* gives off the occasional (but
pungent) whiff of cultural arrogance, and we may feel that Kundera's discourse . . . reveals an aspect of his character that we'd rather not have
known about. . . . In order to become the artist he now is, the Czech nov-
elist had to discover himself a second time, as a European. But what if
that second, grander possibility hadn't been there to be discovered?
What if Broch, Kafka, Musil—all that reading—had never been a part of
his education, or had entered it only as exotic, alien presence? Kundera's
polemical fervor in *The Art of the Novel* annoys us, as American readers,
because we feel defensive, excluded from the transcendent 'idea of the
novel' that for him seems simply to have been there for the taking. (If
only he had cited, in his redeeming version of the novel's history, a few
more heroes from the New World's culture.) Our novelists don't discover
cultural values within themselves; they invent them." (5)

Now consider Morrison's response to this statement:

I was refreshed by Rafferty's comments. With the substitution of certain
phrases, his observations and the justifiable umbrage he takes can be ap-
propriated entirely by Afro-American writers regarding their own exclusion from the "transcendent 'idea of the novel.'" For the present turbu-
lence seems not to be about the flexibility of a canon, its range among
and between Western countries, but about its miscegenation. (6)

In the course of these two statements Morrison positions herself as a mediating door between the competing forces of the defenders of the canonical
faith and the more insurgent intellectual voices involved in the present
canon polemic. She makes the discussion slightly more palatable (or in her
words "not endangering" [4]) for the more conservative interlocutors who
may be reluctant to enter this debate. She places all of her readers at ease by

creating, via the figure of Rafferty, a sympathy for American literature against European arrogance and European exclusion of American literature from its definition of canonical texts (here represented by Kundera). It is a swift, unifying, and almost patriotic "call to arms." It enlists our sympathies as Americans, and we feel slighted. The crucial move comes, however, at the close of her discussion of Kundera when Morrison draws the parallel that what Kundera (Europe) is doing to American literature is like what American literature is doing to African American literature. It is an established rhetorical tactic (initially putting the reader at ease only to make more stark the realization to which you want him or her to come) that proves effective here.[4] The way this rhetorical gesture functions at the level of racial and cultural identity politics should not go unmentioned here either. By establishing herself, in the eyes of her American reading audience, as the critical voice that points out Kundera's Eurocentrism to the detriment of American literature, Morrison also positions herself to be the recipient of the admiration that this critical "call to arms" creates. This then allows her to metonymically enlist those same sympathies for the ways African American literature may suffer from the exclusion of the traditional American literary canon. It is, after all, Morrison (as African American artist-critic) who is able to read the connection between European literature and American literature that Rafferty makes for its applicability to the relationship between American literature and African American literature.

This reading of the rhetorical use to which Morrison puts Rafferty is reminiscent of the kind of analysis she performs on white American literature in *Playing in the Dark: Whiteness and the Literary Imagination*. In this text, Morrison outlines a discussion of what she calls "American Africanisms." She considers the Africanist presence in the fiction of white American writers and argues that African Americans are "serviceable" both in these texts and in the lives of the white characters who populate these novels. Morrison demonstrates how the Africanist presence is "serviceable" both to address larger identity questions these white writers or characters may be confronting, and to provide access for these same writers and characters to the realm of permissive lawlessness, seditiousness, and danger that is not available when one deals solely in white bodies. Morrison offers minstrelsy as a representative metaphor to demonstrate this point:

> In minstrelsy, a layer of blackness applied to a white face released it from law. Just as entertainers, through or by association with blackface, could render permissible topics that otherwise would have been taboo, so American writers were able to employ an imagined Africanist persona to articulate and imaginatively act out the forbidden in American culture. (66)

According to Morrison, the representation of these "serviceable black bodies" (28) accomplishes much for white writers, including what she calls the "economy of stereotype" (67). That is, by invoking a black body in their texts, these writers enact a complex system of signs (that depend upon the reader's pre-programmed complicity in thinking stereotypically about "blackness"), which "allows the writer a quick and easy image without the responsibility of specificity, accuracy, or even narratively useful description" (67). In *Playing in the Dark,* Morrison rehearses this assertion with a variety of literary examples, from Poe and Melville to Cather and Hemingway, which proves its power and insightfulness.

The kind of analysis Morrison performs on white American literature in *Playing in the Dark* (via the issue of the serviceability of black bodies) suggests a way of reading the similar rhetorical moves she makes in "Unspeakable Things Unspoken" in "writing" the figure of Rafferty. If white American writers—and in some cases their white characters—enlist black bodies to economize stereotype and to "imaginatively act out the forbidden in American culture," then Morrison makes use of Rafferty's rhetorical serviceability in "Unspeakable Things Unspoken" to legitimize her critical voice in an academy where the artist-critic dichotomy has been concretizing for quite some time.

Let us now move from this discussion of how Morrison essentializes professional position in the academy to take up her deployment of racial essentialism for the purpose of authorizing her speech about African Americans. I trust that the comparative use of the preceding discussion will become even more evident as I proceed. As subject, Morrison, in the words of Barbara Johnson that appear in my second epigraph, "takes nourishment from more than one source" (43). Johnson's statement becomes even more valuable to our reading of the way Morrison addresses herself to the race question. If one reason that Morrison can claim superiority over the critic, as shown in the earlier discussion of her professional essentializing, has to do with her positionality (i.e., where she stands as she activates the network of discourse), then the same is true of her deployment of racial essentialism as a way of authorizing her speech about African American subjects. Before going too far in this direction, however, I should provide a brief meditation on Morrison's position inside what I will here call "racialized discourse"—an understanding of which will serve to illuminate the complexity of Morrison's rhetorical moves in regard to racial essentialism.

Obvious examples of racialized discourse are the all-too-popular catchall phrases or calls to unity like "blacks" and "the black community" often employed by popular media and in a variety of political discussions. These kinds of terms function as totalizing descriptors or appellations. They serve to make us think (if even for the moment and for the very sake of discourse itself) that "the black community" is knowable, totalizable, locatable, and certainly separate from or other than the speaker (black or non-black in some cases).[5] The use of such terminology, then, represents not only a false will to power on the part of the speaker who appropriates such language, but carries with it extremely high political stakes as well. Such labels deny the heterogeneity among African Americans (class, gender, educational level, sexuality, etc.) and easily seduce us into the language of stereotypes by characterizing in a facile manner the entirety of the experiences of African American people. Further, these labels implicitly assume something called a "white community" that rarely, if ever, gets spoken of in such terms, since it is a priori the norm, the originary against which all else must compare.

I am reminded here of a dialogue I had some time ago as a graduate student at UCLA with another African American male graduate student and an African American male undergraduate. Our conversation, as is often the case among African Americans, eventually settled on the problems facing "the black community." We vigorously catalogued the issues in a manner that seemed almost ritualistic and all too facile, when the uninitiated undergraduate chimed in with a query that is understood as forbidden in polite intellectual discourse of this sort: "So, what can we do about any of this?" As the weight of his question settled upon us, we each fell uncharacteristically silent. There we sat on the steps of Perloff Hall, three well-educated, young, African American men, feeling powerless to answer this question in a way that would challenge the perfunctory, superficial responses often spoken in such situations. The silence, I am convinced in this case, had much to do with the way we had constructed our positionality in this scenario. The very fact that we have the leisure to engage in such conversation, that we can outline the problems in such eloquent fashion, while finding it impossible to include ourselves in the categories we listed (since few of them directly effected the lives of us interlocutors—drugs, access to education, poverty . . .) demonstrates a disjuncture or discontinuity between the speaking black subject in this case and those in "the black community" who are being spoken about.[6]

My use of the term "racialized discourse" is consciously employed as opposed to "racial discourse" or simply "race" in order that the reader might remain aware of the very constructedness of this discourse. The discourse is not simply "racial" because that implies an ontology or essence of something that we can know as "race." It is not simply "race" because this neglects the critical role of language in the construction of such discourse. The only way that even the fiction of the category "race" can be called into existence is if, as Walter Benjamin says in another context, it is supported by an elaborate language (187).[7] In other words, no race without a representational discourse, and no discourse without language. My use of the term "racialized discourse" is an attempt to circumvent these problems. The contrived past participle form "racialized" signifies a political operation on language that makes it appear racially determined (which assumes an existence for "race"). One of the goals of this construction "racialized discourse," then, is the thematization of the disjuncture between "racialized discourse" (as construct and mediated representation) and "race" (as essence or experience).

I find Paul de Man's "The Rhetoric of Temporality" useful in pointing out the ways in which racialized discourse functions allegorically to define and construct "race," while also demonstrating the inherent politicality of allegory itself. The one caveat I will issue here is that while I am unquestionably invested in understanding the constructedness or inventedness of race (that is, what some poststructuralists have called "race" under "erasure"), I also insist that it is politically irresponsible to speak of race in this way without a consistent awareness of the oppressive material and political manifestations of such socio-linguistic constructs on the lives of people of color (i.e., the "real" human pain and suffering people endure). It is for these same oppressive, material and political reasons, I am convinced, that we must inevitably speak the terms of "racial identification" in order to articulate our racial struggle even though we are aware of the risk that these terms may also be turned and used to serve the agenda of our oppressors.

In "The Rhetoric of Temporality" de Man provides an understanding of the development and interrelatedness of symbol, allegory, and irony in literary discourse. Instead of the interrelation of these critical tropes, however, it is de Man's distinctions among the three by way of the temporality of their structure that concerns me here. Among these, allegory is of particular interest because its structure includes an illusory and fictitious center that I maintain is also characteristic of racialized discourse. The paradigm of allegory laid out by de Man provides not only a way to explore "the curious dialectic between formal language use and the inscription of metaphorical racial differences," but also provides a way of looking analytically at the politicality of the deep structure of racialized discourse itself.[8]

He characterizes allegory by saying it "appears . . . dryly rational and dogmatic in its reference to a meaning that it does not itself constitute" (189). In this way allegory, not claiming to know its origins or identification, "designates primarily a distance in relation to its own origin, and, renouncing the nostalgia and desire to coincide, it establishes its language in the void of this temporal difference" (207). The allegorical sign "points to something that differs from its literal meaning and has as its function the thematization of this difference" (209). Allegory has its existence "entirely within an ideal time that is never here and now but always a past or an endless future." Allegory is a "successive mode capable of engendering duration as the illusion of a continuity that it knows is illusionary" (226).

Given de Man's understanding of allegory, how can this function paradigmatically for a deeper understanding of the allegorical structure of racialized discourse? For racialized discourse to function allegorically, we must first ask what abstract quality or phenomenon is being allegorized. In this case, "race" would seem the simple response that turns out, of course, not to be as simple as we might at first imagine. When we recognize the very process of allegorization as the thematization or calling into existence of something that, because of its abstract or illusory nature, has never been represented, then the politicality of allegory begins to come into focus.[9] So even in its inception, racial allegory (and with it racialized discourse) is about choices—the choice to focus on skin color, the choice to make it signify immutable difference, and the choice to call it into existence as a critical category in the first place—and is, therefore, thoroughly and inescapably political.

Again, de Man maintains that allegory "appears dryly rational and dogmatic in its reference to a meaning that it does not itself constitute." A similar case could certainly be made for racialized discourse. Recall the earlier examples ("blacks" and "black community"), which presuppose a category called "race" and a locatable, totalizable "community" of some sort. Such phrases are used in a manner that gives an assumed, unproblematic ontology to a referent that they in themselves do not and cannot constitute. While even the most cursory study of any language would reveal this to be the case, racialized discourse seduces its speakers into an often-unwitting compliance with the assumptions inherent in that discourse. This is precisely what the propagation of the racial allegory depends upon—a kind of selective amnesia, a collective forgetting. It is in that forgetting of the assumptions and origins of racialized discourse (i.e., that racialized discourse is predicated upon a fallacious, contrived assumption of difference) that the agenda of the dominant culture's hegemony and the normalization and defensibility of "whiteness" can be located.[10]

Paul de Man also asserts that the allegorical sign "points to something that differs from its literal meaning and has as its function the thematization of that difference." This and more can be said of the racial allegory. Racialized discourse functions not only to thematize the difference between the literal meaning of the sign and the racial meaning being pointed to by the same sign; since the sign has no real literal meaning (in the sense that the "blackness" of the sign is a convenient contrivance), the discourse is engaging in creating meaning out of what de Man calls "the void of temporal difference." Again, what is at stake has less to do with any kind of real differences between "races," and more to do with buttressing the agenda of the dominant culture and the defensibility of "whiteness." In cases where the racialized discourse is employed in a black-black dialectic, this discursive practice alters little. The speaking black subjects assume superiority and power over those spoken about via language.[11] Although in most cases these speakers possess good intentions, the risk involved is that the same discourse that enables such well-intended articulations will also sustain the articulations of those who may not be so well intended.

The understanding of racialized discourse, as I have outlined it in this essay, also represents an intervention into poststructuralist discourses centered around the critique of the sign of "experience."[12] For I remain convinced that experience can still be called upon as "grounds" for epistemological claims both without critical apology and without being dismissed as essentialist in the prevailing, denigrating sense of the term. I want to preserve a space for "experience" as a way of authorizing certain speech forms over others on issues where systematic human pain and suffering are involved. I contend that even in the realm of mediation, the "experience" of "race" for whites and for people of color is different. The *status of experience* inside racialized discourse need not be viewed as being any more privileged than the *critique of experience* from inside that discourse need be. This allegorical paradigm helps us to better perceive the linguistic and ideological forces at work that mediate experience. It also enables us to see how we are conditioned, prepared, or overdetermined (white or non-white) by racialized discourse to read our "experience" in certain racialized ways. That is to say, to reformulate Morrison's words in another context, in the future when we speak of the status of experience either as subjects relying upon the political value of its "authority" and "authenticity" (although fictive and mediated), or as subjects whose desire it may be to destabilize or deauthorize its reliability, all necks are on the line. Neither the "author" of experience nor its "critics" stand on ground that is more or less stable than the other. Indeed, what a rigorous critique of racialized discourse does is to call us back to the recognition that none of our "experiences"—white or non-white—inside racialized discourse exist outside that discourse. This does not, then, serve to deauthorize experience as a useful category at all. On the contrary, it calls us to recognize how mediated and constructed experience (in my understanding of racialized discourse) operates, even in a staunchly poststructuralist and social constructionist context, "as a more sophisticated form of essentialism," which is the same point Fuss argues about constructionism in *Essentially Speaking* (xii).

The final point of interest that de Man makes about allegory has to do with its temporality, when he argues that it has its existence "entirely within an ideal time that is never here and now but always a past or an endless future." It is a "successive mode capable of engendering duration as the illusion of a continuity that it knows is illusionary." The example of Pecola Breedlove in Morrison's and *The Bluest Eye* is illustrative here. Pecola is a little black girl who through racial experience has come to think of herself as ugly, unworthy, and displaced in a society where the image of beauty is the little yellow-haired, blue-eyed, white girl. The novel traces Pecola's journey into insanity as she pursues her desire to have "the bluest eyes"—the symbol of whiteness that she believes will make her beautiful. Morrison writes: "So it was. A little black girl yearns for the blue eyes of a little white girl, and the horror at the heart of her yearning is exceeded only by the evil of fulfillment" (158). The language through which the narrator articulates Pecola's plight is taken from the mouths of the speakers and creators of racialized discourse. As far as Pecola knows, racialized discourse (if, indeed, we can count her as aware of it as such) has always been around and will always be around. The real tragedy, then, is that Pecola, like all of us, has been seduced into believing that "race" is and always has been "real." That is the quality of racialized discourse that is most pernicious and elusive—the way it insures its continued existence through a fabricated past, reaching back to the beginning of time, and an interminable future. It is for these reasons that the here and now is taken care of, because "race" constitutes a "frozen metaphor" in "ideal time."[13]

Let me now return to Morrison and the question of racial essentialism. Consider again the epigraph by Morrison that opens this essay, the epigraph in which she makes initial use of the first person plural voice. The rhetorical, indeed, the performative use to which Morrison puts the first person plural is simultaneously problematic, politically useful, and undoubtedly essentialist. Morrison's use of "we" and "our" is not unlike the example of the use of the term "black community" I discuss earlier. Its veiled, or not so veiled, attempt at a unity, which is finally evasive, is one response (and arguably the most politically expedient response) available to African Americans trying to speak/think their experience inside a racialized discourse.

Johnson's remarks on the use of the "shifter" "we" are also instructive here:

The pronoun "we" has historically proven to be the most empowering and shiftiest shifter of them all. It is through the "we" that discourses of false universality are created. With its cognitive indeterminacy and its performative authority, it is both problematic and unavoidable for the discourses of political opposition. For this structure of the stressed subject with an indeterminate predicate may well be the structure necessary for empowerment without essentialism. At the same time, it is an empowerment always in danger of presuming too much. But, then, can there be empowerment without presumption? (43)

I am in full agreement with Johnson, to a point. Indeed, the indeterminacy of the "shifter" is tantamount to the process of empowerment. Even de Man, citing Schlegel, makes a similar claim, defining freedom as "the unwillingness of the mind to accept any stage in its progression as definitive, since this would stop what he [Schlegel] calls its 'infinite agility'" (220). I part ways with Johnson where she states that this kind of use of the shifter is a method of avoiding essentialism. On the contrary, it may be a way of avoiding an *explicit* essentialism, but it hardly escapes lapsing into an *implicit* essentialism. In order for the indeterminate "shifter" even to signify empowerment via its indeterminacy on the particular order (especially here in Morrison's case), it must be read as implicitly signifying, generally speaking of course, some configuration of an essentially African American referent.

One cannot help also noticing, in the epigraph by Morrison, her use of the term "experience." In fact, with little alteration, this epigraph might well serve as a diversity mission statement for any number of universities at the present time. As the move in the academy has been from the absence to the presence of African Americans, the emphasis in this passage is on the move from imagining and theorizing about African Americans to African Americans imagining and theorizing themselves. When we speak in terms of the value of diversity or pluralism, the language of difference, experience, and culture are synonymous with these topics. And since we surely do not mean melanin when we speak of the values of diversity, one can imagine little else that we might be referring to if not the value of different experiences and cultural perspectives (shaped by experience). Consider Morrison's statement: "We are the subjects of our own narrative, witness to and participants in our own experience, and . . . in the experience of those with whom we have come in contact." What is interesting about this statement is how Morrison complicates racial experience even as she is essentializing it, effectively demonstrating that essentialism cannot always be read as uncritical or facile. For to say that African Americans are "witness to and participants in our own experience" is to posit experience as something we are both determined by and determining, both inside and outside of. And it most certainly, according to this statement, is something over which we have ownership. In other words, our experience is shaped by our perspective (the way we read the world). And our perspective is shaped by the overdeterminacy of racialized discourse in which we are all caught up or "interpellated" as subjects, to use that language. The latter part of Morrison's statement is no less complicated when she states that we are also participants "in the experience of those with whom we have come in contact." Read in all its richness, this statement testifies to the fact that, not only do African Americans have racial "experience," but white Americans do as well. They, too, have learned to read race according to their experience, which African Americans play no small part in constructing.

By the time Morrison reaches the section of her essay in which she gives her reading of *Sula,* she has provided us with a context in which to understand her use of the racial descriptor "black":

> I always thought of Sula as quintessentially black, metaphysically black, if you will, which is not melanin and certainly not unquestioning fidelity to the tribe. She is new world black and new world woman extracting choices from choicelessness, responding inventively to found things. Improvisational. Daring, disruptive, imaginative, modern, out-of-the-house, outlawed, unpolicing, uncontained and uncontainable. (25)

The "quintessential blackness" to which Morrison refers here is neither, as I say, facile nor uncritical. It is "metaphysical," constructed, overdetermined, and informed by experience. The adjectives used to describe Sula's blackness (and, indeed, her black femaleness) are quite similar to the adjectives used earlier in Morrison's essay to describe the language of African American literature: "Daring, disruptive, imaginative, modern . . . unpolicing" (11). This similarity is suggestive of the relationship that obtains between racial experience and racialized discourse.

Morrison's use of the shifter, as described above, is only one way that African American intellectuals use essentialism to authorize their critical voices. Another well-established method is through anecdote—the relating of "experience." Testifying and storytelling are methods of self-disclosure that legitimize the critical project as somehow more authentic, bearing a direct relationship to "experience." While contemporary examples of this are numerous—for example, consider Patricia Williams's *The Alchemy of Race and Rights,* any number of essays by bell hooks, or Houston Baker's introduction to *Long Black Song,* and not to mention my own use of testimonial earlier in this essay—one of the most illustrative examples is presented in the preface of Cornel West's *Race Matters,* which I will discuss at some length in the next chapter.

For now, however, let's turn to Patricia Williams, who is extremely relevant to our case. In *The Alchemy of Race and Rights,* Williams relates a story of how a sales clerk at Benetton's discriminated against her by denying her access to the store (whose entrance was secured by a buzzer, a common feature in many New York shops). In addition to publishing her story in a law review journal, she occasionally uses it in speaking engagements. She cites some of the questions she is often asked in the wake of its telling:

> Am I not privileging a racial perspective, by considering only the black point of view? Don't I have an obligation to include the "salesman's side" of the story? Am I not putting the salesman on trial and finding him guilty of racism without giving him a chance to respond or cross-examine me? Am I not using the store window as a "metaphorical fence" against the potential of his explanation in order to represent my side as "authentic"? How can I be sure I'm right? What makes my experience the real black one anyway? Isn't it possible that another black person might

disagree with my experience? If so, doesn't that render my story too empirical and subjective to pay any attention to? (50–51)

In a footnote to her text, Williams replies to these questions in the following way:

These questions question my ability to know, to access, to be objective. And of course, since anything that happens to me is inherently subjective, they take away my power to know what happens to me in the world. Others, by this standard, will always know better than I. And my insistence on recounting stories from my own perspective will be treated as presumption, slander, paranoid hallucination, or just plain lies.

Recently I got an urgent call from Thomas Grey of Stanford Law School. He had used the piece [the Benetton's article] in his jurisprudence class, and a rumor got started that the Benetton's story wasn't true that it was . . . a lie that was probably the product of a diseased mind trying to make all white people feel guilty. At this point, I realized it almost didn't make any difference whether I was telling the truth or not—that the greater issue that I had to face was the overwhelming weight of a disbelief that goes beyond mere disinclination to believe and becomes active suppression of anything I might have to say. The greater problem is a powerfully oppressive mechanism for denial of black self-knowledge and expression. And this denial cannot be separated from the simultaneously pathological willingness to believe certain things about blacks—not to believe them, but things about them. (242)

In addition to outlining the institutional risks involved for African Americans trying to speak about and theorize their experiences, Williams also points out that the major risk of vigorous destabilizations of "experience" is that they can ultimately become political tools to silence and deauthorize African American experience. The danger, then, is that since the fundamental way of identifying racism is by narrating its instances, by deauthorizing the witness it could become virtually impossible to ever name "the beast" at all. This is one reason I think it is important that African American intellectuals continue to learn new ways of strategizing and essentializing in racialized discourse. Because what is at stake is nothing less than the ability to narrate our own stories, witness our own experience.

Morrison's characterization of the function of language in African American literature may be a fitting close for now to a project that is very much still in progress for me, and stands as a source of continual interest. She writes:

And in Afro-American literature itself the question of difference, of essence, is critical. What makes a work "Black"? The most valuable point of entry into the question of cultural (or racial) distinction, the one most fraught, is its language—its unpoliced, seditious, confrontational, manipulative, inventive, disruptive, masked and unmasking language. Such a penetration will entail the most careful study, one in which the impact of Afro-American presence on modernity becomes clear and is no longer a well kept secret. (11)

Notice the adjectives used here to characterize the function of the language of the African American text—unpoliced, seditious, confrontational, and so forth. They are all words that express craftiness and resistance. This is because the language is in many ways the quintessential site of the recurring confrontation with the other. The language of the African American text itself stands as an emblem of the Herculean struggle to represent an experience that the language is not intended to accommodate. It is the attempt to write the seemingly unwritable, to speak the unspeakable.

So it is in an attempt to represent one's experience in a language that is not intended to do that work that a strategic essentialism becomes an almost indispensable tool.[14] Why? Simply put: It allows us to speak categorically in a discourse that seems to demand and respect labels. It enables us to speak to and about a people whose individual lives may be markedly different, but who nonetheless suffer from a common form of racial hegemony. It permits us to hold up the possibility of a unity, albeit fictitious, that makes our burdens more manageable because the load is shared. It empowers us to be able to speak (through the discourse available to us) about the oppressive material and political manifestations of a racialized hegemony on our lives. And, finally, for our purposes in literary studies, it makes possible the development of a critical discourse that centers these concerns in the study of our literature.

9 Cornel West and the Rhetoric of Race-Transcending

West is a black John Dewey, in the sense that Dewey was a serious thinker who spoke to the issues of the day—a model that has been sorely missing from the American scene. In an earlier progressive era, Dewey could be a professional philosopher as well as a widely read writer in magazines like *The New Republic* and *The Nation*. West aspires to such a model. And while doing so he shares a deep commitment to radical democracy, transcending what's called the politics of identity or the politics of difference.

—Richard Bernstein, quoted in Anderson, "The Public Intellectual"

I'm really troubled by Cornel West right now. He's been my buddy and my friend, but all of a sudden, he's talking about race transcending. I think the moment you say race transcending, white people get all wet: "Does that mean we're not gonna have to deal with black people talking about blackness or racism?" It's really deep.

Like, this white boy called me up and said, "Cornel West isn't like you. He's not busy trying to present himself as some kind of radical, left commie, and he's getting all the play, right now. And he's still saying what he used to say." But it's not true that he's saying what he used to say. That introduction to *Race Matters* (West's latest book), is all about his elegant car and how he can't drive it through Harlem, and it could have been written by any white man saying he can't drive through Harlem. And I thought that was fucked. But, yeah, he's making hundreds of thousands of dollars, now.

—bell hooks, quoted in Hardy, "Whitewashing Black Beauty"

There can be little doubt that Cornel West is one of the most prolific schol-ars in academia and one of the most widely discussed professional intellec-tuals by mainstream media today. Indeed, few academics have distinguished themselves in such disparate venues as *Emerge,* the *Today Show, Nightline,* a special interview with Bill Moyers, the *Yale Law Journal,* and the *Nation.* How-ever, the very fact of such wide-ranging appeal raises several pressing ques-tions. What exactly has given rise to West's uncharacteristic popularity (i.e., uncharacteristic of professional academics)? Is there something in the sub-stance of West's work that has excited and captured the imagination of both the media and America's literate public? Or is West's popularity attributable to a black vernacular style and mode of self-presentation that West has per-fected and, indeed, commodified in a cultural market where such "authen-ticity" appears to be in vogue?

While all of these factors probably play some role in the rising popularity West enjoys, this essay focuses primarily on the second of these questions—that is, what it is in the substance of West's work that might have captured the imagination of the media and literate America. This essay concerns itself with West's participation in the highly controversial discourse of "race-tran-scending," chiefly as it is treated in one of his latest critical interventions—*Race Matters.*

Race Matters is the first text West has written for a more mainstream and less academic audience. Accordingly, the language and prose style are sim-pler: there are no footnotes, bibliographies, or indexes. While his efforts at reaching an audience beyond academia are laudable, the very style of the text is what can be most frustrating for more academic readers accustomed to footnotes, fine distinctions, and minimal ambiguities. One of my own de-fenses for the use and value of contemporary critical discourse (particularly that which is influenced by the language of poststructuralism) is that it al-lows us as readers to render insightful and subtle readings of texts without sacrificing their complexity. In other words, complex ideas require a critical discourse that can accommodate their nuances and ambiguities. I say this at the outset to suggest that translating a complex idea like race-transcending into the context of a general-audience text like *Race Matters* may be the very problem that creates the kind of ambiguity that allows for such different readings of West as those of Bernstein and hooks with which I began this study.

With this introduction, the remainder of the essay is organized as follows. In part II, I elaborate on what West means by race-transcending and argue that he is not bent—as some would have us believe—on ignoring race or rendering racial experiences insignificant. Instead, West is concerned with constructing a transdisciplinary theory that transcends the limitations of present-day racial discourses, which are necessarily socially, politically and historically contingent. In part III, I focus on one of West's earliest works, *Prophesy Deliverance! An Afro-American Revolutionary Christianity,* to illustrate how West's theory of race-transcending is very much connected to his more general theory of context liberation. Specifically, I argue that "race-transcending" (as West uses the term) is concerned with context transformation, even as it recognizes the context limitation(s) of transformative politics. Central to West's theory is the notion that if we cannot *imagine* a world free of racism, we cannot construct a theory to eradicate it. Finally, in part IV, I conclude with a discussion of West's popularity as a public and interdisciplinary intellectual figure and proffer some suggestions regarding how we should "read" his work.

Racializing Race-Transcending: A Commentary on *Race Matters*

Contrary to the contentions of both hooks and Bernstein, *Race Matters* is not a text about race-transcending in the sense of transcending difference or identity or in the sense of denying the importance of race. In other words, "race-transcending" for West is in no way synonymous with the "unracial." In fact, a close reading of the text, particularly its preface, provides much evidence to the contrary.

The preface to *Race Matters* opens with West describing one of his and his wife's biweekly trips to New York from Princeton last September. His thoughts move from the two lectures he had given that day—one on Plato and the other on Du Bois—to speculation about whether he and his wife would have time to visit their favorite restaurant to relax after their appointments. After dropping off his wife, West parks his car and stands on the corner of 60th and Park to catch a cab to Harlem for the photo shoot for the cover of *Race Matters*. While attempting to hail a cab, he experiences what many other African Americans *experience* and what many others (only) *see* and *recognize*. West, who "waited and waited and waited" on that street corner, is refused by ten cabs. He records his feelings in this way:

After the ninth cab refused me, my blood began to boil. The tenth taxi refused me and stopped for a kind, well-dressed, smiling female fellow citizen of European descent. As she stepped in the cab, she said, "This is ridiculous, is it not?"

Ugly racial memories of the past flashed through my mind. Years ago, while driving from New York to teach at Williams College, I was stopped on fake charges of trafficking cocaine. When I told the police officer I was a professor of religion, he replied "Yeh, and I'm the Flying Nun. Let's go nigger!" I was stopped three times in my first ten days in Princeton for driving too slowly on a residential street with a speed limit of twenty-five miles per hour. . . . Needless to say these incidents are dwarfed by those like the Rodney King beating. . . . Yet memories cut like a merciless knife at my soul as I waited on that godforsaken corner. Finally I decided to take the subway; I walked three long avenues, arrived late, and had to catch my breath as I approached the white male photographer and the white female cover designer. I chose not to dwell on this everyday experience of black New Yorkers. And we had a good time talking, posing, and taking pictures. (x–xi)

The most interesting element of this anecdote is West's precise recognition of what is being experienced: the taxi drivers racially "reading" him as *black* and, therefore, unreliable and even dangerous as a potential customer. West is able to make this recognition because he has experienced a similar pattern of signs before. This event triggers his racial history and causes him to recall other "ugly racial memories," which in turn informs his understanding of his present experience. Even so, it is West's awareness of the poststructuralist's suspicion of experience that explains the curious appearance of the white female witness to his story.[1, 2]

Upon first reading, I was bewildered by the appearance of this "kind, well-dressed, smiling female fellow citizen of European descent." What rhetorical value did her presence have for the story? How did her comments—"This is really ridiculous, is it not?"—signify? The pains to which West goes to carefully and concisely describe the woman are suggestive of how we are to read her. She is white, well-dressed, and taking a cab. This description suggests that she is not poor and, therefore, unreliable as a witness. She is also "smiling." This is a clue that she is sympathetic to what is happening on that street corner, even as she may feel a bit nervous or guilty herself about the situation. In any event, she is cast as the credible witness who can legitimize his experience because she reads it apart from West's potentially "biased" or "overly sensitive" racialized reading. While the essentializing gestures West deploys here are effective and politically necessary, they do run the risk of again locating the woman's ability to be a credible, unbiased witness in her whiteness. This is, however, the kind of risk that one must take to authorize and to legitimize oneself in racialized discourse.

But West does not use the white woman to render the scene "unracial." That race matters for West is clear from his description of his trip back to Princeton from New York with his wife:

As we rode back to Princeton, above the soothing black music of Vaughn Harper's Quiet Storm on WBLS, 107.5 on the radio dial, we talked about what *race* matters have meant to the American past and of how much race *matters* in the American present. And I vowed to be more vigilant and virtuous in my efforts to meet the formidable challenges posed by Plato and Du Bois. For me, it is an urgent question of power and morality; for others, it is an everyday matter of life and death. (xvi)

The very first line signifies this moment as culturally and performatively "black." When West says that they listened to the "soothing black music," the statement is not gratuitous. The music is "black" (the blackness is performed in the "Quiet Storm"—a programming segment, usually at night, featuring "slow jams"—which seems to be a fixture of numerous black radio stations across the country); and the "black music" is "soothing" (which is a specific cultural function of black music and other forms of cultural expression in response to harsh racial realities).[3] In the paragraph preceding the quote above, West writes:

> When I picked up Elleni, I told her of my hour spent on the corner. . . .
> We talked about our fantasy of moving to Addis Ababa, Ethiopia. . . . I
> toyed with the idea of attending the last day of revival led by the Rev. Je-
> remiah Wright of Chicago at Rev. Wyatt T. Walker's Canaan Baptist
> Church of Christ in Harlem. But we settled for Sweetwater's. And the ugly
> memories faded in the face of soulful music, soulful food, and soulful
> folk. (xi)

Significantly, when West describes the event that caused these "ugly racial memories" to surface, he is principally alone; he is in a situation in which the only thing the cab driver sees when reading him is his race; and he is essentially powerless to do anything about it. However, when he describes the setting in which these "ugly memories" begin to fade, he is in the company of his wife; they fantasize about moving to Ethiopia; they toy with the idea of attending a revival service; and end up going to a soul food restaurant.

Several factors contribute to the setting that causes the "ugly memories" to recede. It is the restorative and soothing power of "community." West is in the understanding, empathizing company of his wife and later of the people at Sweetwater's. He calls up romantic views of Africa, and he and his wife muse on the idea of moving to Ethiopia.[4] He invokes the institution of the black church where a literal "revival" is in progress. And finally they decide to eat at a soul food restaurant. This configuration of signifiers serves to refocus and recontextualize West away from the larger white society where he cannot always shield himself from the ills of racism, into a space that is, for the moment, culturally and affirmatively black. It is in this socially constructed space that the weary "race man" can find temporary reprieve from racialist reality.[5]

In addition to the preface, two of the essays in *Race Matters* are also useful in discussing how West articulates this idea of race-transcending in the text: chapter 3, "The Crisis of Black Leadership" and chapter 4, "Demystifying the New Black Conservatism." In chapter 3, West groups present-day black political leaders into three categories: "race-effacing managerial leaders, race-identifying protest leaders, and race-transcending prophetic leaders." A brief description of all three is in order, since important to understanding how West defines race-transcending is an understanding of what it gets defined in relation to.

Race-effacing managerial leaders include the Tom Bradleys (first African American mayor of Los Angeles) and Wilson Goodes (first African American mayor of Philadelphia) of black America. They tried to reach a large white constituency while maintaining a loyal black one. "This type survives on pure political savvy and thrives on personal diplomacy. This kind of candidate is the lesser of two evils in a political situation where the only other electoral choice is a conservative (usually white) politician" (39). This type of leader stifles progressive growth and silences the "prophetic voices" in the black community by "casting the practical mainstream as the only game in town" (39).

Race-identifying protest leaders "view themselves in the tradition of Malcolm X, Martin Luther King, Jr., Ella Baker, and Fannie Lou Hamer. Yet they are usually self-deluded." In reality they operate more in the tradition of Booker T. Washington, "confining themselves to the black turf, vowing to protect their leadership status over it, and serving as power brokers with powerful nonblack (usually white economic or political elites) to 'enhance' this black turf." They often fail to remember that even in the 1950s Malcolm X's project was international in scope, and "after 1964 his project was transracial—though grounded in the black turf" (39).

As for race-transcending prophetic leaders, there are few in contemporary black America:

> Harold Washington was one. The Jesse Jackson of 1988 was attempting to be another—yet the opportunism of his past weighed heavily on him. To be an elected official and prophetic leader requires personal integrity and political savvy, moral vision and prudential judgment, courageous defiance and organizational patience. The present generation has yet to produce such a figure. We have neither an Adam Clayton Powell, Jr. nor a Ronald Dellums. (40)

In addition to his discussion of black political leadership, West outlines the current situation of African American intellectual leadership. He categorizes black intellectuals as follows: "race-distancing elites, race-embracing rebels, and race-transcending prophets" (42). Since the definitions are so similar in character to those offered in his discussion of black political leaders, for the purposes of this essay I will focus primarily on the latter category:

> There are few race-transcending prophets on the current black intellectual scene. James Baldwin was one. He was self-taught and self-styled, hence beholden to no white patronage system. He was courageous and prolific, a political intellectual. . . . He was unswerving in his commitment to fusing the life of the mind (including the craft of writing) with

the struggle for justice and human dignity regardless of the fashions of the day or the price he had to pay. With the exception of Toni Morrison, the present generation has yet to produce such a figure. We have neither an Oliver Cox nor a St. Claire Drake. This vacuum continues to aggravate the crisis of black leadership—and the plight of the wretched of the earth deteriorates. (43)

In both descriptions of black political leadership and black intellectual leadership, what is most notable rhetorically are the terms he uses in opposition to "race-transcending." In the former case, "race-transcending" is *opposed* to "race-effacing" and "race-identifying." In the latter, it gets defined in relation to "race-distancing" and "race-embracing." Significantly, in both cases the first and second terms are opposites of each other, diametrically opposed in their relationship to the primary term "race": we either efface race or identify with race, distance ourselves from race or embrace race. What these terms have in common is that they are each always already engaged with the pre-existing discourse on "race." Each term assumes a relationship to the "what-is," the established boundaries of the racialized world. While "race-transcending" may be in a similar rhetorical predicament, it does offer more liberating possibilities precisely because of its relationship to the pair of terms preceding it in both cases. To be race-transcending is neither to be race-effacing nor race-identifying. It is not race-distancing nor is it race-embracing. To say that it mediates between these decidedly polar opposite terms would be to give too much significance to the dialectic created by them. Instead, what race-transcending accomplishes for West is the creation of an imaginary space from which we can begin to perceive and critique the limits of this kind of reliance on "race," as well as how we position ourselves in relation to the politics of race. I say "imaginary" here because the term "transcending" for West still recognizes its own reliance on a relationship to the primary term "race." This reliance is similar to that which obtains with the other pair of terms to which "race-transcending" is relating. Put another way, while race-transcending prophets recognize the significance of racial history and the oppressive, material impact of a racialized discourse on the lives of people of color, they do not allow these realities to become the limit of their cultural, political, intellectual and philosophical critiques. This is a point that I will return to later in the essay.

In chapter 4 of *Race Matters,* "Demystifying the New Black Conservatism," West's analysis of black conservatives and neo-conservatives is hard hitting and insightful. I mention it here because the course he charts in his critique of black conservatism takes us closer to a more practical understanding of his idea of race-transcending. One of the texts West considers in this chapter is Glen Loury's forthcoming *Free at Last.* West outlines the three arguments Loury puts forward in *Free at Last* in this way:

> First, he holds that black liberals adhere to a victim-status conception of black people that results in blaming all personal failings of black people on white racism. Second, he claims that black liberals harbor a debilitating loyalty to the race that blinds them to the pathological and dysfunctional aspects of black behavior. Third, Loury argues that black liberals truncate intellectual discourse regarding the plight of poor black people by censoring critical perspectives which air the "dirty linen" of the black community—that is, they dub neo-conservatives like Loury as "Uncle Toms" and thereby fail to take his views seriously in an intellectual manner. (50)

West's response to these charges begins in characteristically charitable fashion. He admits that "the hegemony of black liberalism—especially among black academic and political elites—does impose restraints on the quality and scope of black intellectual exchange." West then exposes the flaws in Loury's arguments. Loury ironically deploys the same rhetorical strategies he denounces in his liberal adversaries. He casts black conservatives like himself as victims whose own failings to gain a broad following in African America are attributed to a black liberal conspiracy to discredit them in an ad hominem manner. West points out that this kind of analysis not only implies the gullibility and callousness of the black community, but ignores the likely possibility that the merits of the case put forward by the new black conservatives is unconvincing and unimpressive.

West completes his treatment of Loury's text with a discussion of the uncritical nature of Loury's rejection of blind race loyalty:

> Loury's rejection of blind loyalty to the race is laudable, yet he replaces it with a similarly blind loyalty to the nation. In fact, his major criticism of black liberals and left-liberals is that they put the black community out of step with present-day conservative America because they adopt an excessively adversarial stance to the rest of the country. This criticism amounts not to a deepening and enriching of black intellectual exchange but rather to a defense of new kinds of restrictions in the name of a neo-nationalism already rampant in America—a neo-nationalism that smothers and suffocates the larger American intellectual scene. In this way Loury's neo-conservatism enacts the very "discourse truncation" he claims to be opposing in his foes. His frequent characterizations of left-liberal views as "anachronistic," "discredited," and "idiosyncratic," without putting forth arguments to defend such claims, exemplify this "discourse truncation."
>
> Loury's halfway-house position between the black conservatism of Thomas Sowell and traditional black liberalism is symptomatic of the crisis of purpose and direction among African-American political and intellectual elites.

Loury's thinking, as is the case with much of black political conservative thought, is unambiguously informed by a race-effacing or race-distancing philosophy. Nowhere is this more apparent than in debates concerning affirmative action.

On the topic of the new black conservatives' views of affirmative action, West contends that two considerations cannot be overestimated—the quest for middle-class respectability and the need of black conservatives to gain the respect of their white peers. One could argue from this that black conservatives simply desire the same thing most people do—to be judged by their skills and not their race—and that this informs their critique of affirmative action. As West points out, however, this argument "overlook[s] the fact that affirmative action policies were political responses to the pervasive refusal of most white Americans to judge black Americans on that basis." Additionally, this argument "assumes that without affirmative action programs, white Americans will make choices on merit rather than on race. Yet they have adduced no evidence for this." Indeed, on the topic of job-hiring specifically, West argues that the discourse is truncated by the terms we use to speak about it. He states:

> Most Americans realize that job-hiring choices are made both on reasons of merit and on personal grounds. And it is this personal dimension that is often influenced by racist perceptions. Therefore, the pertinent debate regarding black hiring is never "merit vs. race" but whether hiring decisions will be based on merit, influenced by race-bias against blacks, or on merit, influenced by race-bias, but with special consideration for minorities and women, as mandated by law. In light of actual employment practices, the black conservative rhetoric about race-free hiring criteria (usually coupled with a call for dismantling affirmative action mechanisms) does no more than justify actual practices of racial discrimination. (52)

West also points out that the majority of the black conservatives who level these attacks on affirmative action programs and advocate race-free hiring are themselves beneficiaries of affirmative action. According to West, it is their discomfort with that very fact, and their preoccupation with what their white peers think of them, that leads them to challenge affirmative action rather than the pervasive racism that creates the situation in which they find themselves. West argues that this kind of self-doubt and preoccupation with mainstream acceptance is not unlike the normal self-doubts and insecurities of new arrivals to the middle class. Most of the new black conservatives are first-generation middle-class persons, offering themselves as examples of how well the system works if you are willing to sacrifice and work hard. However, genuine white peer acceptance still preoccupies—and often escapes— them. To this extent, they are still affected by white racism.

The position of African American conservatives on affirmative action presented here represents another example of the way in which race-distancing or race-effacing thought (with its preoccupation with race) overdetermines and limits the ways in which we understand our subjectivity and our potential responses to it. Again, West is closing a door on this approach to racial reasoning to open a door for race-transcending thought.

The several examples from the two chapters discussed above hardly seem the work of a West who is transcending race in the sense of a denial of the importance of race. In fact, in *Race Matters,* West does little else if not persistently to point out the importance of race in almost every subject he discusses (and he discusses an impressive number of topics). Given his emphasis on the importance of race, then, one must search elsewhere to understand fully the significance of West's rhetoric of race-transcending as it functions in *Race Matters.* For this, we will need to turn briefly to consider West's earlier work in *Prophesy Deliverance!*

Liberating Racial Critiques

In the introduction to *Prophecy Deliverance!* West outlines his understanding of "prophetic Christianity." He argues that, like Marxism, "prophetic Christianity" insists upon both this—worldly liberation and other-worldly salvation. West expands upon what he means by this as follows: "For Christians, the realm of history is the realm of the pitiful and the tragic. It serves as the context for passive persons who negate and transform what is and for the active persons who reject and change prevailing realities."

This statement illustrates that transcendence for West has little to do with ignoring the significance of, or moving beyond the material realities of, in this case, human history (and in the context of *Race Matters,* racial oppression). It has far more to do with taking note of and critiquing the way we position ourselves as social subjects in relationship to the conditions brought on by human history. It is a way of constructing a space for at least some individual human agency. West makes the point in *Prophesy Deliverance!* in this way:

> The pitiful are those who remain objects of history, victims manipulated by evil forces; whereas the tragic are those persons who become subjects of history, aggressive antagonists of evil forces. Victims are pitiful because they have no possibility of achieving either penultimate liberation or ultimate salvation; aggressive antagonists are tragic because they fight for penultimate liberation, and in virtue of their gallant struggle against the limits of history they become prime candidates for ultimate salvation. In this sense, to play a tragic role in history is positive: To negate and transform what is, yet run up against the historical limits of such negation and transformation, is candidacy for transcending those limits. (18)

In ecclesiastical terms, we might call this a philosophy of "pressing toward the mark for the prize of the high calling."[6] And while one may never reach "the mark" in this world or on this side of the eschaton, the real testament to the will to ameliorate one's condition is in the "pressing." For even when the reach exceeds the grasp, the very act of contesting the limits of the "what is" creates liberating possibilities that could not have otherwise been imagined.[7] For the purposes of this essay, if we substitute "racialized discourse" where "history" appears in West's statements, we begin to arrive at a more meaningful understanding of West's rhetoric of race-transcending.

West himself relates the contribution of prophetic Christian thought as a source for African American critical thought in the following way:

> First, it [prophetic Afro-American thought] confronts candidly the tragic character of human history (and the hope for ultimate transhistorical tri-

umph) without permitting the immensity of what is and must be lost to call into question the significance of what may be gained. In this way it allows us to sidestep what Baudelaire called "the metaphysical horror of modern thought" and take more seriously the existential anxiety, political oppression, economic exploitation, and social degradation of actual human beings. Second, prophetic Afro-American Christian thought elevated the notion of struggle (against the odds!)—personal and collective struggle regulated by the norms of individuality and democracy—to the highest priority. To be a prophetic Afro-American Christian is to negate what is and transform prevailing realities against the backdrop of the present historical limits. In short, prophetic Afro-American Christian thought imbues Afro-American thinking with the sobriety of tragedy, the struggle for freedom and the spirit of hope. (*Prophesy* 19–20)

West is not speaking here of any facile notion of transcendence. Instead, he is admonishing us that even as we take seriously the material conditions and circumstances that impact our daily lives, we must not allow our thinking to be limited by those conditions. In other words, "race" does matter; it has a recognizably oppressive impact on our lives. In order to respond to that, however, we must not fall into the trap of accepting wholeheartedly the terms of racialized discourse as the "what is." For when we do, we run the risk ourselves of becoming agents of the very same discourse that oppresses us. Part of the oppression, then, becomes the ways in which our acceptance of racial history and of racialized discourse impoverishes the progressive and liberating possibilities we might otherwise imagine.

To recapitulate this in West's language: those who refuse to transcend race and the history of racial constructions are pitiful and doom themselves to the political limits imposed by racialized discourse. They cannot *imagine* a world free of racism; they force themselves into accepting narrowly defined identity constructions (like many constructions of black nationalism), which restrict and inhibit the progressive coalitions they might otherwise imagine or in which they might otherwise participate.

It is clear from West's treatment of "prophetic Christianity" that his rhetoric of "race-transcending" is less an appeal to whites who may be "tired of hearing about race" and want to move "beyond" it, and more a caveat to progressive "freedom fighters" (to use West's language), who in their zeal to redress race matters may make the fatal error of beginning with the pre-established terms of racialized discourse and racialized history. In this sense, it would be more accurate to describe West as a "race" transcender (i.e., a person who sees race as a discourse, a social construction), rather than a "race transcender" (a person who ignores the material realities that the hegemonic use of such constructions bring to bear on the lives of people of color).

This does not mean, however, that West's use of race-transcending in *Race Matters* is unproblematic. Indeed, the appearance of the term "race-transcending" in the context of a general-audience text like *Race Matters* (where it does not receive its fullest articulation) may be precisely what leaves it open to ambiguity and, hence, misreading. This is the extent to which I have some sympathy for hooks's reading of West. To use a term like "race-transcending" at all (given the popular connotations of the term as a "moving over or beyond") in a political climate rife with rightist and reactionary sentiment is to open oneself to both genuine and sometimes willful misreadings.

Conclusions

I want to conclude by returning to the issue with which I began—West's uncharacteristic popularity as a public intellectual figure. One of the major problems with doing critical work on West at present is that one feels as if one is writing in a vacuum because most of the work that has been done about West (with the exception of book reviews) has been more on the phenomenon of "Cornel West" than on his work.

One might be led to ask whether it is the sweeping range of issues that West addresses in his work that makes him difficult to label, characterize, or treat in ways that are customary to academic discourse. One might ask additionally who is best suited to evaluate his scholarship. Is it the literary critic armed with her spectrum of theoretical tools and a finely tuned sense of the function of language and rhetoric? Is it the philosopher who can tease out, for our consideration, the larger systems of thought that West employs? Perhaps it is the sociologist, who can evaluate the enormous amount of statistical data upon which many of the general claims West makes about African Americans are based? Or better still, is it the anthropologist, with his seasoned skills of cultural analysis and ethnographically informed sense of African American culture who is best suited to address the variety of claims being made by West? In this sense, ironically enough, it may be that the very thing that has, at least in part, created his popularity (the appeal of his breadth, which characterizes the transdisciplinarity of African Americanist scholars), is also the thing that appears daunting in the face of conventional academic commentary.

I would contend, however, that the intellectual work of Cornel West is too vital to the African American intelligentsia, and to all students and scholars of African America, for us to simply draw back in the face of the task before us. Cornel West must not only be read as a cultural icon, a "public intellectual"; he must be read for his philosophical, intellectual, and social import. For West has contributed much, and has much still to contribute, to the contemporary discourses on the meaning of poststructuralist thought for African Americans, the role and place of African American intellectuals in this postmodern world, and the socioeconomic problems currently crippling African Americans.

If Henry Louis Gates Jr. represents the intellectual model that demonstrates the utility of poststructuralist thought (and more broadly, Western philosophy) for African American literary discourse, and if Patricia Williams illuminates the uses and power in taking personal experience and personal narration seriously as forms of analysis, then Cornel West holds up a powerful new model for transdisciplinary African American intellectual practice for our consideration. In the final analysis, regardless of how we may read the media phenomenon that is "Cornel West," it is my hope that this essay might stand as a humble call for further serious intellectual evaluation of West's public scholarly model and the specifics of his impressive body of work. What can it teach us? What is the meaning of the breadth of his analysis? And finally, what might the appearance on the intellectual scene of this transdisciplinary scholarly approach signal for the direction of African American critical thought at this moment in our history?

10 Can the Queen Speak?

Sexuality, Racial Essentialism, and the Problem of Authority[1]

The gay people we knew then did not live in separate subcultures, not in the small, segregated black community where work was difficult to find, where many of us were poor. . . . Sheer economic necessity and fierce white racism, as well as the joy of being there with black folks known and loved, compelled many gay blacks to live close to home and family. That meant, however, that gay people created a way to live out sexual preferences within the boundaries of circumstances that were rarely ideal no matter how affirming. In some cases, this meant a closeted sexual life. In other families, an individual could be openly expressive, quite out.

. . . Unfortunately, there are very few oral histories and autobiographies which explore the lives of black gay people in diverse black communities. This is a research project that must be carried out if we are to fully understand the complex experience of being black and gay in this white-supremacist, patriarchal, capitalist society. Often we hear more from black gay people who have chosen to live in predominately white communities, whose choices may have been affected by undue harassment in black communities. We hear hardly anything from black gay people who live contentedly in black communities.

—bell hooks, *Talking Back*

I speak for the thousands, perhaps hundreds of thousands of men who live and die in the shadows of secrets, unable to speak of the love that helps them endure and contribute to the race. Their ordinary kisses of sweet spit and loyalty are scrubbed away by the propaganda makers of the race, the "Talented Tenth" . . .

The Black homosexual is hard pressed to gain audience among his heterosexual brothers; even if he is more talented, he is inhibited by his silence or his admissions. This is what the race has depended on in being able to erase homosexuality from our recorded history. The "chosen" history. But the sacred constructions of silence are futile exercises in denial. We will not go away with our issues of sexuality. We are coming home.

It is not enough to tell us that one was a brilliant poet, scientist, educator, or rebel. Whom did he love? It makes a difference. I can't become a whole man simply on what is fed to me: watered-down versions of Black life in America. I need the ass-splitting truth to be told, so I will have something pure to emulate, a reason to remain loyal.

—Essex Hemphill, *Ceremonies*

The fundamental question driving this essay is: Who speaks for "the race," and on what authority? In partial answer to this query, I have argued elsewhere that African American intellectuals participate, even if out of political necessity, in forms of racial essentialism to authorize and legitimate their positions in speaking for or representing "the race."[2] This essay is in some ways the culmination of a tripartite discussion of that argument. Of course, the arguments made here and in those earlier essays need not be limited solely to the field of African American intellectuals. Indeed, the discursive practices described in these essays are more widely disseminated. Nevertheless, because I am quite familiar with African American intellectualism and am actively invested in addressing that body of discourse, it makes sense that I locate my analysis of racial essentialism in the context of a broader discussion of how we have come to understand what "black" is.

My essay moves from an examination of African American intellectuals' efforts to problematize racial subjectivity through black anti-racist discourse to a critique of their representation, or lack thereof, of gays and lesbians in that process. I will further have occasion to observe the political process that legitimates certain racial subjects and qualifies them to speak for (represent) "the race," and excludes others from that very possibility. I use three exemplary reading sites to formulate this analysis. First, I examine bell hooks's essay, "Homophobia in Black Communities." I then move to an exchange, of sorts, between essays by the controversial black psychiatrist Frances Cress Welsing and the late black gay poet, essayist, and activist Essex Hemphill, "The Politics Behind Black Male Passivity, Effeminization, Bisexuality and Homosexuality" and "If Freud Had Been a Neurotic Colored Woman: Reading Dr. Frances Cress Welsing," respectively. Finally, I consider two moments from the documentary on the life and art of James Baldwin entitled *James Baldwin: The Price of the Ticket.*

In her oft-cited intervention into the 2 Live Crew controversy of a few years ago, "Beyond Racism and Misogyny: Black Feminism and 2 Live Crew," Kimberlé Williams Crenshaw asserts that the danger in the misogyny of the group's lyrics cannot simply be read as an elaborate form of cultural signifying, as Henry Louis Gates Jr. argues in his defense of 2 Live Crew. On the contrary, Crenshaw maintains that such language is

> no mere braggadocio. Those of us who are concerned about the high rates of gender violence in our communities must be troubled by the possible connections between such images and violence against women. Children and teenagers are listening to this music, and I am concerned that the range of acceptable behavior is being broadened by the constant propagation of antiwoman imagery. I'm concerned, too, about young Black women who together with men are learning that their value lies between their legs. Unlike that of men, however, women's sexual value is portrayed as a depletable commodity: By expending it, girls become whores and boys become men. (30)

My concerns are similar in kind to those of Crenshaw. Having come of age in a small rural black community where any open expression of gay or lesbian sexuality was met with derision at best and violence at worst; having been socialized in a black Baptist church that preached the damnation of "homosexuals"; having been trained in an African American studies curriculum that provided no serious or sustained discussion of the specificity of African American lesbian and gay folk; and still feeling—even at the moment of this present writing—the overwhelming weight and frustration of having to speak in a race discourse that seems to have grown all too comfortable with the routine practice of speaking about a "black community" as a discursive unit wholly separate from black lesbians and gay men (evidenced by the way we always speak in terms of the relationship of black gays and lesbians to the black community or how we speak of the homophobia of the black community, etc.); all of this has led me to the conclusion that as a community of scholars who are serious about political change, healing black people, and speaking truth to black people, we must begin the important process of undertaking a truly more inclusive vision of "black community" and of race discourse. As far as I am concerned, any treatment of African American politics and culture, and any theorizing about the future of black America, indeed, about any black religious practice or critique of black religion that does not take seriously the lives, contributions, and presence of black gays and lesbians (just as we take seriously the lives of black women, the black poor, black men, the black middle class, etc.), or any critique that does no more than to render token lip service to black gay and lesbian experience is a critique that not only denies the complexity of who we are as a representationally "whole people," but denies the very "ass-splitting truth" that Essex Hemphill referred to so eloquently and so very appropriately in *Ceremonies*.

I mean this critique quite specifically. Too often, African American cultural critique finds itself positing an essential black community that serves as a point of departure for commentary. In other cases, it assumes a kind of monolith in general when it calls upon the term "black community" at all. Insofar as the position of such a construct might be deemed essential to the critical project, it is not that gesture to which I object. Rather, it is the narrowness of the vision for what is constitutive of that community that is most problematic. If we accept the fact that the term "community," regardless of the modifier which precedes it, is always a term in danger of presuming too much, I favor making sure that our use of the term accounts for as much of what it presumes as possible.

At present, the phrase "the black community" functions as a shifter or floating signifier. That is, it is a term whose meaning shifts in accordance with the context in which it is articulated. But at the same time the phrase is also most often deployed in a manner that presumes a cultural specificity that works as much on a politics of exclusion as it does on a politics of in-clusion. There are many visions and versions of the black community that get posited in scholarly discourse, popular cultural forms, and in political dis-course. Rarely do any of these visions include lesbians and gay men, except perhaps as an afterthought. I want to see a black anti-racist discourse that does not need to maintain such exclusions in order to be efficacious.

Insofar as there is a need to articulate a black anti-racist discourse to ad-dress and to respond to the real and present dangers and vicissitudes of racism, essential to that discourse is the use of the rhetoric of community. Perhaps in the long term it would be best to explode all of the categories hav-ing to do with the very notion of "black community" and all of the inclu-sions and exclusions that come along with it. That is a project the advent of which I will be among the first to applaud. However, in the political mean-time, my aim here is to take seriously the state of racial discourse, especially black anti-racist discourse and the accompanying construct of "the black community," on the very irksome terms in which I have inherited it.

As I think again on the example of the exchange between Crenshaw and Gates over the misogyny charges against 2 Live Crew, it also occurs to me that similar charges of homophobia or heterosexism could be waged against any number of rap or hip-hop artists, though this is a critique that seems to have been given very little attention.[3] If similar charges could be made, could not, then, similar defenses of heterosexism be mounted as well? The argu-ment would go something like this: What appears to be open homophobia on the part of black rap and hip-hop artists is really engaged in a complicated form of cultural signifying that needs to be read not as homophobia, but in the context of a history of derisive assaults on black manhood. This being the case, what we really witness when we see and hear these artists participate in what appears to be homophobia is an act involved in the project of the reclamation of black manhood that does not really mean the literal violence that it performs. This is, in fact, similar to the logic used by bell hooks in her essay "Homophobia in Black Communities" when she speaks of the contradiction that is openly expressed homophobia among blacks:

> Black communities may be perceived as more homophobic than other communities because there is a tendency for individuals in black communities to verbally express in an outspoken way anti-gay sentiments. I talked with a straight black male in a California community who acknowledged that though he has often made jokes poking fun at gays or expressing contempt, as a means of bonding in group settings, in his private life he was a central support person for a gay sister. Such contradictory behavior seems pervasive in black communities. It speaks to ambivalence about sexuality in general, about sex as a subject of conversation, and to ambivalent feelings and attitudes toward homosexuality. Various structures of emotional and economic dependence create gaps between attitudes and actions. Yet a distinction must be made between black people overtly expressing prejudice toward homosexuals and homophobic white people who never make homophobic comments but who have the power to actively exploit and oppress gay people in areas of housing, employment, etc. (122)

Her rhetoric here is at once to be commended for its critique of the claims by many that blacks are more homophobic than other racial or ethnic groups, and to be critiqued as an apology for black homophobia. For hooks to offer as a rationale for black homophobia, as in her anecdote of the "straight black male in a California community," the fact that "bonding" (since it is unspecified, we can assume both male and racial bonding here) is the reason he participates in homophobic "play," is both revealing and inexcusable. This is precisely the kind of play that, following again the logic of Crenshaw, we cannot abide given the real threats that still exist in the form of discrimination and violence to gays and lesbians. While hooks may want to relegate systemic discrimination against gays and lesbians to the domain of hegemonic whites, anti-gay violence takes many forms—emotional, representational, and physical—and is not a practice exclusive to those of any particular race. Furthermore, it seems disingenuous and naive to suggest that what we say about gays and lesbians and the cultural representations of gays and lesbians do not, at least in part, legitimate—if not engender—discrimination and violence against gays and lesbians.

The rhetorical strategy that she employs here is a very old one, indeed, wherein blacks are blameless because "powerless." The logic implied by such thinking is that because whites constitute a hegemonic racial block in American society that oppresses blacks and other people of color, blacks can never be held wholly accountable for their own sociopolitical transgressions. Since this is sensitive and volatile territory upon which I am treading, let me take some extra care to make sure that I am properly understood. I do not mean to suggest that there is not a grain of truth in the reality of the racial claims made by hooks and sustained by a history of black protest. However, it is only a grain. And the grain is, after all, but a minute particle on the vast shores of discursive truth. For me, any understanding of black oppression that makes it possible, and worse permissible, to endorse at any level sexism, elitism, or heterosexism is a vision of black culture that is finally not politically consummate with liberation. We can no more excuse black homophobia than black sexism. One is as politically and, dare I say, morally suspect as the other. This is a particularly surprising move on the part of hooks when we consider that in so many other contexts her work on gender is so unrelenting and hard hitting.[4] So much is this the case that it is almost unimaginable that hooks would allow for a space in which tolerance for black sexism would ever be tenable. This makes me all the more suspect of her willingness not just to tolerate but to apologize for black homophobia.

There is still one aspect of hooks's argument that I want to address here, which is her creation of a dichotomy between black gays and lesbians who live in black communities and those who live in predominately white communities. It is raised most clearly in the epigraph with which I began this essay. She laments that "often we hear more from black gay people who have chosen to live in predominately white communities, whose choices may have been affected by undue harassment in black communities. We hear hardly anything from black gay people who live contentedly in black communities" (122). This claim about the removal of black gays and lesbians from the "authentic" black community is quite bizarre for any number of reasons. Is it to say that those who remain in black communities are not "unduly harassed"? Or is it that they can take it? And is undue harassment the only factor in moves by black gays and lesbians to other communities? Still, the statement is problematic even beyond these more obvious curiosities in that it plays on the kind of authenticity politics that are under critique here. She faults many black middle-class gays and lesbians, and I dare say many of her colleagues in the academy who live in "white communities," in a way that suggests that they are unable to give us the "real" story of black gays and lesbians. What of those experiences of "undue harassment" that she posits as potentially responsible for their exodus from the black community? Are those narratives, taking place as they do in hooks's "authentic" black community, not an important part of the story of black gay and lesbian experience, or are those gays and lesbians unqualified because of the geographical locations from which they speak? It appears that the standard hooks ultimately establishes for "real" black gay commentary here is a standard that few black intellectuals could comfortably meet any more—a by-product of the class structure in which we live. In most cases the more upwardly mobile one becomes, the whiter the circles in which one inevitably finds oneself circulating—one of the more unfortunate realities of American society.[5]

The logic used by hooks on black homophobia is dangerous not only for the reasons I have already articulated, but also because it exists on a continuum with that of thinkers like Frances Cress Welsing. They are not, of course, the same; but each does exist in a discursive field that makes the other possible. Therefore, hooks's implied logic of apology played out to its fullest conclusion bears a great deal of resemblance to Welsing's own heterosexist text.

Welsing's sentiments are exemplary of and grow out of a black cultural nationalist response to gay and lesbian sexuality, which has most often read homosexuality as "counter-revolutionary."[6,7] She begins first by dismissing the entirety of the psychoanalytic community that takes its lead from Freud. Freud is dismissed immediately by Welsing because he was unable to deliver his own people from the devastation of Nazi Germany. To Welsing, this "racial" ineffectualness renders moot anything that Freud (or any of his devotees) might have to say on the subject of sexuality. The logic is this: since the most important political element for black culture is that of survival, and Freud didn't know how to provide that for his people, nothing that Freud or his devotees could tell us about homosexuality should be applied to black people. The idea of holding Freud responsible for not preventing the Holocaust is not only laughable, but it denies the specific history giving rise to that event. Furthermore, if we use this logic of victim-blaming in the case of the Jews and Freud, would it not also follow that we would have to make the same critique of slavery? Are black Africans and the tribal leaders of West Africa, then, not also responsible for not preventing the enslavement of blacks? It is precisely this sort of specious logic that makes a very articulate Welsing difficult and frustrating when one tries to take her seriously.

But take her seriously we must, since Welsing continues to speak and to command quite a following among black cultural nationalists. We have to be concerned, then, about the degree to which Welsing's heterosexist authentication of blackness contributes to the marginalization of black gays and lesbians. For Welsing, black Africa is the site of an "originary" or "authentic" blackness. At the beginning of her essay, Welsing makes the following statement:

Black male passivity, effeminization, bisexuality and homosexuality are being encountered increasingly by Black psychiatrists working with Black patient populations. These issues are being presented by family members, personnel working in schools and other social institutions or by Black men themselves. Many in the Black population are reaching the conclusion that such issues have become a problem of epidemic proportion amongst Black people in the U.S., although it was an almost non-existent behavioral phenomenon amongst indigenous Blacks in Africa. (81)

From the beginning, Welsing describes homosexuality in a language associated with disease. It is a "problem of epidemic proportion" that seems to be spreading among black people. This rehearses a rhetorical gesture I mentioned earlier by speaking of the black community as an entity wholly separate from homosexuals who infect its sacrosanct authenticity. Of course, it goes without saying that Welsing's claim that homosexuality "was an almost non-existent behavioral phenomenon amongst indigenous Blacks in Africa" is not only unsupported by anthropological study, but it also suggests the biological or genetic link, to use her language, that non-indigenous blacks have to indigenous black Africans.[8] Welsing more than adopts an Afrocentric worldview in this essay by positing Africa as the seat of all real, unsullied, originary blackness. In this way she casts her lot with much of black cultural nationalist discourse, which is heavily invested in Afrocentrism. For further evidence of this, we need look no further than Welsing's own definition of "Black mental health":

The practice of those unit patterns of behavior (i.e., logic, thought, speech, action and emotional response) in all areas of people activity: economics, education, entertainment, labor, law, politics, religion, sex and war—which are simultaneously self- and group-supporting under the social and political conditions of worldwide white supremacy domination (racism). In brief, this means Black behavioral practice which resists self- and group-negation and destruction. (82)

Here, as elsewhere, Welsing prides herself on being outside of the conceptual mainstream of any currently held psychiatric definitions of mental illness. She labels those the "'European' psychoanalytic theories of Sigmund Freud" (82). She seems here to want to be recognized for taking a bold, brazen position as solidly outside any "mainstream" logic. This is because all such logic is necessarily bad because it is mainstream, which is to say, white. One, then, gets the sense that homosexuality too is a by-product of white supremacy. And further, that if there were no white supremacy, homosexuality would, at best, not exist or, at worst, be somehow okay if it did. The overriding logic of her argument is the connection between white supremacy and homosexuality. The latter is produced by the former as a way to control black people. Hence, it follows that the only way to be really black is to resist homosexuality.

From this point on, Welsing's essay spirals into an ever-deepening chasm from which it never manages to return. For example, she argues that it is "male muscle mass" that oppresses a people. Since white men understand this fact and the related fact of their genetic weakness in relation to the majority of the world's women (women of color), they are invested in the effeminization and homosexualization of black men (83–84). She also states that the white women's liberation movement—white women's response to the white male's need to be superior at least over them—has further served to weaken the white male's sense of power, "helping to push him to a *weakened* and *homosexual* stance" (my emphasis—the two are synonymous for Welsing). Feminism, then, according to Welsing, leads to further "white male/female alienation, pushing white males further into the homosexual position and . . . white females in that direction also" (85–86). Finally, she suggests that it is black manhood that is the primary target of racism, since black men, of course, are the genetically superior beings who can reproduce not only with black women, but who can also reproduce with white women. And since the offspring of such unions, according to Welsing's logic, are always black (the exact opposite of the result of such sexual pairings for white men and black women), black manhood is the primary target of a white supremacist system. Welsing's words are significant enough here that I quote her at some length:

> Racism (white supremacy) is the dominant social system in today's world. Its fundamental dynamic is predicated upon the genetic recessive deficiency state of albinism, which is responsible for skin whiteness and thus the so-called "white race." This genetic recessive trait is dominated by the genetic capacity to produce any of the various degrees of skin melanation—whether black, brown, red or yellow. In other words, it can be annihilated as a phenotypic condition. Control of this potential for genetic domination and annihilation throughout the world is absolutely essential if the condition of skin whiteness is to survive. "White" survival is predicated upon aggressiveness and muscle mass in the form of technology directed against the "non-white" melanated men on the planet Earth who constitute the numerical majority. Therefore, white survival and white power are dependent upon the various methodologies, tactics and strategies developed to control all "non-white" men, as well as bring them into cooperative submission. This is especially important in the case of Black men because they have the greatest capacity to produce melanin and, in turn, the greatest genetic potential for the annihilation of skin albinism or skin whiteness. (83)

This passage demonstrates, to my mind, the critical hazards of privileging the category of race in any discussion of black people. When we give "race," with its retinue of historical and discursive investments, primacy over other signifiers of difference, the result is a network of critical blindnesses that prevent us from perceiving the ways in which the conventions of race discourse get naturalized and normativized. These conventions often include, especially in cases involving—though not exclusive to—black cultural nationalism, the denigration of homosexuality, and the accompanying peripheralization of women. Underlying much of race discourse, then, is always the im-

214

plication that all "real" black subjects are male and heterosexual. Therefore, in partial response to the query with which I began this essay, only these subjects are best qualified to speak for or to represent the race.

Unfortunately, Welsing does not stop there. She continues her discussion of black manhood to a point where what she means by the appellation far-and-above exceeds her mere genetic definition. Though she never clearly defines what she intends by black manhood, we can construct a pretty clear idea from the ways that she uses the term in her argument. "The dearth of black males in the homes, schools and neighborhoods," Welsing proclaims,

> leaves Black male children no alternative models. Blindly they seek out one another as models, and in their blindness end up in trouble—in juvenile homes or prisons. But fate and the dynamics of racism again play a vicious trick because the young males only become more alienated from their manhood and more feminized in such settings. (89)

It is clear from this statement that black manhood is set in opposition to femininity and is something that is retarded by the influence of women, especially in female-headed households. She describes the effect of effeminizing influences on black men as the achievement of racist programming. This achievement is, in part, possible because of the clothing industry as well, according to Welsing: "The white run clothing industry is all too pleased to provide the costumes of feminine disguise for Black male escape. However, they never would provide uniforms or combat gear if customers were willing to pay $1000 per outfit" (89). She also faults television as "an important programmer of behavior in this social system" that "plays a further major role in alienating Black males (especially children) from Black manhood" (89). The examples she cites are Flip Wilson's persona Geraldine and Jimmy Walker's character J. J. on the 1970s television series *Good Times*. "These weekly insults," she maintains, "to Black manhood that we have been programmed to believe are entertainment and not direct racist warfare, further reinforce, perhaps in the unconscious thinking of Black people, a

215

loss of respect for Black manhood while carrying that loss to even deeper levels" (90). Most telling, perhaps, is that the clinical method she endorses for "disorders" of "passivity, effeminization, bisexuality, homosexuality" is to have the patients "relax and envision themselves approaching and opposing, in actual combat, the collective of white males and females (without apology or giving up in the crunch)" (91–92). Again, there is an essence to what black manhood is that never receives full articulation, but is only expressed implicitly. But what is implied could be described as monstrous, combative, and even primitive. There is certainly no room for a nurturing view of manhood here. To be a man is to be strong. And strength, in Welsing's logic, is the opposite of weakness, which can only signify at best as effeminacy or passivity and at worst as bisexuality or homosexuality. Still another of the vexatious implications of this logic is that in a world devoid of racism or white supremacy, there would be no black male homosexuality. The result is that black male homosexuality is reducible to being a by-product of racist programming. Once again, this is the function of an argument that privileges race discourse over other forms of difference in its analysis of black oppression.

Let me turn my attention for a moment to Essex Hemphill's response to Welsing's troublesome essay. Hemphill's rhetoric demonstrates how even in a very astute and well-wrought "reading" of Welsing—and it is fair to say that Hemphill "reads" her in both the critical and the more campy sense of the word—the move is never made to critique the structure (and by structure here I mean the implied rules governing the use of) and function of race discourse itself. It is clear to me, as I have tried to demonstrate, that this is precisely what is missing from hooks's logic, which undergirds her discussion of homophobia in black communities as well. Hemphill's response to Welsing is thoughtful, engaging, and identifies the faulty premises upon which Welsing bases her arguments. Still, Hemphill's own essay and rhetoric falls prey to the conventions of race discourse in two very important ways. First, in order to combat Welsing's homophobia/heterosexism, Hemphill himself feels the pressure to legitimize and authorize himself as a speaker on race matters by telling his own authenticating anecdote of black/gay experience at the beginning of his essay:[9]

> In 1974, the year that Dr. Frances Cress Welsing wrote "The Politics Behind Black Male Passivity, Effeminization, Bisexuality, and Homosexuality," I entered my final year of senior high school.
>
> By that time, I had arrived at a very clear understanding of how dangerous it was to be a homosexual in my Black neighborhood and in society. . . . Facing this then-limited perception of homosexual life, I could only wonder, where did I fit in? . . .
>
> Conversely, I was perfecting my heterosexual disguise; I was practicing the necessary use of masks for survival; I was calculating the distance between the first day of class and graduation, the distance between graduation from high school and departure for college—and ultimately, the arrival of my freedom from home, community, and my immediate peers. . . .
>
> During the course of the next sixteen years I would articulate and politicize my sexuality. I would discover that homo sex did not constitute a whole life nor did it negate my racial identity or constitute a substantive reason to be estranged from my family and Black culture. I discovered, too, that the work ahead for me included, most importantly, being able to integrate all of my identities into a functioning self, instead of accepting a dysfunctional existence as a consequence of my homosexual desires. (52–53)

While Hemphill's personal anecdote demonstrates his access to the various categories of identity he claims, it is not a critique of the very idea of the categories themselves. In fact, he plays the "race/sexuality" card in a way that is similar to the way in which Welsing plays the "race" card.

Furthermore, while his critique of Welsing is thorough and extremely insightful, it does not move to critique the methodological fault Welsing makes in her analysis—that is, the fact that much of what is wrong with Welsing's argument is a result of the privileging of "race" over other critical categories of difference. Instead, Hemphill treats Welsing's heterosexism itself as the critical disease instead of as symptomatic of a far more systemic critical illness.

One of the most noteworthy things about Hemphill's anecdotal testimony is that while it insists, and rightly so, upon the integration of what Welsing has established as the dichotomous identities of race and homosexuality, it also participates in a familiar structural convention of race discourse in its necessity to claim the racial identification as a position from which even the black homosexual speaks. In other words, part of the rhetorical strategy enacted by Hemphill in this moment is that of claiming the category of racial authenticity for himself as part of what legitimizes and authorizes the articulation of his corrective to Welsing's homophobic race logic. The net result is the substitution of heterosexist race logic with a homo-positive or homo-inclusive race logic. Still, the common denominator of both positions is the persistence of race as the privileged category in discussions of black identity.

The first clue we get of Hemphill's failure to identify the larger systemic problem of Welsing's argument is when he compares Welsing to Shahrazad Ali:

> Dr. Welsing is not as easily dismissible as Shahrazad Ali, author of the notorious book of internal strife, *The Black Man's Guide to Understanding the Black Woman* (Philadelphia: Civilized Publications, 1989). . . . By dismissing the lives of Black lesbians and gay men, Ali is clearly not advocating the necessary healing Black communities require; she is advocating further factionalization. Her virulently homophobic ideas lack credibility and are easily dismissed as incendiary.

Dr. Welsing is much more dangerous because she attempts to justify *her* homophobia and heterosexism precisely by grounding it in an acute understanding of African American history and an analysis of the psychological effects of centuries of racist oppression and violence (54).

Hemphill is right in his reading of Welsing, though his reading does not go far enough: Ali is not more easily dismissible than Welsing. In fact, Ali's ideas are rooted in a history of sorts, a history shared by Welsing's arguments—that is, the history of race discourse itself that, in its privileging of the dominant category of analysis, has always sustained the derision or exclusion of black gays and lesbians.

Another such moment in Hemphill's essay comes when he identifies what he seems to understand as the central problem of Welsing's text. He writes:

Welsing refutes any logical understanding of sexuality. By espousing Black homophobia and heterosexism—imitations of the very oppressive forces of hegemonic white male heterosexuality she attempts to challenge—she places herself in direct collusion with the forces that continually move against Blacks, gays, lesbians, and all people of color. Thus, every time a gay man or lesbian is violently attacked, blood *is* figuratively on Dr. Welsing's hands as surely as blood is on the hands of the attackers. Her ideas reinforce the belief that gay and lesbian lives are expendable, and her views also provide a clue as to why the Black community has failed to intelligently and coherently address critical, life-threatening issues such as AIDS. (55)

Hemphill's statement is true. Welsing's logic does imitate that of the oppressive forces of white male heterosexuality that she tries to refute. The difference is that Welsing does not view the latter category as crucial to her analysis. The problem with Welsing's argument does not end where Hemphill supposes it does. Much of race discourse, even the discourse of racial liberation, participates in a similar relationship with hegemonic anti-gay forces. This is especially the case, and some might even argue that it is inevitable, when we consider the history and development of black liberationist or anti-racist discourse, with its insistence on the centrality of black masculinity (in the narrowest sense of the term) as the essential element of any form of black liberation. If racial liberationist discourse suggests at best the invisibility of homosexuality and at worst understands homosexuality as racially antagonistic, Dr. Welsing radically manifests one of the more unseemly truths of race discourse for blacks—the demonization of homosexuality.

The critical blindness demonstrated by Hemphill does not alone express the extent of what happens when a gay black man takes up the mantle of race discourse. Another example worth exploring is that of James Baldwin. In the documentary of his life done in 1989, *James Baldwin: The Price of the Ticket,* there are at least two moments to which I want to call attention. The first is a statement made by Amiri Baraka and the second is a statement made by Baldwin himself from interview footage from the *Dick Cavett Show.* I turn to these less literally textual examples to demonstrate that in our more casual or less scripted moments, our subconscious understanding of the realities of race discourse is laid bare even more clearly.

Baraka's regard for Baldwin is well documented by the film. He talks about how Baldwin was "in the tradition" and how his early writings, specifically *Notes of a Native Son,* really impacted him and spoke to a whole generation. In an attempt to describe or account for Baldwin's homosexuality, however, Baraka falters in his efforts to unite the racially significant image of Baldwin that he clings to with the homosexual Baldwin with whom he seems less comfortable. Baraka states the following:

> Jimmy Baldwin was neither in the closet about his homosexuality, nor was he running around proclaiming homosexuality. I mean, he was what he was. And you either had to buy that or, you know, *mea culpa,* go somewhere else.

The poles of the rhetorical continuum that Baraka sets up here for his understanding of homosexuality are very telling and should remind us of the earlier dichotomy set up by bell hooks between homosexuals who live some-what closeted existences in black communities and those who do not. To Baraka's mind, one can either be in the closet or "running around proclaim-ing homosexuality" (the image of the effete gay man and the gay activist col-lide here, it would seem). What makes Baldwin acceptable to enter the pan-theon of race men for Baraka is the fact that his sexual identity is unlocat-able. It is neither here nor there, or perhaps it is everywhere at once, leaving the entire question undecided and undecidable. And if Baldwin is undecided about his sexual identity, the one identity to which he is firmly committed is his racial identity. The rhetorical ambiguity around his sexual identity, ac-cording to Baraka, is what makes it possible for Baldwin to be a race man who was "in the tradition."

Baldwin himself, it seems, was well aware of the dangers of—indeed, the "price of the ticket" for—trying to synthesize his racial and sexual identities. He understood that his efficacy as race man was—at least in part—depend-ent on limiting his public activism to racial politics. The frame of the docu-mentary certainly confirms this in the way it represents Baldwin's own re-sponse to his sexuality. In one interview, he makes the following statement:

> I think the trick is to say yes to life. . . . It is only we of the twentieth cen-tury who are so obsessed with the particular details of anybody's sex life. I don't think those details make a difference. And I will never be able to deny a certain power that I have had to deal with, which has dealt with me, which is called love; and love comes in very strange packages. I've loved a few men; I've loved a few women; and a few people have loved me. That's . . . I suppose that's all that's saved my life.

It may be of interest to note that while making this statement, the camera pans down to Baldwin's hands, which are fidgeting with the cigarette and cigarette holder. This move on the part of the camera undercuts the veracity of Baldwin's statement here and suggests that Baldwin himself does not quite believe all that he is saying. From the 1949 essay "The Preservation of Innocence" that he wrote and published in *Zero,* a small Moroccan journal, Baldwin knows just how profoundly important sexuality is to discussions of race. But the desire registered here for sexuality not to make a difference is important to recognize. When we understand this statement as spoken in a prophetic mode, it imagines a world in which the details of a person's sex life can "matter" as part of a person's humanity, but not have to usurp her authority or legitimacy to represent the race.

If Baldwin's statement here raises the complications of speaking from a complex racial/sexual identity location, the following excerpt from his interview on the *Dick Cavett Show* illustrates this point all the more clearly:

I don't know what most white people in this country feel, but I can only conclude what they feel from the state of their institutions. I don't know if white Christians hate Negroes or not, but I know that we have a Christian church which is white and a Christian church which is black. I know as Malcolm X once put it, "The most segregated hour in America is high noon on Sunday." That says a great deal to me about a Christian nation. It means that I can't afford to trust most white Christians and certainly cannot trust the Christian church. I don't know whether the labor unions and their bosses really hate me. That doesn't matter. But I know that I'm not in their unions. I don't know if the real estate lobby has anything against black people, but I know the real estate lobby keeps me in the ghetto. I don't know if the board of education hates black people, but I know the textbooks they give my children to read and the schools that we go to. Now this is the evidence! *You want me to make an act of faith risking myself, my wife, my woman, my sister, my children on some idealism which you assure me exists in America which I have never seen.* [Emphasis added.]

Interesting for both the rich sermonic quality and the vehement tone for which Baldwin was famous, this passage is also conspicuous for the manner in which Baldwin assumes the voice of representative race man. In the very last sentence, when Baldwin affects the position of race man, part of the performance includes the masking of his specificity, his sexuality, his difference. And in race discourse, when all difference is concealed, what emerges is the heterosexual black man "risking [himself], [his] wife, [his] woman and [his] children." The image of the black man as protector, progenitor, and defender of the race—which sounds suspiciously similar to the image fostered by Welsing and much of black cultural nationalism—is what Baldwin assumes here. The truth of this rhetorical transformation—the hard, difficult, worrisome truth—is that in order to be a representative race man, one must be heterosexual. And what of women? They would appear, in the confines of race discourse, to be ever the passive players. They are rhetorically useful in that they lend legitimacy to the black male's responsibility for their care and protection, but they cannot speak any more than the gay or lesbian brother or sister can. If these are part of the structural demands of race discourse, the erasure of subtlety and black difference, it is time to own up to that truth. As black intellectuals and cultural workers, we have to demand, insist upon, and be about the business of helping to create new and more inclusive ways of speaking about race that do not cause even good, thorough thinkers like hooks, Hemphill, and Baldwin (and there are many others) to compromise their/our own critical veracity by participating in the form of race discourse that has been hegemonic for so long. Race is, indeed, a fiction, an allegory, if you will, with an elaborate linguistic court. Knowing that, more needs to be done to reimagine race; to create new and inclusive mythologies to replace the old, weather-worn, heterosexual masculinity–centered ones; to reconstitute "the black community" as one that includes our various differences as opposed to the monolith to which we inevitably seem to return.

For far too long the field of African American/Afro-American/black studies has thought about race as the primary category of analysis for the work that proceeds from the field. The problem with such work has always been, and continues to be, that African Americans and African American experience are far more complicated than this. And it is time that we begin to understand what that means in the form of an everyday critical and political practice. Race is not simple. It has never been simple. It does not have the history that would make it so, no matter how much we may yearn for that degree of clarity. This is a point I have argued in a variety of venues. The point being, if I am thinking about race, I should already be thinking about gender, class, and sexuality. This statement, I think, assumes the very impossibility of a hierarchy or chronology of categories of identity. The point is not just one of intersection, as we have thought of it for so long; it is one of reconstitution. That is, race is already more than just race. Or put another way, race is always already everything that it ever was, though some of its constitutive aspects may have been repressed for various nefarious purposes or for other strategic ones. Either way, it is never simple, never to be taken for granted. What I say is not revolutionary or revelatory. The theory, in this way, has gotten ahead of the critical practice. Almost all good race theorists these days will recognize the merit of this approach; the point is that the work we produce has not fully caught up. That explains why it is still possible today to query: What does a race theory, of which all of these categories of identity are constitutive, look like? And more importantly, how do the critiques, the work informed by such theory, look different from what we now see dominating the field? I have great hope in the future for the work of scholars like Lindon Barrett who are beginning to theorize racial blackness in relationship to the category of value with all the trappings of desire, commodification, and exchange inherent in that operation. This may be just the kind of critical innovation needed to help us to reconstitute our ideas about "race" and race discourse.[10]

Of course, it is not my intention in these reflections to suggest that there are not good heterosexual "race men" and "race women" on the scene who have progressive views about sexuality and are "down" with their gay and lesbian brothers and sisters. In fact, quite the contrary. In many instances, it adds an extra dimension of cachet and progressivism to hear such heterosexual speakers be sympathetic to gays and lesbians. So long as they are not themselves gay or lesbian, it would appear on the open market to enhance their "coolness" quotient. The issue that needs more attention exists at the level at which we authenticate our authority and legitimacy to speak for the race as representational subjects. In other words, there are any number of narratives that African American intellectuals employ to qualify themselves in the terms of race discourse to speak for the race. And while one routinely witnesses the use of narratives of racial discrimination, narratives of growing up poor and black and elevating oneself through education and hard work, narratives about how connected middle-class black intellectuals are to "the black community" or "the hood," we could scarcely imagine an instance in which narrating or even claiming one's gay or lesbian identity would authenticate or legitimate oneself as a racial representative. And as we see in the case of James Baldwin, when black gays and lesbians do don the racial representational mask, they often do so by effacing (even if only temporarily) their sexual identities.

Given the current state of black anti-racist discourse, it is no wonder that even at the time of this writing there is only one book-length critical, literary investigation of the work of James Baldwin, by Trudier Harris;[11] it is no wonder that Langston Hughes's biographer, even in 1986, felt the need to defend him against the "speculation" surrounding his homosexuality; it is no wonder that even to this day we can still say with Cheryl Clark and bell hooks that there exists no sustained sociological study of black lesbians and gays;[12] and it is no wonder that among the vanguard of so-called black public intellectuals there is the notable near absence of openly gay and lesbian voices. Lamentable though this state of affairs may be, we cannot deny that part of the responsibility for it has much to do with the limits of black anti-racist discourse: that is, what it is still considered appropriate to say about race, and the policing of who speaks for the race.

Notes

Notes to Chapter 1

1 Griffin, "Black Feminist and Du Bois," 28–40.

2 Carbado, McBride, and Weise, eds., *Black Like Us*.

3 Gross, "Examining the Politics of Respectability in African-American Studies."

4 At the time of this writing, an announcement of the conference listing the names of the participants could be found archived online at http://www.unc.edu/~epjohnso/bqs.html.

5 I am thankful to Susan Manning at Northwestern University for engaging me in this very productive conversation.

6 The original subtitle was "A Century of Queer African American Literature." It was changed in response to concerns and discussion over the term "queer."

7 This is in part the goal of one of my next book projects, tentatively titled *Poetics, Politics, and Phillis Wheatley*.

8 Some of the most visible exemplars of this kind of work, to name but a few, include literary and cultural critics Phillip Brian Harper and Robert Reid-Pharr and political scientist Cathy Cohen.

9 Judging by the 1949 essay, "The Preservation of Innocence," that he wrote and published in *Zero*, a small Moroccan journal, Baldwin knows just how profoundly

important sexuality is to discussions of race. But the desire registered here for sexuality not to make a difference is important to recognize. When we understand this statement as spoken in a prophetic mode, it imagines a world in which the details of a person's sex life can "matter" as part of a person's humanity but not have to "matter" in terms that usurp their authority or legitimacy to represent the race.

10 Carby, *Race Men.*

11 Black women, in this regard, would appear, in the confines of race discourse, to be ever the passive players. They are rhetorically useful in that they lend legitimacy to the black male's responsibility for their care and protection, but they cannot speak any more than the gay or lesbian brother or sister can. The gendered portion of this critique has long been argued by black feminist critics since at least the early 1970s with the likes of Toni Cade Bambara up to the more recent works of Hazel Carby, Valerie Smith, E. Frances White, Farah Griffin, and many others.

12 Read by Cole in Karen Thorsen's 1989 film *James Baldwin: The Price of the Ticket.*

13 Ross, "White Fantasies of Desire," 25.

14 "Wandering" is a euphemism utilized by Gertrude Stein in *Melanctha* to signal wayward or promiscuous sexuality.

15 Following is the Oxford English Dictionary entry for "racism": "1936 L. DENNIS *Coming Amer. Fascism* 109 If . . . it be assumed that one of our values should be a type of racism which excludes certain races from citizenship, then the plan of execution should provide for the annihilation, deportation, or sterilization of the excluded races. 1938 E. & C. PAUL tr. *Hirschfeld's Racism* xx. 260 The apostles and energumens of racism can in all good faith give free rein to impulses of which they would be ashamed did they realise their true nature. 1940 R. BENEDICT *Race: Science & Politics* i. 7 Racism is an *ism* to which everyone in the world today is exposed. 1952 M. BERGER *Equality by Statute* 236 Racism, tension in industrial, urban areas. 1952 *Theology* LV. 283 The idolatry of our time—its setting up of nationalism, racism, vulgar materialism. 1960 *New Left Rev.* Jan./Feb. 21/2 George Rogers saw fit to kow-tow to the incipient racism of his electorate by including a line about getting rid of 'undesirable elements.'"

16 Black queer studies has been defined by Jennifer DeVere Brody and myself in "Plum Nelly" as a critical sensibility which draws "its influences from sources such as identity politics, cultural studies, feminist and gender studies, race theory, gay and lesbian studies, masculinity studies and queer studies." Its primary goal is the push "for a greater degree of specificity in both the questions being formulated and on the conclusions being reached at the margins of American society" (286).

17 The very language of this phrase is caught up in the primacy of race in the discussion of racial identity. But for now it will have to suffice.

Notes to Chapter 4

1. See Hill and Jordan, eds., *Race, Gender, and Power in America,* and Morrison, ed., *Race-ing Justice, En-Gendering Power* for a wealth of such informative essays on the Hill-Thomas hearings.

2 See note in Williams, *The Alchemy of Race and Rights,* 242.

Notes to Chapter 8

1 I use "anti-essentialist" with a purpose here as opposed to "constructionist" because Morrison never articulates a full-blown argument for constructionism. Rather, she is always guarding against the popular and facile dismissal that is all too often the response to essentialism. See page 3 of "Unspeakable Things Unspoken" for the most notable example of this practice.

2 By "unspeakable" here I intend the sometimes seeming indefensibility of essentialist categories like race in light of much poststructuralist critical work (invested in social constructionism) that has placed "race" under "erasure."

3 This statement is most revealing in that it serves as one example of how Morrison's rhetoric seems to learn from, or be informed by, her critical project as she proceeds. The shrewd enshrining of self here is not unlike the academy's enshrining of traditional canonical texts that Morrison is questioning. That is, if Morrison deconstructs the artist-critic dichotomy to legitimize her critical voice, then academic traditionalists challenge the inclusion of women and "people of color" in the canon to maintain the status of white male domination that obtains in the curriculum and in the membership of the academy as well. While Morrison's rhetorical strategies here seem deconstructive, they still rely on a kind of thinking that essentializes "artist," "critic," and "American literary canon." This may speak to Diana Fuss's larger claim that constructionism really operates as a more sophisticated form of essentialism. (See Fuss's "Introduction" in *Essentially Speaking*.) Whatever the case, Morrison is not beyond using the "master's" rhetorical process, which has obviously worked so well for him, to perform the same kind of legitimizing function on herself.

4 I am thinking here particularly of the rhetorical tactics of Phillis Wheatley and of the many nineteenth-century slave narratives' direct addresses to their readers. Consider also that Morrison's position in this essay by way of audience is complicated in much the same way that the position of the authors of these slave narratives was. She must negotiate the right amount of courting of her traditionalist audience without appearing sycophantic and overly accommodationist to her more progressive audience if she is to be heard.

5 There are at least two ways in which these appellations function for black speakers: 1. as a totalizing way of associating oneself with a monolithic black community (in which all differences that may obtain between the speaker and the various members of that community are erased or subsumed by the political claim to rhetorical unity) and 2. as a way of constructing "the black community" as always "out there" and, therefore, in its separateness from the speaker it functions as the object of study or critique. The following anecdote functions in the latter fashion.

6 I contend that this discontinuity represents the kinds of meaningful heterogeneous strains within "the black community" that are subsumed with such naming (e.g., class). The question of the utility of such appellations then naturally arises, which the following discussion of "racialized discourse" seeks to address.

7 Benjamin says of allegory: "In its fully developed, baroque form, allegory brings with it its own court; the profusion of emblems is grouped around the figural centre, which is never absent from genuine allegories, as opposed to periphrases of concepts."

8 Gates, "Writing 'Race' and the Difference It Makes," 6. Gates's project is to point out that what I have called "racialized discourse" represents "arbitrary constructs, not reports of reality." He historicizes such discourse, locating its nascence in a larger Enlightenment context.

9 For lack of a better term, I use "illusory" here to signify the status of phenomena present in our human experience that we have yet to recognize as such.

10 Recall what de Man says about allegory claiming not to know its origins or identification. It "designates primarily a distance in relation to its own origin, and, renouncing the nostalgia and desire to coincide, it establishes its language in the void of this temporal difference" (207).

11 I intend "speaking" here with all the implications of will to power. While we must recognize that everyone can speak, not everyone is heard. So by speaking black subjects, I mean those who represent and mediate to the institutions of dominant culture. Speaking black subjects are those who at least have such positional entrée.

12 Poststructuralism's critique of experience has a history of its own that is too involved to adequately detail here. Diana Fuss represents the position best, perhaps, when she writes: "the poststructuralist objection to experience is not a repudiation of grounds of knowing *per se* but rather a refusal of the hypostatization of experience as *the* ground (and the most stable ground) of knowledge production" (27). For a more detailed discussion of the issues involved in poststructuralism's critique of "experience" see Fuss's *Essentially Speaking,* chapter 2, "Reading Like a Feminist," and chapter 7, "Essentialism in the Classroom"; Joan W. Scott's essay "Experience" in *Feminists Theorize the Political*; and Teresa de Lauretis's *Alice Doesn't,* chapter 6: "Semiotics and Experience."

13 Nielsen, *Reading Race,* 12.

14 I am thinking here of the closing line of a short, comic film called *Hair Piece* by the African American, female filmmaker, Ayoka Chenzira; the closing line goes something like this: "If you are having difficulty with your comb, perhaps the comb that you are using was not designed with your hair in mind."

Notes to Chapter 9

1 Or more pointedly, West recognizes both the suspicion with which poststructuralism approaches "experience," and how this suspicion functions (even if unintentionally) to legitimize the already extant white suspicion of black racial experiences (i.e., "racial sensibilities").

2 A well-established method through which African American intellectuals use essentialism to authorize their critical voices is anecdote—the relating of "experience." Testifying and storytelling (i.e., the experiential authority to narrate) are methods of self-disclosure that legitimize the critical project as somehow more authentic, bearing a direct relationship to "experience." While contemporary examples of this are numerous (Williams, *The Alchemy of Race and Rights,* and Baker, *Long*

Black Song), West's preface to *Race Matters* is one of the more recent and illustrative examples.

3 Recall the list of African American vocalists that get named in Spike Lee's 1989 film *Do the Right Thing*. The DJ, Mr. Señor Love Daddy, says to all of the singers he names: "We would like to thank you all for making our world a little brighter." See also Alice Walker's 1983 book *In Search of Our Mothers' Gardens*. In the text, Walker explains the valiant, historical struggle of African American women to create art in spite of their simultaneously gendered and racialized circumstances. She exhorts us:

> Listen to the voices of Bessie Smith, Billie Holiday, Nina Simone, Roberta Flack, and Aretha Franklin, among others, and imagine those voices muzzled for life. Then you may begin to comprehend the lives of our "crazy," "Sainted" mothers and grandmothers. (234)

4 For an even more illustrative example of this kind of treatment of Ethiopia and his wedding, see West, *Keeping Faith*.

5 In chapter 8, I argue that African American intellectuals participate in a variety of self-authorizing practices that rely upon a kind of racial essentialism. The authors of these self-authorizing practices often rely upon racial experience to authenticate and legitimize the position from which their critical voices are raised in a (racialized) discourse where they are frequently viewed with doubt and suspicion by the dominant race.

6 Philippians 3:13–14. This section of the King James version of the Bible reads: "Brethren, I count myself not to have apprehended: but *this* one thing *I do,* forgetting those things which are behind and reaching forth unto those things which are before, I press toward the mark for the prize of the high calling of God in Jesus Christ" (emphasis added).

7 This is similar to the workings of ideology in the Marxist sense of the term. That is, when the dominant ideology really works, not only does it teach us how to think, it even limits what we are capable of thinking about. This is the extent to which even our epistemologies are overdetermined. Only when we can recognize the limits set in place by ideology and make those very limits a part of the critique can we discursively "transcend" them. As a more concrete example, I do not think that even a short time ago many of us could have imagined the demise of the former Soviet Union, the dismantling of the Berlin Wall, or the liberation of black South

Africa. Had social subjects not been participating in a kind of transcendent historical thinking, much of this may not have been possible.

Notes to Chapter 10

1 Let me thank Bob E. Myers, Darieck Bruce Scott, and Toni Morrison for listening
to and responding to these ideas in their even more unfinished conversational form.
I also wish to thank Arthur Little, Jonathan Holloway, and Chris Cunningham for
reading and responding to an earlier draft of this essay. And finally let me acknowledge the careful and instructive readings of Kara Keeling, Eric Clarke, and Lindon
Barrett.

2 See chapter 8 and chapter 9.

3 Thinkers like Kobena Mercer at the Black Nations/Queer Nations Conference in
1995 represent one among a few of the exceptions to this claim. Still, such critique
of homophobia has not been a part of the more public debates about the objec-
tionable qualities of rap and hip-hop.

4 See, for example, any number of hooks's essays in *Yearning* and *Black Looks*.

5 This is not to say that those of us who exist (at least professionally) in predominately white circles do not interact with the "black community" as a geo-political
construct. It is to suggest that our interaction is, in a sense, always uneasy because
of the very lower- and working-class specific terms in which any authentic version
of "the black community" has been articulated.

6 For a fuller discussion of how homosexuality is counter-revolutionary, see Eldridge Cleaver's *Soul on Ice*. The chapters entitled "The Allegory of the Black Eu-
nuchs" and "The Primeval Mitosis" are especially noteworthy. In order to relate this
to the earlier discussion of Crenshaw and Gates's exchange over 2 Live Crew, it is interesting to note the point made by Essex Hemphill in his essay on Welsing that she
has been a highly "sought-after public speaker, and in recent years, her ideas have
been embraced in the reemergence of Black cultural nationalism, particularly by rap
groups such as Public Enemy" (53–54).

7 Welsing herself is no exception to this rule. The last sentence of her essay reads
as follows: "Black male bisexuality and homosexuality has been used by the white
collective in its effort to survive genetically in a world dominated by colored people, and Black acceptance of this position does not solve the major problem of our

oppression [read here the race problem] but only further retards its ultimate solution" (92).

8 Even as recently as a few weeks ago at the time of this writing, Welsing appeared on NPR speaking about her famous Cress Theory of race. The theory is based on the genetic inferiority of whites to blacks. Since whites have knowledge of this, they fear genetic annihilation. This fear, according to Welsing, has been the cause of the history of racism as we know it.

9 For some preliminary discussion of anthropological evidence of the existence of homosexual practices among certain African cultures and other peoples of color, see Caplan, ed., *The Cultural Construction of Sexuality*.

10 See chapter 9, where I argue that one of the essentializing gestures in which African American intellectuals participate in order to legitimate themselves as speakers for the race is to relate racially affirming anecdotes from their own experience. Also, in fairness to Hemphill, his use of the anecdotal gesture of self-authorization is somewhat different from the usual race-based model. His narrative authority derives from the simultaneity of his gay and black experience. He insists upon them both. Still, the need to narrate the two side by side, indeed, to narrate his story at all, is interesting to note as a response to Welsing's very problematic position.

11 The state of affairs with regard to Baldwin has changed somewhat since 1997 when this piece was initially written. Several monographs and edited volumes on Baldwin have emerged constituting what I have elsewhere referred to as a Baldwin revival of sorts.

12 The recently published *Black Pride Survey*, which I discuss in the introduction to this book, represents an important beginning in this sense.

Bibliography

Anderson, Jervis. "The Public Intellectual." *New Yorker* 17 Jan. 1994: 39, 40.

Assy, Bethania. "Eichmann, the Banality of Evil, and Thinking in Arendt's Thought." Twentieth World Congress of Philosophy. Boston, Massachusetts. 10–15 August 1998. http://www.bu.edu/wcp/Papers/Cont/ContAssy.htm.

Baker, Houston A., Jr. *Long Black Song: Essays in Black American Literature and Culture.* Charlottesville: U of Virginia P, 1972.

Bakke, Ray. *A Theology as Big as the City.* Downers Grove, IL: Intervarsity, 1997.

Baldwin, James. *Giovanni's Room.* New York: Dell, 1988/1956.

———. "Preservation of Innocence." *Out/Look* 2.2 (Fall 1989): 40–45.

Bambara, Toni Cade. *The Black Woman: An Anthology.* New York: Mentor, 1970.

Battle, Juan, et al. *Say It Loud I'm Black and I'm Proud: Black Pride Survey 2000.* New York: Policy Institute of the National Gay and Lesbian Task Force, 2002.

Benjamin, Walter. *The Origin of the German Tragic Drama.* New York: Verso, 1977.

Bernal, Martin. *Black Athena: The Afroasiatic Roots of Classical Civilization, Volume 1: The Fabrication of Ancient Greece 1785–1985.* New Brunswick, NJ: Rutgers UP, 1987.

Brandt, Eric, ed. *Dangerous Liaisons: Blacks, Gays, and the Struggle for Equality.* New York: New Press, 1999.

Brody, Jennifer DeVere, and Dwight A. McBride. "Introduction" to "Plum Nelly: New Essays in Black Queer Studies." *Callaloo* 23.1 (Winter 2000): 286–88.

Bronski, Michael. "Blatant Male Pulchritude: The Art of George Quaintance and Bruce Weber's *Bear Pond*." *Art Papers* 16.4 (July/August 1992): 26–29.

Caplan, Pat. "Introduction." *The Cultural Construction of Sexuality*. Ed. Pat Caplan. London: Tavistock, 1987. 1–30.

Carbado, Devon, Dwight McBride, and Donald Weise, eds. *Black Like Us: A Century of Lesbian, Gay, and Bi-Sexual African American Fiction*. San Francisco: Cleis Press, 2002.

Carby, Hazel. *Race Men*. Cambridge, MA: Harvard UP, 1998.

Cleaver, Eldridge. *Soul on Ice*. New York: McGraw-Hill, 1968.

Cohen, Cathy. *The Boundaries of Blackness: AIDS and the Breakdown of Black Politics*. Chicago: U of Chicago P, 1999.

Crenshaw, Kimberlé Williams. "Beyond Racism and Misogyny: Black Feminism and 2 Live Crew." *Boston Review* 16.6 (December 1991): 6, 30.

"Demarginalizing the Intersection of Race and Sex: A Black Feminist Critique of Antidiscrimination Doctrine, Feminist Theory, and Antiracist Politics." *The Black Feminist Reader*. Ed. Joy James and T. Denean Sharpley-Whiting. Malden, MA: Blackwell, 2000.

de Lauretis, Teresa. *Alice Doesn't: Feminism, Semiotics, Cinema*. Bloomington: Indiana UP, 1984.

de Man, Paul. "The Rhetoric of Temporality." *Blindness and Insight: Essays in the Rhetoric of Contemporary Criticism*. Minneapolis: U of Minnesota P, 1971/1983. 187–228.

D'Emilio, John. *Lost Prophet: The Life and Times of Bayar Rustin*. New York: Free Press, 2003.

DiCarlo, John. "The Gym Body and Heroic Myth." *Gay and Lesbian Review* (July/August 2001): 14–16.

Dixon, Melvin. "This Light, This Fire, This Time: James Arthur Baldwin." *Out/Look* 2.2 (Fall 1989): 38–39.

Drowne, Kathleen. "'An Irrevocable Condition': Constructions of Home and the Writing of Place in *Giovanni's Room*." *Re-Viewing James Baldwin: Things Not Seen*. Ed. D. Quentin Miller. Philadelphia: Temple UP, 2000. 72–87.

Fisher. Gary. *Gary in Your Pocket: Stories and Notebooks of Gary Fisher.* Ed. Eve Kosofsky Sedgewick. Durham, NC: Duke UP, 1996.

Fuss, Diana. *Essentially Speaking: Feminism, Nature and Difference.* New York: Routledge, 1989.

Gates, Henry Louis, Jr. "Writing 'Race' and the Difference It Makes." *"Race," Writing, and Difference.* Ed. Henry Louis Gates Jr. Chicago: U of Chicago P, 1985. 1–20.

———. "To the Editor." *Boston Review* 17.1 (February 1992): 11–12.

Glenn, Evelyn Nakano. *Unequal Freedom: How Race and Gender Shaped American Citizenship and Labor.* Cambridge: Harvard UP, 2004.

Goldstein, Lauren. "The Alpha Teenager." *Fortune* 140.12 (December 1999): 201–3.

Graves, Florence George. "The Complete Anita Hill." *Boston Globe Magazine* 19 January 2003.

Griffin, Farah. "Black Feminist and Du Bois: Respectability, Protection, and Beyond." *Annals of the American Academy of Political & Social Science* 568 (March 2000): 28–40.

Gross, Kali N. "Examining the Politics of Respectability in African-American Studies." *The University of Pennsylvania Almanac* 43.28 (1 April 1997). http://www.upenn.edu/almanac/v43/n28/benchmrk.html).

Hardy, Ernest. "Whitewashing Black Beauty: For Cultural Critic & Feminist Theorist bell hooks Role-Playing and Racial Stereotyping Are Still a Drag." *L.A. Village View* 22–28 Oct. 1993: 36–37.

Harper, Phillip Brian. *Are We Not Men? Masculine Anxiety and the Problem of African-American Identity.* New York: Oxford UP, 1996.

Harris, Trudier. *Black Women in the Fiction of James Baldwin.* Knoxville: U of Tennessee Press, 1985.

Hemphill, Essex. *Ceremonies.* San Francisco: Cleis Press, 2000/1992.

Higgenbotham, Evelyn Brooks. *Righteous Discontent: The Women's Movement in the Black Baptist Church 1880–1920.* Cambridge, MA: Harvard UP, 1994.

hooks, bell. *Talking Back.* Boston: South End, 1989.

———. *Yearning: Race, Gender, and Cultural Politics.* Boston: South End 1990.

———. *Black Looks: Race and Representation.* Boston: South End, 1992.

Internet Filter Review. "Pornography Statistics 2003." http://www.internetfilterreview.com/internet-pornography-statistics.html.

Johnson, Barbara. "Nothing Fails Like Success." *A World of Difference*. Baltimore: Johns Hopkins UP, 1987.

———. "'Response' to Henry Louis Gates's 'Cannon-Formation and the Afro-American Tradition: From the Seen to the Told.'" *Afro-American Literary Study for the 1990s*. Ed. Houston A. Baker Jr. and Patricia Redmond. Chicago: U of Chicago P, 1989. 39–44.

Johnson, Phillip. "Is There an Abercrombie & Fitch Cult (and If There Is, Can I Join?)." *Lucire Living* 25 Jan. 2003. http://www.lucire.com/2001/0831ll0.htm.

Jordan, Mark D. *Telling Truths in Church: Scandal, Flesh, and Christian Speech*. Boston: Beacon Press, 2003.

Kelley, Robin D. G. "Playing for Keeps: Pleasure and Profit on the Postindustrial Playground." *The House That Race Built: Black Americans, U.S. Terrain*. Ed. Wahneema Lubiano. New York: Pantheon, 1997. 195–231.

Lee, Spike, dir. *Do the Right Thing*. Universal City Studios, 1989.

Lubiano, Wahneema. "Mapping the Interstices between Afro-American Cultural Discourse and Cultural Studies: A Prologue." *Callaloo* 19.1 (Winter 1996): 68–77.

McBride, Dwight A. "Speaking the Unspeakable: On Toni Morrison, African American Intellectuals and the Uses of Essentialist Rhetoric." *Modern Fiction Studies* 39.3/4 (Fall/Winter 1993): 755–76.

———. "Transdisciplinary Intellectual Practice: Cornel West and the Rhetoric of Race-Transcending." *Harvard Black Letter Law Journal* 11 (Spring 1994): 155–68.

———. "Can the Queen Speak? Racial Essentialism, Sexuality and the Problem of Authority." *Callaloo* 21.2 (Spring 1998): 363–79.

Mendelsohn, Daniel. *The Elusive Embrace: Desire and the Riddle of Identity*. New York: Knopf, 1999.

Morrison, Toni. *The Bluest Eye*. New York: Washington Square, 1970.

———. "Unspeakable Things Unspoken: The Afro-American Presence in American Literature." *Michigan Quarterly Review* 28.1 (Winter 1989): 1–34.

———. *Playing in the Dark: Whiteness and the Literary Imagination*. Cambridge, MA: Harvard UP, 1992.

———, ed. *Race-ing Justice, En-Gendering Power: Essays on Anita Hill, Clarence Thomas, and the Construction of Social Reality*. New York: Pantheon, 1992.

Nielsen, Aldon Lynn. *Reading Race: White American Poets and the Racial Discourse in the Twentieth Century.* Athens: U of Georgia P, 1988.

Painter, Nell. "Black Studies, Black Professors, and the Struggles of Perception." *Chronicle of Higher Education* 15 Dec. 2000: B7.

Pattillo, Mary. *Black Picket Fences: Privilege and Peril among the Black Middle Class.* Chicago: U of Chicago P, 1999.

Rafferty, Terrence. "Articles of Faith." *New Yorker.* 16 May 1988: 110–18.

Rampersad, Arnold. *The Life of Langston Hughes, Volume I: 1902–1941.* New York: Oxford, 1986.

Reid-Pharr, Robert. *Black Gay Man.* New York: New York UP, 2001.

Rose, Tricia. *Black Noise: Rap Music and Black Culture in Contemporary America.* Middletown: Wesleyan UP, 1994.

———. *Longing to Tell: Black Women Talk about Sexuality and Intimacy.* New York: Farrar, Straus & Giroux, 2003.

Ross, Marlon. "White Fantasies of Desire: Baldwin and the Racial Identities of Sexuality." *James Baldwin Now.* Ed. Dwight A. McBride. New York: New York UP, 1999. 13–55.

———. "Some Glances at the Black Fag: Race, Same-Sex Desire, and Cultural Belonging." *Canadian Review of Comparative Literature* 28.1/2 (March/June 1994): 193–219.

Scarry, Elaine. *On Beauty and Being Just.* Princeton, NJ: Princeton UP, 1999.

Scott, Joan W. "Experience." *Feminists Theorize the Political.* Ed. Judith Butler and Joan W. Scott. New York: Routledge, 1992. 22–40.

Smith, Valerie. *Not Just Race, Not Just Gender: Black Feminist Readings.* New York: Routledge, 1998.

Spivak, Gayatri. "Can the Subaltern Speak?" *Marxism and the Interpretation of Culture.* Ed. Cary Nelson and Lawrence Grossman. Urbana: U of Illinois P, 1988. 271–313.

Standley, Fred L., and Louis H. Pratt, eds. *Conversations with James Baldwin.* Jackson: U of Mississippi P, 1989.

Thomas, Kendall. "'Ain't Nothin' Like the Real Thing': Black Masculinity, Gay Sexuality, and the Jargon of Authenticity." *The House That Race Built: Black Americans, U.S. Terrain.* Ed. Wahneema Lubiano. New York: Pantheon, 1997. 116–35.

Thorsen, Karen, dir. *James Baldwin: The Price of the Ticket.* Nobody Knows Productions, 1989.

Tropiano, Stephen. "Post-*Ellen* Blues: (Or Lack of?) Gay and Lesbian Characters on Prime Time." *Pop Matters* 16 Oct. 2002. http://www.popmatters .com/columns/tropiano/021016.shtml.

Troup, Quincey, ed. *James Baldwin: The Legacy.* New York: Simon & Schuster, 1989.

Walker, Alice. *In Search of Our Mothers' Gardens: Womanist Prose.* San Diego: Harcourt Brace Jovanovich, 1983.

Warner, Michael. *The Trouble with Normal: Sex, Politics, and the Ethics of Queer Life.* Cambridge, MA: Harvard UP, 1999.

Welsing, Frances Cress. "The Politics Behind Black Male Passivity, Effeminization, Bisexuality and Homosexuality." *The Isis Papers: The Keys to the Colors.* Chicago: Third World, 1991. 81–92.

West, Cornel. *Keeping the Faith: Philosophy and Race in America.* New York: Routledge, 1993.

———. *Prophesy Deliverance! An Afro-American Revolutionary Christianity.* Philadelphia: Westview Press, 1982.

———. *Prophetic Fragments.* Grand Rapids, MI: Eerdman's Publishing, 1988.

———. *Race Matters.* Boston: Beacon Press, 1993.

White, E. Frances. *Dark Continent of Our Bodies: Black Feminism and the Politics of Respectability.* Philadelphia: Temple UP, 2001.

Williams, Patricia. *The Alchemy of Race and Rights: Diary of a Law Professor.* Cambridge, MA: Harvard UP, 1991.

Wolcott, Victoria. *Remaking Respectability: African American Women in Interwar Detroit.* Chapel Hill: U of North Carolina P, 2001.

Wu, Frank. *Yellow: Race in America Beyond Black and White.* New York: Basic Books, 2002.

Index

Abercrombie & Fitch, 1, 59–88, 127
  A&F look, 67, 78–80
  A&F Quarterly, 62, 65, 66, 70–72, 78, 86
  Abercrombie Look Book: Guidelines for Brand Representatives of Abercrombie & Fitch, 66, 67, 69–71, 78
  Brand Representatives, 66, 67, 70, 71, 78–80, 81
  Corporate culture, 62, 76, 80, 107
Abercrombie, David T., 62
Advertising Age, 64
Advocate, 130
Aesthetics, 64, 70, 100
Affirmative action, 5, 84, 99, 100, 143, 151, 154, 155, 157–160, 195–197
African American community, 1, 11, 22, 27, 36–38, 53
African American conservatives, 197

African American intellectuals, 163, 164, 166, 181, 183, 201, 204, 225
African American Literature and Culture Society, 14
African American studies, 1, 2, 6–11, 13–15, 36, 38, 40, 41, 43, 53–58, 164, 206
African Americanist, 3, 10, 35, 36, 54, 201
Africanist, 170, 171
Afro-American, 42, 54, 56, 57, 163, 164, 166, 169, 183, 187, 198, 199, 223
Afrocentrism, 212
Alchemy of Race and Rights, The, 138, 282
Alcott & Andrews, 65
Alexander, Elizabeth, 104
Allegory, 174–177, 223
  Allegorical, 175–177
Allegorization, 175

America, 3, 35, 40, 42, 43, 46, 47, 49, 68, 69, 111, 140, 146, 151, 152, 168, 186, 191, 192, 194, 195, 201, 204, 206, 222
   American dream, 23, 27, 72, 152
   American literature, 14, 39, 53, 166, 170, 171, 181, 183
America On-Line (AOL), 111
American Decency Association, 61
Arendt, Hannah, 75
Ariel Mutual Funds, 17
Art of th Novel, The, 166, 168, 169
Artist-critic dichotomy, 168, 171
Asian American, 7, 72, 77, 78, 82
Asian Pacific American Legal Center, 77
Atlantic Monthly, 22
Authenticity, 177, 186, 210, 212
   Authentic blackness, 43
   Racial authenticity, 218
Authority, 13, 42, 151, 164, 165, 177, 178, 204, 222, 225

Baker, Ella, 192
Baker, Houston A., 14, 181
Baldwin, James, 35, 36, 38–48, 52, 53, 56–58, 156, 192, 205, 220–223, 225
Banana Republic, 72–74
Baraka, Amiri, 44, 45, 220, 221
Bare-back, 113
Barrett, Lindon, 224
Bath house, 88
Baudelaire, Charles, 199
B-Boy Blues, 42
Bear Pond, 59
Bear witness, 4, 49, 92, 93, 99, 105, 112, 137, 145, 163, 179, 180, 183, 189, 208
Beckford, Tyson, 73
Benetton, 138, 181, 182
Benjamin, Walter, 173
Bernal, Martin, 166

Bernstein, Richard, 185
Bigger Thomas, 43
Billy Budd, 95, 96
Bisexuality, 46, 211, 216
Black anti-racist discourse, 3, 43, 46, 204, 207, 225
Black Athena, 166
Black community, 2, 18–20, 23, 99, 172, 173, 175, 178, 191, 194, 195, 203, 205–207, 210, 212, 219, 223, 225
Black cultural nationalism, 199, 211, 212, 214, 223
Black Gay Man, 93, 97, 98
Black liberation, 99, 219, 220
Black Like Us: A Century of Lesbian, Gay, and Bi-Sexual African American Fiction, 29, 38, 39
Black manhood, 102, 208, 213–216
Black masculinity, 102, 103, 105, 220
Black Man's Guide to Understanding the Black Woman, The, 218
Black Picket Fences, 25
Black queer studies, 2, 36, 37, 38, 39, 43, 57, 58
Black studies, 2, 12, 17, 54, 57, 58, 99, 223
Black Women in the Fiction of James Baldwin, 42
Blatino, 102, 104
Bling bling, 97
Bluest Eye, The, 177
Boston Globe Magazine, 136
Bourgeois sensibility, 21, 23, 25, 28
Bowers v. Hardwick, 59
Bradley, Tom, 191
Brady, James, 64
Brand, 5, 60, 62, 65–67, 70–72, 74, 78–83, 85, 86, 93, 103, 125, 158
   Branding, 60, 75

Brawley, Tawana, 138, 139
Brody, Jennifer DeVere, 39
Bronski, Michael, 59
Byrd, James, 156

California Assembly Bill 101, 153
Callaloo, 39, 43
Calvin Klein, 65
Canon, 166–170
    Canon-building, 166
Capital, 26, 27, 62, 69, 89, 91, 97, 118
    Capitalism, 97
    Capitalist, 144, 203
Carby, Hazel V., 46
Cather, Willa, 171
Cha-Cha queen, 122
Chat rooms, 111
Choco-holics, 122, 124
Chocolate queens, 122
Chu, Austin, 77
Circuit scene, 89
Civil unions, 5, 85
CLA Journal, 14
Clark, Cheryl, 64, 225
Clinton, William Jefferson, 158
Closet, 44, 51, 220, 221
    Closeted, 203, 221
CNN, 22, 73
Code, 69, 71, 88, 92, 127
    Code of silence, 19, 88, 92, 93
    Coded language, 80
    Coded moniker, 71
Cohen, Cathy, 11
Cole, William, 47
College Language Association, 14
Columbine shootings, 59
Coming out, 120, 127, 130, 149, 150
Commodity, 103, 118, 205
    Commodify, 72, 86, 224

Conservative Republicanism, 158
Constructionism, 177
    Constructionist, 177
Cox, Oliver, 193
Credibility, 137, 139, 218
Crenshaw, Kimberlé Williams, 135, 136, 142, 205, 207, 209
Critical theory, 41, 135
Cruising, 119
Cultural signifying, 205, 207
Cultural studies, 13, 14, 41, 43, 56
Cycle of poverty, 145

D'Emilio, John, 99
Dahmer, Jeffrey, 126
Deconstruction, 56, 163, 168
Dehumanization, 126
Dellums, Ronald, 192
Dern, Laura, 152
Derrida, Jacques, 164
Dewey, John, 185
DiCarlo, John, 88
Dinesen, Isak, 163
Dinge queen, 122, 124
Discourse, 8, 35, 36, 44, 46, 53–57, 68, 80, 98, 101, 112, 141, 144, 146, 159, 160, 163–169, 172–178, 183, 184, 186, 187, 193, 195, 196, 199–201, 204, 206, 207, 212, 214, 216, 219, 220, 223, 225
    Critical discourse, 40, 164, 165, 184, 186
    Discursive practices, 204
    Intellectual discourse, 166, 173, 194
    Political discourse, 157, 207
    Race discourse, 10, 44, 206, 214, 216, 218–220, 223–225
    Racialized discourse, 43, 140, 172–181, 183, 189, 194, 198–200

Scholarly discourse, 207
Discrimination, 4, 19, 62, 73, 77, 84,
    153, 157, 209
    Discriminatory, 78–80
    Linguistic discrimination, 127
Diversity, 7, 8, 11, 12, 13, 15, 23, 57, 73,
    156, 179
Dominance, 85, 98, 99
Douglass, Frederick, 12
"Down low," the, 61, 110
Drowne, Kathleen, 41

Earhart, Amelia, 64
Effiminacy, 216
Eichmann in Jerusalem, 75
Elitism, 76, 209
*Elusive Embrace: Desire and the Riddle of
    Identity, The*, 111
E-mail, 111
Emancipation Proclamation, 145
Emerge, 186
Emerson, Ralph Waldo, 154
Empire-building, 166
English studies, 10, 112
Epistemology, 4, 9, 139
    Epistemological, 93, 139, 176
Essentialism, 165, 166, 172, 177, 179–
    181, 204
    Anti-essentialist, 165
    Essentialist, 136, 165, 176, 178
    Essentialist black body, 136
    Essentialist rhetoric, 163
    Essentializing, 39, 43, 166, 172, 180,
        183, 189
    Strategic essentialism, 183
*Essentially Speaking: Feminism, Nature and
    Difference*, 165
Ethnic studies, 7, 8, 10, 68
Expatriate, 43

Experience, 12, 21, 24–26, 28, 41, 48,
    67, 76, 80, 81, 86, 91, 93, 94, 98, 100,
    101, 103, 106, 117, 118, 120, 121,
    130, 131, 135–137, 141, 142, 151,
    163–165, 174, 176–183, 188, 189,
    201, 203, 206, 210, 217, 223

Falwell, Jerry, 160
Faulkner, William, 168
Federated Department Stores, Inc., 65
Femininity, 215
Feminist movement, 136
Fetish, 88, 103, 104, 124
    Fetishistic, 102, 105, 109, 110, 112,
        124
    Fetishization, 104
Films
    Barber Shop, 22
    Basic Instinct, 71
    Best Man, The, 22
    Boiler Room, 117
    Cabaret, 74
    Exorcist, The, 139
    Forrest Gump, 157
    Four Weddings and a Funeral, 21
    Get on the Bus, 22
    James Baldwin: The Price of the Ticket,
        40, 205, 220
    Jungle Fever, 18
    Next Best Thing, The, 21
    Philadelphia, 21, 152, 191, 218
    Two Can Play That Game, 22
    Wall Street, 117
Fisher, Gary, 94, 96–99
Fitch, Ezra, 62
Fraternity, 82, 84, 85
Freud, Sigmund, 205, 211, 213
Fugitive Slave Law, 154
Fuss, Diana, 165, 177

Gable, Clark, 64
Gang bang, 104, 108
Garbo, Greta, 64
Gary in Your Pocket, 94, 98
Gates, Henry Louis, Jr., 14, 42, 163, 201, 205, 207
Gay bar, 111, 112, 125, 128
Gay liberation movement, 40
Gay marketplace of desire, 2, 60, 84, 88, 92, 100, 101, 103, 104, 109, 110, 116–118, 120, 122–127, 131
Gay personals ads, 65, 88, 92, 106, 110, 112, 113, 116, 117, 130
Gender, 1, 2, 3, 5, 8–11, 14, 43, 57, 58, 68, 88, 92, 135–137, 140, 172, 205, 209, 224
Gender affect, 88
Gender studies, 8, 10
Genre, 130
Glenn, Evelyn Nakano, 68
Go Tell It on the Mountain, 47
Goesinya, Peter, 106
Goldstein, Lauren, 59
Gomez-Montejano, Juancarlos, 77
Gonzalez, Eduardo, 73, 77
Goode, Wilson, 191
Grey, Thomas, 138, 182
Griffin, Farah, 37
Guest, Churchill, Winston Frederick, 64
Gutierrez, Encarnacion, 77

Hamer, Fannie Lou, 192
Harassment, 203, 210
    Sexual, 4, 137, 139, 141
Hardy, James Ear, 42
Harlem Renaissance, 14, 57
Harper, Vaughn, 189
Harris, Trudier, 42, 225

Hatch, Orin, 139
Hegel, Georg Wilhelm Friedrich, 98
Hegemony, 43, 124, 146, 176, 183, 184, 194
    Counter-hegemonic, 56
    Hegemonic, 57, 112, 136, 160, 200, 209, 219, 223
Helms, Jesse, 104
Hemingway, Ernest, 64, 171
Hemphill, Essex, 3, 35–38, 204–206, 216–220, 223
Henderson, Mae G., 14, 39
Hepburn, Katherine, 64
Herman, Edward, 75
Heteronormativity, 50–52, 129
Heterosexism, 76, 207, 209, 216, 218, 219
Heterosexist, 18, 29–31, 35, 36, 38, 96, 211, 218
Heterosexual, 5, 20, 35, 46, 50, 91, 92, 99, 122, 129, 151, 152, 203, 215, 217, 223, 224
Heterosexual marketplace of desire, 92
Higgenbotham, Evelyn Brooks, 38
Hill, Anita, 39, 95, 135–137, 139, 140–142
Hip-hop, 73, 97, 105, 207
    Culture, 97, 105
HIV, 113, 131
Hobson, Mellody, 17
Holocaust, 75, 211
Homo thug, 88, 122, 127
Homophobia, 20, 21, 91, 131, 206–210, 216, 218, 219
Homosexuality, 35, 40, 44, 46, 90, 158, 203, 208, 211–214, 216, 218, 220, 221, 225
hooks, bell, 181, 185, 187, 200, 203, 205, 208–211, 216, 221, 223, 225

Horatio Alger, 68
Hughes, Langston, 14, 39, 225
Hugo, Victor, 145
Humanity, 20, 43, 61, 89, 96, 131, 144, 148, 222
Hurston, Zora Neale, 14

Identity, 19, 26, 27, 36, 37, 39, 40, 43–46, 48, 49, 57, 68, 85, 93, 94, 97, 98, 135, 156, 157, 165, 170, 185, 187, 199, 217, 218, 221, 222, 224, 225
    Identification, 142, 151, 174, 175, 218
    Identity constructions, 46, 199
    Identity politics, 39, 93, 170
    Modes of identification, 91
Ideology, 8, 22, 37, 41, 46, 51, 63, 64, 68, 72, 85, 140, 141, 158, 159
    Ideological, 27, 38, 52, 68, 69, 98, 109, 139, 159, 177
    Ideologues, 140
Ileto, Joseph, 156
Indeterminacy, 178, 179
Instinct, 130
Interdisciplinary, 41, 187
Interpellated, 180
Interpellation, 140, 142
Interracial, 102–104, 106, 108, 109
Intersectionality, 135, 136, 142

Jackson, Jesse, 12, 146, 192
Jefferson, Thomas, 98
Jeffries, Michael, 65, 83
Johnson, Barbara, 39, 55, 56, 159, 163, 172, 178, 179
Johnson, E. Patrick, 39
Johnson, Lyndon, 158
Jones, Star, 17
Jordan, Mark D., 1

Karl Lagerfeld, 65
Kelley, Robin D. G., 109
Kennedy, John F., 64
Kennedy, Randall, 156
King, Martin Luther, Jr., 12, 144–146, 192
King, Rodney, 143, 144, 146–148, 188
Klein, Naomi, 59
Knowles, Beyoncé, 17
Kuhn, Thomas, 10
Kundera, Milan, 166, 168, 169, 170

Latinos, 77, 78, 84, 113, 122
Law, 7, 76, 77, 137
Lawrence v. Texas, 85
Lee, Spike, 18, 22, 42
LGBT, 5, 21, 23, 85
Liberalism, 84, 85, 87, 140, 194, 195
Lieff, Cabraser, Heimann & Bernstein, 77
Lieno, David, 83
Lifestyle marketing, 65, 86
Locke, Alain, 14, 39, 57
Long Black Song, 181
Lorde, Audre, 93
Los Angeles Times, 137
Los Angeles uprising, 143
Lost Prophet: The Life and Times of Bayard Rustin, 99
Loury, Glenn, 194, 195
Lu, Jennifer, 77
Lubiano, Wahneema, 56, 57

Malcolm X, 12, 192, 222
Mandingo fantasy, 122, 127
Mapplethorpe, Robert, 104
Marriage, 5, 20, 85
Marsh, Lisa, 86
Marxism, 197

Media, 12, 19, 22, 66, 136, 137, 143, 144, 150, 172, 186, 201
Meese, Ed, 59
Melville, Herman, 95, 171
Mendelsohn, Daniel, 111
Minority, 139, 156, 157, 196
Miscegenation, 169
Misogyny, 205, 207
Monogamy, 50, 128, 129
Montoya, Johan, 77
Moore, Darrell, 11
Mores, 101, 117, 152
Morrison, Toni, 163–172, 177–181, 183, 193
Moyers, Bill, 186
Mr. T, 71
Multiculturalism, 156

Nation, 185
Nazi, 75, 83, 211
Neo-Conservatives, 194
New black conservatism, 191, 194
New Criticism, 112
New Republic, 185
New York Post, 86, 139
New York Times, 22, 61, 139, 160
New York Times Magazine, 61
New Yorker, 64, 168, 188
Newsweek, 17, 19, 20
Nightline, 186
No Logo, 59
Norm, 31, 92, 124, 125, 138, 172, 199
Normative, 10, 109, 136
Notes of a Native Son, 44, 220

Objectivity, 57
Ocampo, Anthony, 77
Ontology, 173, 175
Other, 141

Out, 130, 149, 150
Outing, 22, 40
Overdetermine, 43, 96, 103, 155, 177, 180

Painter, Nell Irvin, 53–55
Paradigm shift, 10
Passivity, 211, 216
Patriarchy, 38, 140, 203
Paul Harris, Inc., 65
Peary, Robert, 64
People of color, 6, 72, 77, 84, 85, 146, 155–159, 174, 177, 194, 200, 209, 219
Performative, 127, 178
Perot, Ross, 158
Plato, 188, 190
Playing in the Dark: Whiteness and the Literary Imagination, 170, 171
Pleasure, 36, 61, 93, 101, 103, 104, 109, 131
Pluralism, 179
Poe, Edgar Allen, 171
Political right, the, 5, 59, 69, 84, 99, 111, 128, 143, 155, 157, 158, 159
Politics of exclusion, 207
Politics of inclusion, 207
Pornography, 88, 92, 101–103, 105, 106
Pornographic films
Black & White, 102
Black and Horny, 102
Black Brooklyn Beef, 102
Black Cowboys and Studs, 102
Black Drills & White Holes, 102, 106
Black Gomorrah, 102
Black Heat, 102
Black Hot Rods, 102
Black Jocks and Spanish Cocks, 102
Black Men in Black, 102

Black Patrol, 102
Black Power White Surge, 102
Black Sex Pack, 102
Black Street Fever, 102
Black Tricks White Treats, 106
Blacker the Berry Sweeter the Juice, 102
Blatino Gang Bang, 102
Fantasies of White and Black, 106
White Movers Black Shakers, 106, 109
Porter, Cole, 64
Poststructuralism, 14, 163–166, 176,
    177, 186, 189, 201
Power, 10, 22, 31, 45, 55, 91, 93, 96,
    104, 105, 107–109, 117, 124, 126,
    127, 130, 138, 147, 153, 167, 168,
    171, 172, 176, 182, 190–192, 201,
    208, 213, 214, 221
Privacy, 29, 85, 92, 106, 111, 117
Promise Keeper men, 106
Prophetic Christianity, 197, 198, 200
Prophetic Fragments, 140
Prophetic leader, 191, 192
Prophetic mode, 222
Proposition 54, 101
Psychoanalytic, 211, 213
Public intellectual, 12, 22, 155, 200, 201,
    225
Public sphere, 155

Quaintance, George, 59
Queer, 2, 14, 36–40, 43, 46, 57, 58, 71,
    85, 97, 99, 101, 130, 131
Queer studies, 2, 36, 39, 43, 57, 58
Queer theory, 2, 101
Queerness, 129
Quindlen, Anna, 160

Race, 1–13, 15, 17, 18, 23, 35–37, 39,
    40, 42–47, 54–58, 68, 71, 75, 78, 87,
88, 91, 92, 97, 99–101, 103, 104, 114,
    120, 126, 130, 135–137, 140, 141,
    151, 155, 156, 158, 160, 163–166,
    168, 172–175, 177, 178, 180, 185–
    187, 189–200, 203–206, 209, 214–
    225
Race man, 12, 42, 44, 45, 46, 99, 191,
    221–224
Racial authenticity, 218
Racial discrimination, 36, 131, 151,
    196, 225
Racial essentialism, 164, 165, 167,
    171, 172, 178, 203, 204
Racial inequality, 101
Racial profiling, 93
Racial whiteness, 120, 125
Racialist, 86, 122, 191
Racialized, 43, 69, 100, 109, 117, 140,
    155, 160, 172–178, 180, 181, 183,
    184, 189, 193, 194, 198–200
Racism, 4, 6, 35, 56, 72, 76, 86, 96,
    100, 117, 120, 124, 131, 138, 145,
    157, 181, 182, 185, 187, 191, 194,
    196, 197, 199, 203, 207, 212, 213,
    215, 216
Racist, 1, 4, 8, 31, 38, 54, 64, 66, 80,
    85–87, 96, 112, 117, 118, 122,
    123, 130, 164, 196, 207, 215, 216,
    219, 225
Racist programming, 215, 216
Race Matters, 181, 185–188, 191, 194,
    197, 198, 200
Race-transcending, 185–187, 191–194,
    197, 198, 200
Prophets, 192, 193
Rafferty, Terrence, 168–171
Ralph Lauren, 65, 72, 73
Polo, 73
Rap, 71, 207

Rape, 104, 139, 141
Rastafarianism, 70
Reagan, Ronald, 59
  Reagan era, 146
Reid-Pharr, Robert, 93, 94, 97–99
Representation, 20–22, 38, 41, 46, 53,
  55, 57, 72, 98, 99, 103, 128, 130, 131,
  157, 171, 174, 204, 209
Republican, 83–85
Respectability, 38, 46, 84, 93, 99, 106,
  195
  Black respectability, 13, 37, 38
  Politics of respectability, 22, 38
Reverse discrimination, 4, 5, 87, 143,
  151, 157
Rhetoric, 12, 36, 55, 68, 101, 135, 143,
  154, 157, 160, 196–198, 200, 201,
  207, 208, 216
  Rhetorical strategy, 54, 158, 164, 165,
    168, 194, 209, 218
  Rhetorical value, 189
Rice queen, 122
Riggs, Marlon, 42, 155
Robertson, Pat, 151
Rockwell, Norman, 64
Rolling Stone, 64
Rose, Tricia, 123
Rustin, Bayard, 99

Say It Loud, I'm Black and I'm Proud: Black
  Pride Survey 2000, 19, 20, 131
Scarry, Elaine, 100
Schlegel, Friedrich Von, 179
Scott, Jill, 18
Sedgewick, Eve Kosofsky, 94, 97
Self-hatred, 96
Sex clubs, 88
Sexism, 37, 76, 209
Sex-object choice, 100

Sexual preference, 203
Sexuality, 1–3, 5, 8, 9, 11, 14, 15, 20, 22,
  35, 36, 39, 40, 43, 45, 46, 48, 50–52,
  57–59, 76, 84, 85, 89, 91, 92, 96, 99,
  103, 104, 110, 122, 123, 129, 133,
  136, 150–152, 160, 172, 203–205,
  208, 211, 217, 219, 221–224
Sexualized, 43, 48, 59, 71, 109
Shahrazad Ali, 218, 219
Shame, 37, 49, 61, 88, 112
Signification, 68, 71, 110, 191, 207, 214
  Shifting signifier, 141, 178, 179, 181,
    207
  Transcendental signified, 164
Simple truth, 18, 76, 155, 158
Singleton, John, 22
Sisyphus, 144
Skin albinism, 214
Slavery, 37, 69, 100, 144, 145, 211
Social contract, 147
Social terrain, 91
Sound bite, 19, 158
Sowell, Thomas, 195
Specter, Arlen, 137
Spillers, Hortense, 14
Stereotype, 72, 95, 102, 103, 122, 171,
  172
Stone, Sharon, 71
Subculture, 203
Subjectivity, 2, 25, 37, 39, 40, 57, 98,
  197, 204
  Subject, 8, 12, 25, 27, 28, 55, 135,
    141, 163, 172, 173, 197, 208, 211
  Subject position, 25, 135, 141
Sula, 180

"Talented Tenth," 35, 37, 203
Television Shows
  Boy Meets Boy, 21, 127, 130

Cosby Show, The, 22
Dick Cavett Show, 45, 220, 222
Ellen, 130, 149–153
Good Times, 215
Queer as Folk, 21
Queer Eye for the Straight Guy, 21, 129
Sex and the City, 21
Six Feet Under, 21
Spin City, 21
Today Show, 22, 186
Will and Grace, 21
Thomas, Clarence, 10, 135–138, 140–142, 182, 195
Thornton, Bill Bob, 151
Thorsen, Karen, 40
Transdisciplinary, 41, 43, 187, 201, 202
Trouble with Normal, The, 92
Truth-telling, 92, 99
2 Live Crew, 205, 207

U.S. Congress, 147
U.S. Senate Judiciary Committee, 137
U.S. Supreme Court, 99, 135, 137, 159
Uncle Tom, 194

Victim-status, 194
Violence, 61, 143, 144, 145, 155–157, 160, 205, 208, 209, 219
Virtual blackness, 105

Walker, David, 12
Walker, Jimmy, 215
Walker, Wyatt T., 190
Warner, Michael, 92

Washington, Booker T., 12, 192
Washington, Harold, 192
Waters, Maxine, 143, 146
Watts Riots, 144
Weber, Bruce, 59, 65, 72, 73
"Welcome table," 37
Welsing, Frances Cress, 205, 210–220, 223
West, Cornel, 24, 42, 65, 80, 120, 140, 149, 150, 152, 181, 185–202, 211
West Hollywood, 120, 149, 150, 152
White community, 172
White House, 147, 158
White master, 97, 98
White privilege, 84, 100
White supremacy, 87, 100, 212, 213, 214, 216
White supremacist, 30, 156, 214
Whiteness, 1, 26, 27, 44, 47, 48, 64, 66, 68, 69, 76, 84, 97, 117–120, 124–127, 156, 176, 177, 189, 214
Cultural whiteness, 72, 156
Masculine whiteness, 68, 69
Whiteness studies, 48
Whitman, Walt, 19, 97
Williams, Patricia, 138, 181, 201
Williams, Tennessee, 11
Wilson, Flip, 215
Winfrey, Oprah, 151
Wood, Corrine, 61
Wright, Jeremiah, 190
Wright, Richard, 42
Wu, Angeline, 77
Wu, Frank H., 159

About the Author

Dwight A. McBride is chair of the Department of African American Studies and Leon Forrest Chair of African American Studies at Northwestern University. He is editor of *James Baldwin Now* (NYU Press 1999), author of the Hurston-Wright Legacy Award–nominated *Impossible Witnesses: Truth, Abolitionism, and Slave Testimony* (NYU Press 2001), and coeditor of the Lambda Literary Award–winning *Black Like Us: A Century of Lesbian, Gay, and Bi-Sexual African American Fiction* (2003). He lives in Chicago, Illinois and Saugatuck, Michigan.